THE
COMPLETE
SCHOOL
ATLAS

HOLT, RINEHART AND WINSTON

Harcourt Brace & Company

Austin • New York • Orlando • Chicago • Atlanta • San Francisco • Boston • Dallas • Toronto • London

Photo Credits

Front and Back Cover: Inset, Ralph Mercer/Tony Stone Images; Background, Frank Curry.

Title Page: Ralph Mercer/Tony Stone Images.

Pages 37–70, Douglas Mazonowicz/Bruce Coleman, Inc.

Requests for permission to make copies of any part of the work should be mailed to: Permissions Department, Holt, Rinehart and Winston, Inc., 6277 Sea Harbor Drive, Orlando, Florida 32887-6777.

For permission to reprint copyrighted material, grateful acknowledgment is made to the following sources:

Macmillan Publishing Company: Adapted from map, "United States: Ethnic Population, 1980's" from *We the People: An Atlas of America's Diversity* by James Paul Allen and Eugene James Turner. Copyright © 1988 by Macmillan Publishing Company.

Printed in the United States of America

ISBN 0-03-095267-0

2 3 4 5 6 7 030 97 96 95 94

CONTENTS

WORLD HISTORY 71

AMERICAN HISTORY 101

Introduction

*T*he **Complete School Atlas** is a valuable source of geographical, historical, and statistical information. This classroom and research source has many useful features to aid you in your study:

> ▶ a **Skills Handbook** that explains how to read and to use different kinds of maps

> ▶ a selection of up-to-date physical and political maps of the world and the continents

> ▶ a **World Geography** section that contains information about various regions of the world, including full-color thematic maps that show economic, climate, and population characteristics

> ▶ easy-to-understand **World History** and **American History** maps that lead you from early world civilizations to the American Revolution and on to the turbulent changes of the twentieth century

> ▶ an **Appendix** that provides important statistical information about the countries of the world

> ▶ an **Index** that helps you locate places and directs you to maps about specific historical events

The Complete School Atlas packs a great deal of up-to-date information into one source. This easy-to-use atlas is a valuable resource for students and teachers trying to understand our ever-changing world.

SKILLS HANDBOOK

CONTENTS

Using an atlas requires the ability to understand how maps are created and how they are used. This Skills Handbook explains how to read and understand the maps in this atlas. You also will find examples of maps you will see on pages 41–70 of this atlas. These thematic maps are only some examples of the many kinds of maps you will find in this atlas and elsewhere.

MAPPING THE EARTH

The Globe

A **globe** is a scale model of the earth. It is useful for looking at the entire earth or at large areas of the earth's surface. The earth's land surface is organized into seven large landmasses, called **continents**, which are pictured in the four maps in **Figure 1**. Landmasses smaller than continents and completely surrounded by water are called **islands**. Geographers also organize the earth's water surface into parts, the largest of which is the world **ocean**. Geographers divide the world ocean into four oceans: the Pacific Ocean, the Atlantic Ocean, the Indian Ocean, and the Arctic Ocean. Lakes and seas are smaller bodies of water.

Figure 2 is a diagram of a globe. The pattern of lines that circle the earth in east-west and north-south directions is called a **grid**. The intersection of these imaginary lines helps us find the location of places on the earth. Some mapmakers label the lines with letters and numbers. The grid on many maps and globes, however, is made up of lines of **latitude** and **longitude**.

Lines of latitude are drawn in an east-west direction and measure distance north and south of the **equator**. The equator is an imaginary line that circles the globe halfway between the North Pole and the South Pole. Lines of latitude are called **parallels** because they are

NORTHERN HEMISPHERE

INDIAN OCEAN
ASIA
EUROPE
AFRICA
ARCTIC OCEAN
+ North Pole
PACIFIC OCEAN
ATLANTIC OCEAN
Equator
NORTH AMERICA

SOUTHERN HEMISPHERE

SOUTH AMERICA
Equator
PACIFIC OCEAN
ATLANTIC OCEAN
+ South Pole
ANTARCTICA
AUSTRALIA
INDIAN OCEAN
AFRICA

WESTERN HEMISPHERE

North Pole
NORTH AMERICA
ATLANTIC OCEAN
180°
Equator
PACIFIC OCEAN
SOUTH AMERICA
ANTARCTICA
South Pole

EASTERN HEMISPHERE

North Pole
EUROPE
ASIA
AFRICA
Equator
ATLANTIC OCEAN
INDIAN OCEAN
AUSTRALIA
Prime Meridian
ANTARCTICA
South Pole

▲ **Figure 1: The hemispheres**

always parallel to the equator. Parallels north of the equator are labeled with an *N*, and those south are labeled with an *S*.

Lines of longitude are drawn in a north-south direction and measure distance east and west of the **prime meridian**. The prime meridian is an imaginary line that runs through Greenwich, England, from the North Pole to the South Pole. Lines of longitude are called **meridians**.

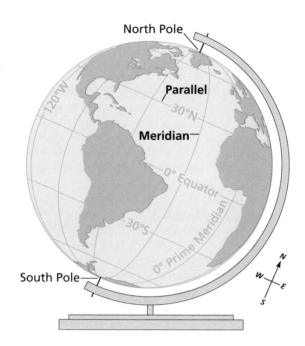

▼ **Figure 2: Globe**

Parallels measure distance from the equator, and meridians from the prime meridian, in **degrees**. The symbol for degrees is °. Degrees are further divided into minutes, for which the symbol is '. There are 60 minutes in a degree.

Lines of latitude range from 0°, for locations on the equator, to 90°N or 90°S, for locations at the North Pole or South Pole. Lines of longitude range from 0° on the prime meridian to 180° on a meridian in the mid-Pacific Ocean. Meridians west of the prime meridian to 180° are labeled with a *W*. Those east of the prime meridian to 180° are labeled with an *E*.

Looking at the globe, you can see that the equator divides the globe into two halves, or **hemispheres**. See **Figure 1**. The half north of the equator is the Northern Hemisphere. The southern half is the Southern Hemisphere.

The prime meridian and the 180° meridian divide the world into the Eastern Hemisphere and the Western Hemisphere. Because the prime meridian separates parts of Europe and Africa into two different hemispheres, some mapmakers divide the Eastern and Western hemispheres at 20° W. This places all of Europe and Africa in the Eastern Hemisphere.

MAP-MAKING

A map is a flat diagram of all or part of the earth's surface. An **atlas** is an organized collection of maps in one book. **M**apmakers have different ways of presenting a round earth on flat maps. These different ways are called **map projections**. Because the earth is round, all flat maps have some distortion. Some flat maps distort size, especially at high latitudes. Those maps, however, might be useful because they show true direction and shape. Some maps, called equal-area maps, show size in true proportions but distort shapes. **M**apmakers must choose the type of map projection that is best for their purposes. Many map projections are one of three kinds: cylindrical, conic, or flat-plane.

▶ **Figure 3a: Paper cylinder**

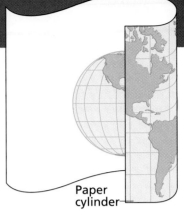

Cylindrical projections are designed from a cylinder wrapped around the globe. See **Figure 3a**. The cylinder touches the globe only at the equator. The meridians are pulled apart and are parallel to each other instead of meeting at the poles. This causes landmasses near the poles to appear larger than they really are. **Figure 3b** is a Mercator projection, one type of cylindrical projection. The Mercator projection is useful for navigators because it shows true direction and shape. The Mercator projection for world maps, however, emphasizes the Northern Hemisphere. Africa and South America are shown to be smaller than they really are.

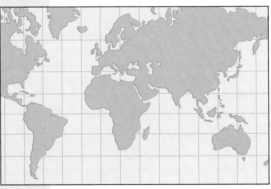

▲ **Figure 3b: Mercator projection**

▼ **Figure 4a: Paper cone**

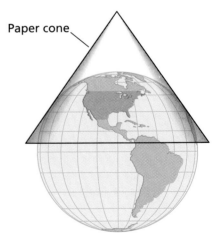

Conic projections are designed from a cone placed over the globe. See **Figure 4a**. A conic projection is most accurate along the lines of latitude where it touches the globe. It retains almost true shape and size. Conic projections are most useful for areas that have long east-west dimensions, such as the United States. See the map in **Figure 4b**.

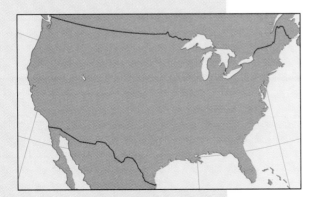

◀ **Figure 4b: Conic projection**

Paper

Flat-plane projections are designed from a plane touching the globe at one point, such as at the North Pole or South Pole. See **Figures 5a** and **5b**. A flat-plane projection is useful for showing true direction for airplane pilots and ship navigators. It also shows true area, but it distorts true shape.

▲ **Figure 5a: Flat plane**

◀ **Figure 5b: Flat-plane projection**

The Robinson projection is a compromise between size and shape distortions. It often is used for world maps, such as the map on pages 38–39. The minor distortions in size at high latitudes on Robinson projections are balanced by realistic shapes at the middle and low latitudes.

▼ **Figure 6a: Great-circle route**

NORTH AMERICA
Great-circle route
EUROPE
Lisbon
40°N Philadelphia
ATLANTIC OCEAN
AFRICA
PACIFIC OCEAN
SOUTH AMERICA

MERCATOR PROJECTION

Drawing a straight line on a flat map will not show the shortest route between two locations. Remember, maps represent a round world on a flat plane. The shortest route between any two points on the earth is a **great-circle route**. See **Figures 6a** and **6b**. Any imaginary line that divides the earth into equal parts is a great circle. The equator is a great circle. Airplanes and ships navigate along great-circle routes.

ASIA
PACIFIC OCEAN
North Pole +
EUROPE
AFRICA
Great-circle route
Lisbon
NORTH AMERICA
Philadelphia
ATLANTIC OCEAN

FLAT-PLANE PROJECTION

◀ **Figure 6b: Great-circle route**

N
W — E
S

Medellín
Magdalena
Bogotá
Meta River
Cali
COLOMBIA
Orinoco River
Guaviare River
PACIFIC
Paramaribo
Kourou
Devil's Island (Fr
Cayenne
SURINAME
FRENCH GUIANA
GUYANA
GUIANA
HIGHLAND

11

Map Essentials

In some ways, maps are like messages sent out in code. Mapmakers provide certain elements that help us translate these codes to understand the information, or message, they are presenting about a particular part of the world. Almost all maps have several common elements: **directional indicators**, **scales**, and **legends**, or keys. **Figure 7**, a map of East Asia, has all three elements.

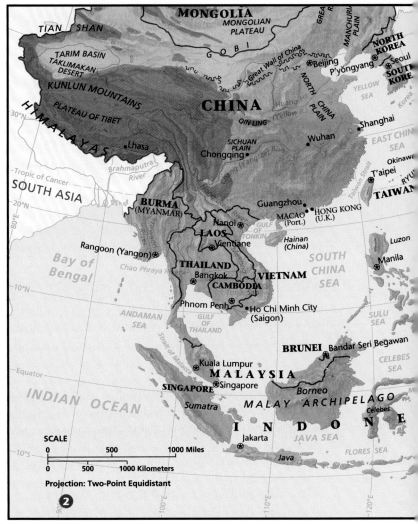

▲ **Figure 7: East Asia—Physical–Political**

A directional indicator shows which directions are north, south, east, and west. Some mapmakers use a "north arrow," which points toward the North Pole. Remember, "north" is not always at the top of a map. The way a map is drawn and the location of directions on that map depend on the perspective of the mapmaker. Many maps in this atlas indicate direction by using a **compass rose ❶**. A compass rose has arrows that point to all four principal directions, as shown in **Figure 7**.

Mapmakers use scales to represent distances between points on a map. Scales may appear on maps in several different forms. The maps in this atlas provide a line scale ❷. The scales give distances in miles and kilometers (km).

To find the distance between two points on the map in **Figure 7**, place a piece of paper so that the edge connects the two points. Mark the location of each point on the paper with a line or dot. Then, compare the distance between the two dots with the map's line scale. The number on the top of the scale gives the distance in miles. The number on the bottom gives the distance in kilometers. Because the distances are given in intervals, you will have to approximate the actual distance on the scale.

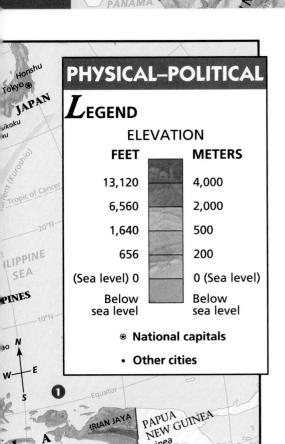

PHYSICAL–POLITICAL

*L*EGEND

ELEVATION

FEET		METERS
13,120		4,000
6,560		2,000
1,640		500
656		200
(Sea level) 0		0 (Sea level)
Below sea level		Below sea level

⊛ **National capitals**

• **Other cities**

❸

The legend ❸, or key, explains what the symbols on the map represent. Point symbols are used to specify the location of things, such as cities, that do not take up much space on a large-scale map. Some legends, such as the one in **Figure 7**, show which colors represent certain elevations. Other maps might have legends with symbols or colors that represent things such as roads, economic resources, land use, population density, and climate.

Inset maps are sometimes used to show a small part of a larger map. Mapmakers also use inset maps to show areas that are far away from the areas shown on the main map. Maps of the United States, for example, often include inset maps of Hawaii. (See the map on page 41.) That state is too far from the other 49 states to accurately represent the true distance on the main map. Subject areas in inset maps can be drawn to a scale different from the scale used on the main map.

WORKING WITH MAPS

The maps on pages 16–36 include two kinds of maps: physical and political. On pages 41–70 you will find four kinds of maps. First is a physical–political map. Each of these maps is followed by a series of three thematic maps. These climate, population, and economic maps provide different kinds of information about each region of the world.

Mapmakers often combine physical and political features into one map. Physical–political maps, such as the one in **Figure 7** on pages 12 and 13, show important physical features in a region, including major mountains and mountain ranges, rivers, oceans and other bodies of water, deserts, and plains. Physical–political maps also show important political features, such as national borders, state and provincial boundaries, and capitals and other main cities.

▼ **Figure 8:**
East Asia — Climate

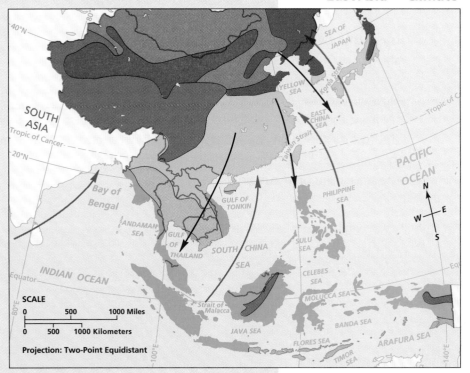

Mapmakers use climate maps to show dominant weather patterns in certain areas. Climate maps in this atlas use color to show the various climate regions of the world. See **Figure 8**. Colors that identify climate types are found in a legend that accompanies each map. Boundaries between climate regions do not indicate an abrupt change in dominant weather conditions between two climate regions. Instead, boundaries approximate areas of gradual change between two climate regions.

PANAMA

GULF
OF
PANAMA

VENEZUELA

ATLANTIC

⊛ Georgetown

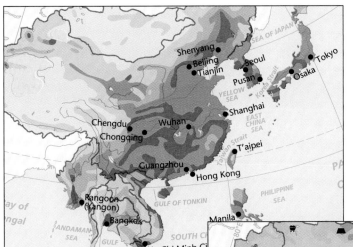

▲ Figure 9:
East Asia—Population

Population maps show where people live in a particular region and how crowded, or densely populated, regions are. Population maps in this atlas use color to show population density. See **Figure 9**. Each color represents a certain number of people living within a square mile or square kilometer. The population maps also use symbols to show metropolitan areas with populations of a particular size. These symbols and the color categories are identified in a legend.

Economic maps show the important resources of a region. See **Figure 10**. Various symbols and colors are used to show information about economic development, such as where major industry is located or where agricultural or ranching activities are most common. The meanings of each symbol and color are shown in a legend.

◀ Figure 10: East
Asia—Economy

Most of the maps after page 70 of this atlas are historical maps. Each map shows historical events or political conditions as they existed at a particular time in the past. These maps use a variety of tools to provide information. These tools include colors and various symbols that show such things as important events and places. Historical maps have legends that help you to understand the information the maps contain.

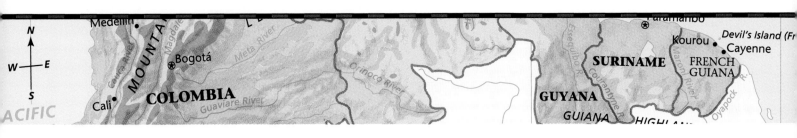

WORLD AND REGIONAL MAPS

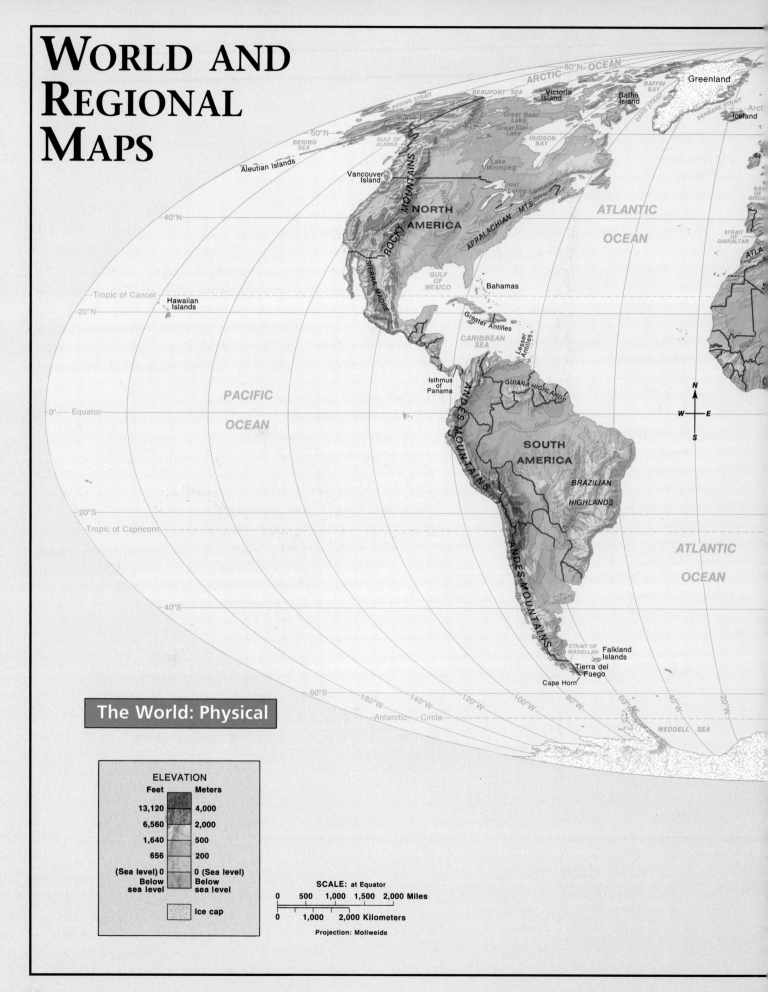

The World: Physical

ELEVATION

Feet	Meters
13,120	4,000
6,560	2,000
1,640	500
656	200
(Sea level) 0	0 (Sea level)
Below sea level	Below sea level

Ice cap

SCALE: at Equator

0   500   1,000   1,500   2,000 Miles

0   1,000   2,000 Kilometers

Projection: Mollweide

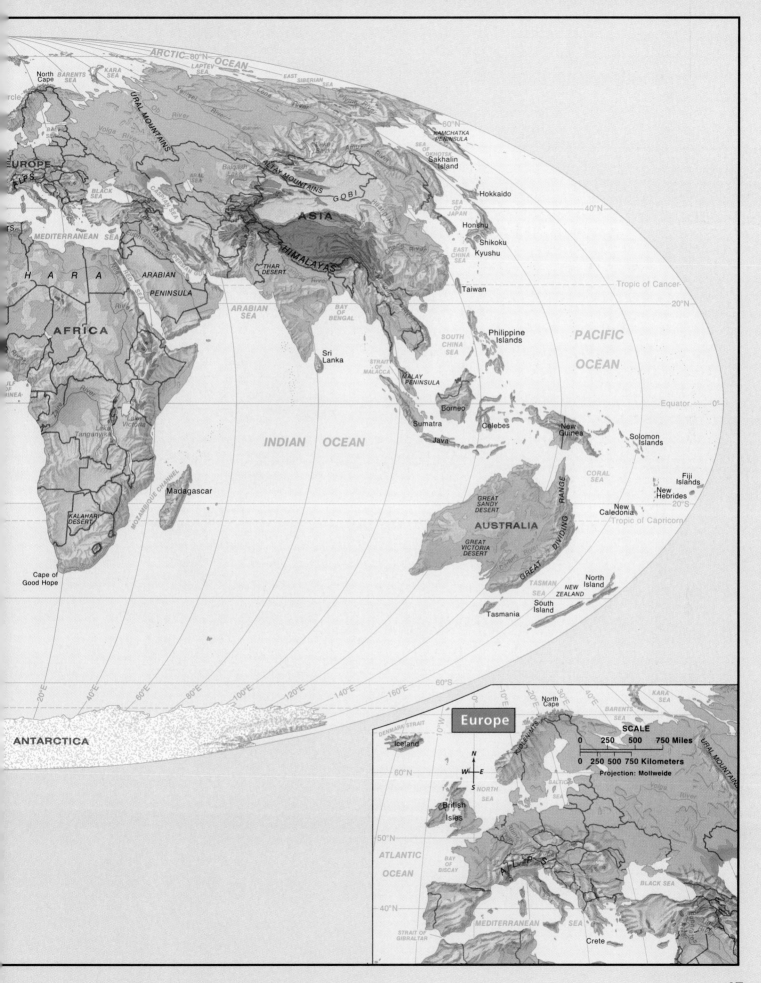

ARCTIC 80°N OCEAN

North Cape
BARENTS SEA
KARA SEA
LAPTEV SEA
EAST SIBERIAN SEA
URAL MOUNTAINS
Ob River
Yenisei
Lena River
Olenek River
Kolyma River
60°N

EUROPE
ALPS
BALTIC SEA
Volga River
ARAL SEA
Balqash Lake
Lake Baikal
Amur River
ALTAY MOUNTAINS
GOBI
ASIA

KAMCHATKA PENINSULA
SEA OF OKHOTSK
Sakhalin Island

BLACK SEA
CASPIAN SEA
Euphrates River
Tigris River
Persian Gulf
Huang He
HIMALAYAS
Chang River
40°N
SEA OF JAPAN
Hokkaido
Honshu
Shikoku
Kyushu
EAST CHINA SEA

MEDITERRANEAN SEA
HARA
ARABIAN PENINSULA
RED SEA
THAR DESERT
Taiwan
Tropic of Cancer
20°N

AFRICA
Nile River
ARABIAN SEA
BAY OF BENGAL
Sri Lanka
STRAIT OF MALACCA
MALAY PENINSULA
SOUTH CHINA SEA
Philippine Islands
PACIFIC OCEAN

GULF OF GUINEA
Zaire River
Lake Victoria
Lake Tanganyika
INDIAN OCEAN
Sumatra
Borneo
Java
Celebes
New Guinea
Equator 0°
Solomon Islands

Madagascar
MOZAMBIQUE CHANNEL
CORAL SEA
New Hebrides
Fiji Islands
New Caledonia

KALAHARI DESERT
GREAT SANDY DESERT
AUSTRALIA
GREAT VICTORIA DESERT
GREAT DIVIDING RANGE
Darling River
Tropic of Capricorn
20°S

Cape of Good Hope
TASMAN SEA
NEW ZEALAND
North Island
South Island
Tasmania

20°E 40°E 60°E 80°E 100°E 120°E 140°E 160°E 60°S

ANTARCTICA

Europe

North Cape
Iceland
DENMARK STRAIT
KARA SEA
BARENTS SEA
URAL MOUNTAINS
30°E 40°E
60°N
50°N
40°N

SCALE
0 250 500 750 Miles
0 250 500 750 Kilometers
Projection: Mollweide

N
W E
S

British Isles
NORTH SEA
BALTIC SEA
Volga River

ATLANTIC OCEAN
BAY OF BISCAY
ALPS
BLACK SEA

STRAIT OF GIBRALTAR
MEDITERRANEAN SEA
Crete

The World: Political

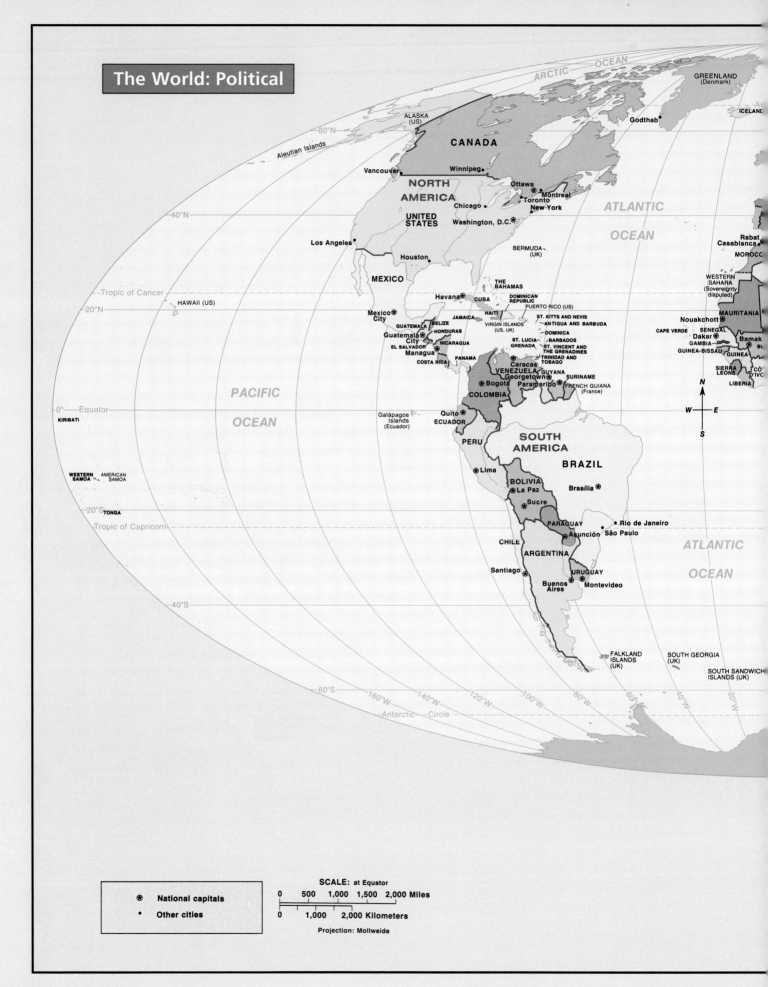

National capitals ⊛
Other cities •

SCALE: at Equator

0   500   1,000 1,500 2,000 Miles

0   1,000   2,000 Kilometers

Projection: Mollweide

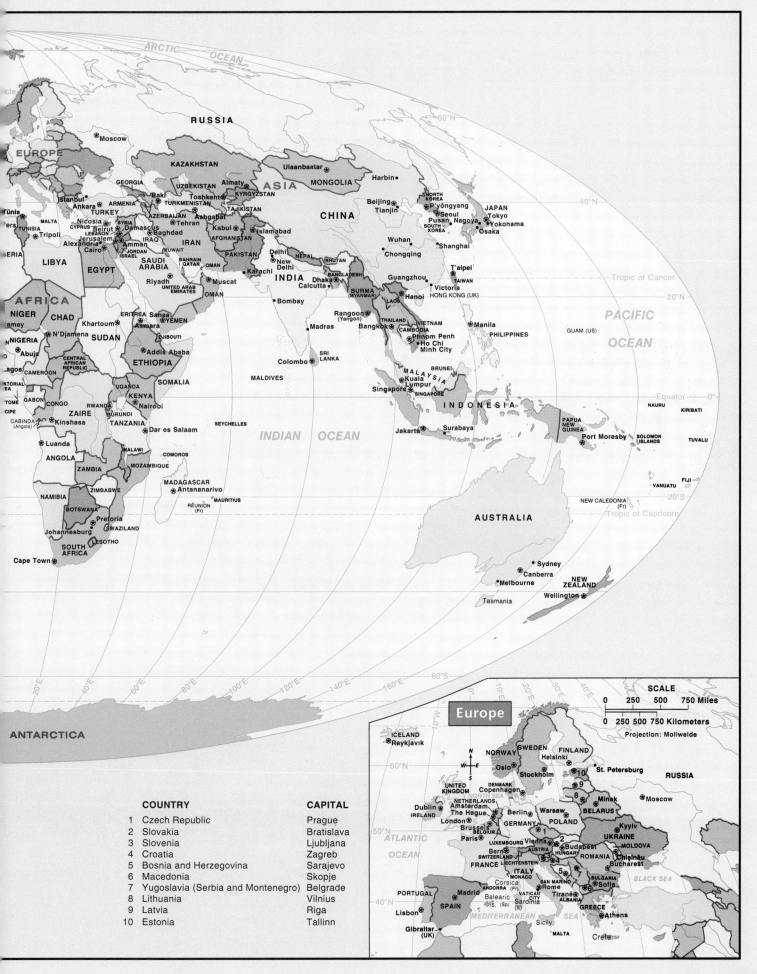

ARCTIC OCEAN

RUSSIA

⊛ Moscow

EUROPE

KAZAKHSTAN

GEORGIA

Ulaanbaatar ⊛

ASIA

MONGOLIA

Harbin •

NORTH KOREA

60°N

UZBEKISTAN

Almaty •

Toshkent ⊛

KYRGYZSTAN

Istanbul •

Ankara ⊛

ARMENIA

Bakı ⊛

TURKMENISTAN

Beijing •

Tianjin •

P'yŏngyang ⊛

JAPAN

Tokyo •

40°N

Tünis

MALTA

TURKEY

AZERBAIJAN

Ashgabat ⊛

TAJIKISTAN

CHINA

Seoul ⊛

Pusan •

Nagoya •

Yokohama •

ers

TUNISIA

⊛ Tripoli

CYPRUS

Nicosia ⊛

SYRIA

Beirut ⊛

Damascus ⊛

Tehran ⊛

Kabul ⊛

AFGHANISTAN

Islamabad ⊛

SOUTH KOREA

Osaka •

LEBANON

IRAQ

Baghdad ⊛

IRAN

Alexandria •

Jerusalem ⊛

Amman ⊛

ISRAEL

JORDAN

KUWAIT

PAKISTAN

Delhi •

New Delhi ⊛

NEPAL

BHUTAN

Wuhan •

Chongqing •

Shanghai •

ERIA

LIBYA

EGYPT

Cairo ⊛

SAUDI ARABIA

BAHRAIN

QATAR

OMAN

Karachi •

INDIA

BANGLADESH

Dhaka ⊛

Calcutta •

Guangzhou •

T'aipei ⊛

TAIWAN

Tropic of Cancer

AFRICA

NIGER

CHAD

Riyadh ⊛

Muscat ⊛

UNITED ARAB EMIRATES

OMAN

Bombay •

BURMA (MYANMAR)

Victoria •

HONG KONG (UK)

20°N

amey

NIGERIA

Abuja ⊛

Khartoum ⊛

N'Djamena ⊛

SUDAN

ERITREA

Sanaa ⊛

Asmara ⊛

YEMEN

DJIBOUTI

Madras •

Rangoon (Yangon) ⊛

Bangkok ⊛

THAILAND

LAOS

Hanoi •

VIETNAM

CAMBODIA

Manila ⊛

PHILIPPINES

GUAM (US)

PACIFIC OCEAN

agos

CAMEROON

CENTRAL AFRICAN REPUBLIC

Addis Ababa ⊛

ETHIOPIA

SOMALIA

Colombo •

SRI LANKA

MALDIVES

Phnom Penh ⊛

Ho Chi Minh City •

BRUNEI

TORIAL EA

GABON

SÃO TOMÉ

CIPE

CONGO

ZAIRE

RWANDA

BURUNDI

UGANDA

KENYA

Nairobi •

TANZANIA

SEYCHELLES

MALAYSIA

Kuala Lumpur ⊛

Singapore •

SINGAPORE

INDONESIA

NAURU

KIRIBATI

Equator 0°

CABINDA (Angola)

Kinshasa ⊛

Luanda ⊛

Dar es Salaam •

INDIAN OCEAN

Jakarta •

Surabaya •

PAPUA NEW GUINEA

Port Moresby ⊛

SOLOMON ISLANDS

TUVALU

ANGOLA

MALAWI

ZAMBIA

COMOROS

MOZAMBIQUE

MADAGASCAR

Antananarivo ⊛

RÉUNION (Fr)

MAURITIUS

FIJI

VANUATU

NEW CALEDONIA (Fr)

20°S

NAMIBIA

ZIMBABWE

BOTSWANA

Pretoria ⊛

SWAZILAND

Johannesburg •

LESOTHO

SOUTH AFRICA

Cape Town •

AUSTRALIA

Tropic of Capricorn

• Sydney

Canberra ⊛

NEW ZEALAND

• Melbourne

Tasmania

Wellington ⊛

20°E 40°E 60°E 80°E 100°E 120°E 140°E 160°E 60°S

ANTARCTICA

COUNTRY	CAPITAL
1 Czech Republic	Prague
2 Slovakia	Bratislava
3 Slovenia	Ljubljana
4 Croatia	Zagreb
5 Bosnia and Herzegovina	Sarajevo
6 Macedonia	Skopje
7 Yugoslavia (Serbia and Montenegro)	Belgrade
8 Lithuania	Vilnius
9 Latvia	Riga
10 Estonia	Tallinn

SCALE

0 250 500 750 Miles

0 250 500 750 Kilometers

Projection: Mollweide

Europe

ICELAND

Reykjavík ⊛

NORWAY

SWEDEN

FINLAND

Helsinki ⊛

60°N

Oslo ⊛

Stockholm ⊛

10 ⊛

St. Petersburg •

9 ⊛

RUSSIA

UNITED KINGDOM

DENMARK

Copenhagen ⊛

NORTH SEA

8 ⊛

Minsk ⊛

⊛ Moscow

Dublin ⊛

IRELAND

NETHERLANDS

Amsterdam ⊛

The Hague ⊛

Berlin ⊛

Warsaw ⊛

POLAND

BELARUS

London ⊛

Brussels ⊛

BELGIUM

GERMANY

1

Kyyiv ⊛

UKRAINE

50°N

ATLANTIC OCEAN

Paris ⊛

LUXEMBOURG

Vienna ⊛

2

Budapest ⊛

HUNGARY

MOLDOVA

Bern ⊛

SWITZERLAND

AUSTRIA

3

4

ROMANIA

Chișinău ⊛

Bucharest ⊛

FRANCE

LIECHTENSTEIN

ITALY

5

7

BULGARIA

Sofia ⊛

BLACK SEA

Corsica

San Marino

Rome ⊛

6

Tiranë ⊛

ALBANIA

PORTUGAL

ANDORRA

VATICAN CITY

Madrid ⊛

SPAIN

Balearic Is. (Sp)

Sardinia (It)

GREECE

Athens ⊛

40°N

Lisbon ⊛

Gibraltar (UK)

MEDITERRANEAN SEA

Sicily

MALTA

Crete

19

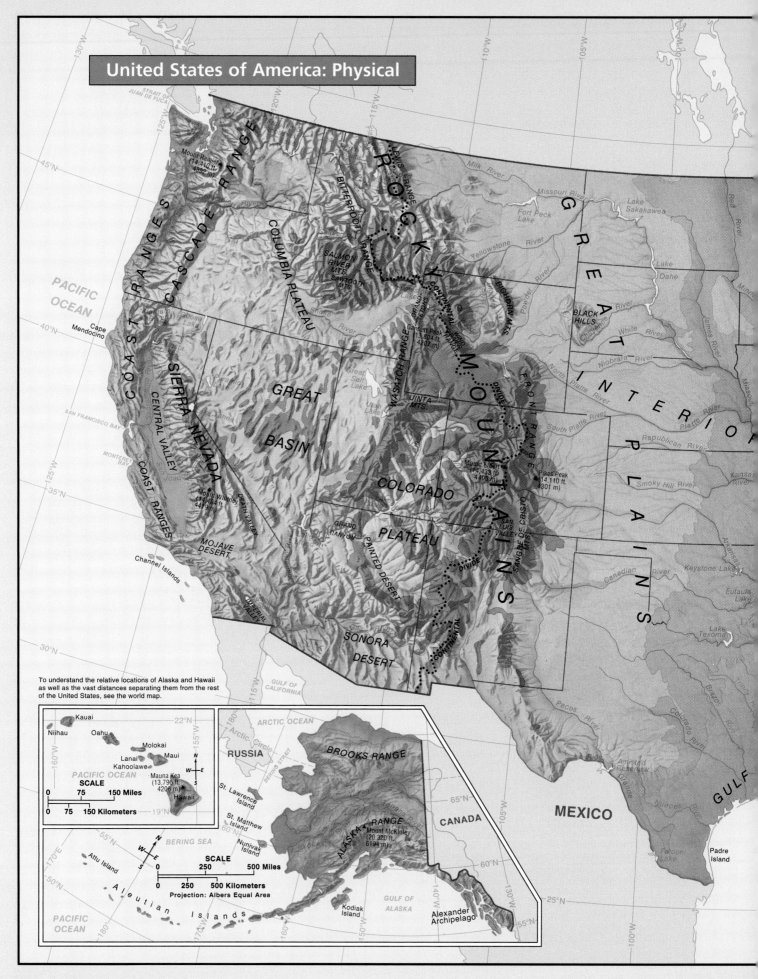

United States of America: Physical

To understand the relative locations of Alaska and Hawaii as well as the vast distances separating them from the rest of the United States, see the world map.

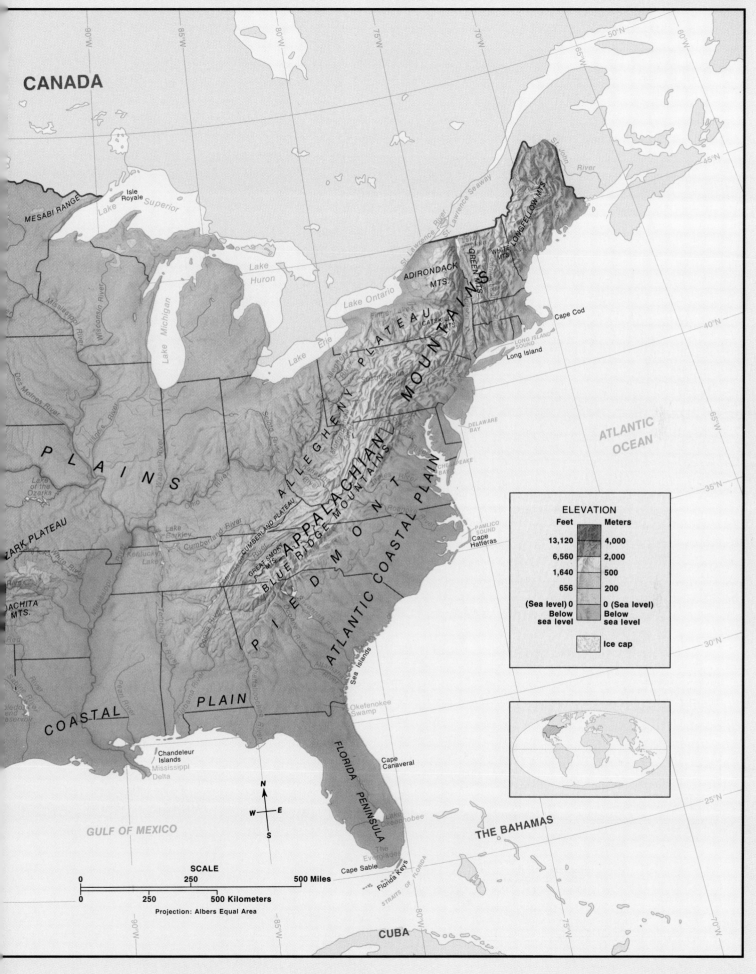

CANADA

MESABI RANGE

Isle Royale

Lake Superior

Lake Huron

Lake Michigan

Mississippi River

Wisconsin River

Des Moines River

P L A I N S

Lake of the Ozarks

OZARK PLATEAU

OUACHITA MTS.

Illinois River

Wabash River

Ohio River

Lake Barkley

Cumberland River

Kentucky Lake

Tennessee River

White River

Red River

C O A S T A L   P L A I N

Sabine River

Toledo Bend Reservoir

Pearl River

Mississippi Delta

Chandeleur Islands

GULF OF MEXICO

N
W   E
S

Alabama River

Tombigbee River

Coosa River

Chattahoochee River

Flint River

Okefenokee Swamp

FLORIDA PENINSULA

Lake Okeechobee

The Everglades

Cape Sable

Florida Keys

STRAITS OF FLORIDA

Cape Canaveral

Sea Islands

ATLANTIC COASTAL PLAIN

P I E D M O N T

BLUE RIDGE MOUNTAINS

GREAT SMOKY MTS.

CUMBERLAND PLATEAU

A P P A L A C H I A N

A L L E G H E N Y   P L A T E A U

M O U N T A I N S

Lake Erie

Lake Ontario

Finger Lakes

Susquehanna River

Mohawk River

Delaware River

Potomac River

CATSKILL MTS.

ADIRONDACK MTS.

St. Lawrence River

St. Lawrence Seaway

St. Lawrence River

GREEN MTS.

WHITE MTS.

LONGFELLOW MTS.

St. John River

Cape Cod

LONG ISLAND SOUND

Long Island

DELAWARE BAY

CHESAPEAKE BAY

PAMLICO SOUND

Cape Hatteras

Roanoke River

ATLANTIC OCEAN

THE BAHAMAS

CUBA

ELEVATION

Feet	Meters
13,120	4,000
6,560	2,000
1,640	500
656	200
(Sea level) 0	0 (Sea level)
Below sea level	Below sea level

Ice cap

SCALE

0   250   500 Miles

0   250   500 Kilometers

Projection: Albers Equal Area

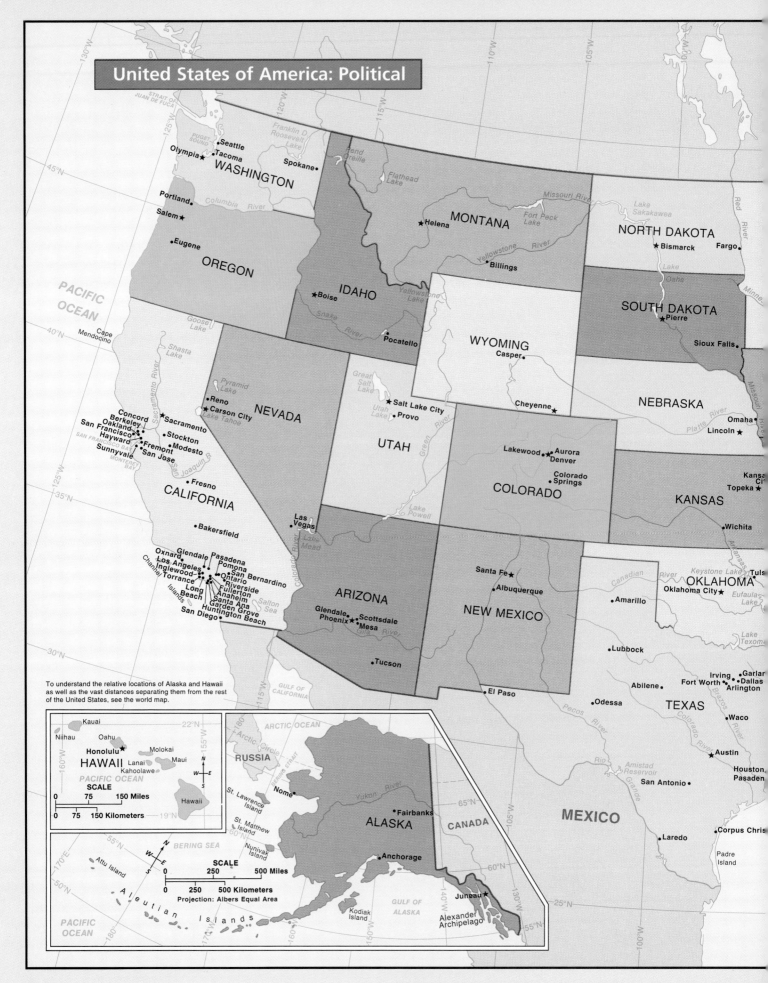

United States of America: Political

WASHINGTON
Seattle
Tacoma
Olympia ★
Spokane

Portland
Salem ★
Eugene

OREGON

PACIFIC OCEAN

Cape Mendocino

Shasta Lake

Pyramid Lake

Reno
Carson City ★
Lake Tahoe

NEVADA

Concord
Berkeley
Oakland
San Francisco
Hayward
Sunnyvale
Fremont
San Jose

Sacramento
Stockton
Modesto

Fresno

CALIFORNIA

Bakersfield

Oxnard
Glendale Pasadena
Los Angeles Pomona
Inglewood San Bernardino
Torrance Ontario
Long Riverside
Beach Fullerton
Anaheim
Santa Ana
Garden Grove
Huntington Beach
San Diego

Channel Islands

MONTANA
Helena
Billings

Flathead Lake
Fort Peck Lake
Missouri River
Yellowstone River

IDAHO
Boise ★
Pocatello
Snake River
Yellowstone Lake

NORTH DAKOTA
Bismarck ★
Fargo
Lake Sakakawea

SOUTH DAKOTA
Pierre ★
Sioux Falls
Lake Oahe

WYOMING
Casper
Cheyenne ★

NEBRASKA
Omaha
Lincoln

Great Salt Lake
Salt Lake City ★
Provo
Utah Lake

UTAH

Green River

COLORADO
Lakewood
Aurora
Denver
Colorado Springs

Lake Powell

KANSAS
Kansas City
Topeka ★
Wichita

Las Vegas
Lake Mead

ARIZONA

Glendale Scottsdale
Phoenix ★ Mesa

Tucson

Santa Fe ★
Albuquerque

NEW MEXICO

El Paso

OKLAHOMA
Oklahoma City ★

Amarillo

Lubbock

Abilene
Odessa

TEXAS

Irving Garland
Fort Worth Dallas
Arlington

Waco

Austin ★

Houston
Pasaden

San Antonio

Laredo

Corpus Christ

Padre Island

Canadian River
Keystone Lake
Tulsa
Eufaula Lake

Arkansas River
Lake Texoma

Brazos River
Colorado River

Rio Grande
Amistad Reservoir
Pecos River

MEXICO

To understand the relative locations of Alaska and Hawaii as well as the vast distances separating them from the rest of the United States, see the world map.

Kauai
Niihau
Oahu
Honolulu ★
Molokai
Lanai Maui
Kahoolawe

HAWAII
PACIFIC OCEAN

SCALE
0   75   150 Miles
0   75   150 Kilometers

Hawaii

ARCTIC OCEAN
Arctic Circle

RUSSIA

St. Lawrence Island
St. Matthew Island

Nome

Nunivak Island

ALASKA

Fairbanks

Anchorage

Yukon River

CANADA

Juneau ★

Alexander Archipelago

GULF OF ALASKA

Kodiak Island

BERING SEA

Attu Island

Aleutian Islands

PACIFIC OCEAN

SCALE
0   250   500 Miles
0   250   500 Kilometers
Projection: Albers Equal Area

PUGET SOUND
STRAIT OF JUAN DE FUCA

Columbia River
Franklin D. Roosevelt Lake
Pend Oreille

SAN FRANCISCO BAY
MONTEREY BAY

San Joaquin
Sacramento River
Goose Lake

Colorado River

Salton Sea

GULF OF CALIFORNIA

Platte River
Minne...
Missouri

Red River

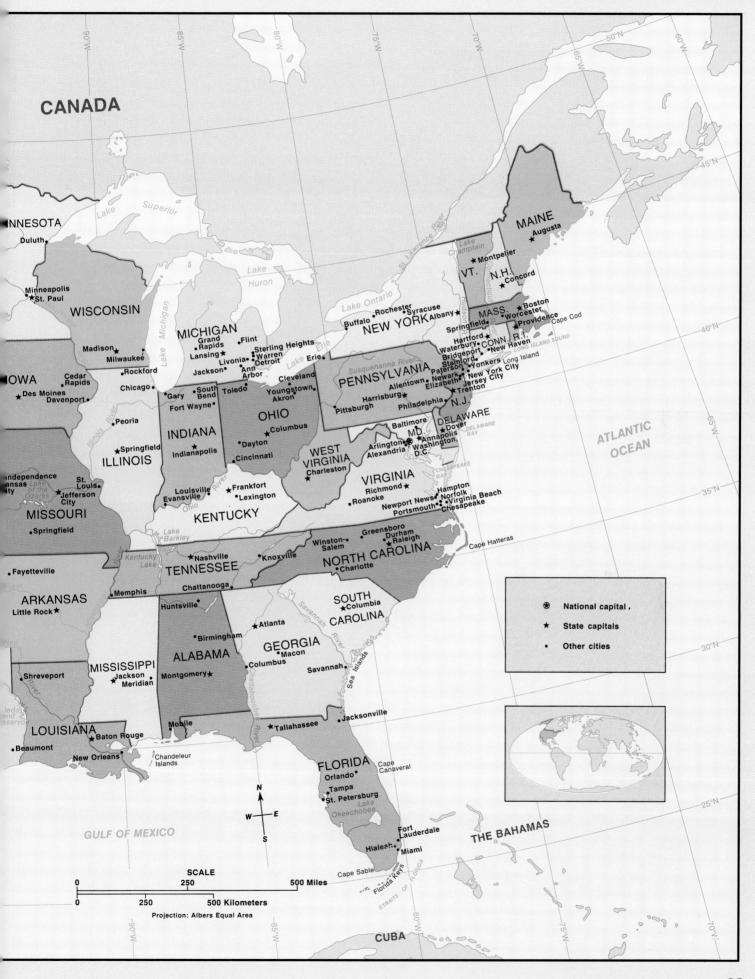

CANADA

MINNESOTA
Duluth

Minneapolis
St. Paul

WISCONSIN

Madison
Milwaukee
Rockford

IOWA
Cedar Rapids
Des Moines
Davenport

Chicago

MICHIGAN
Grand Rapids
Lansing
Jackson
Ann Arbor
Flint
Sterling Heights
Livonia
Warren
Detroit

Peoria

Gary
Fort Wayne
South Bend
Toledo

Cleveland

Youngstown
Akron

Springfield

INDIANA
Indianapolis

OHIO
Columbus

Dayton
Cincinnati

ILLINOIS

Independence
Kansas City
St. Louis
Jefferson City

MISSOURI
Springfield

Louisville
Evansville

Frankfort
Lexington

KENTUCKY

Lake Barkley

WEST VIRGINIA
Charleston

PENNSYLVANIA
Pittsburgh
Harrisburg
Allentown
Philadelphia

VIRGINIA
Richmond
Roanoke
Newport News
Portsmouth
Hampton
Norfolk
Virginia Beach
Chesapeake

Baltimore
Arlington
Alexandria
Annapolis
Washington D.C.
MD.
DELAWARE
Dover

N.J.
Trenton
Elizabeth
Newark
Paterson
Jersey City
New York City
Yonkers
Long Island

NEW YORK
Buffalo
Rochester
Syracuse
Albany
Springfield
Hartford
Waterbury
Bridgeport
Stamford
New Haven

CONN. R.I.
MASS.
Worcester
Boston
Providence
Cape Cod

VT. N.H.
Montpelier
Concord

MAINE
Augusta

Lake Champlain

Fayetteville

Memphis

Nashville
Knoxville
Chattanooga

TENNESSEE

Winston-Salem
Greensboro
Durham
Raleigh

NORTH CAROLINA
Charlotte

ARKANSAS
Little Rock

Huntsville

SOUTH CAROLINA
Columbia

Atlanta

MISSISSIPPI
Jackson
Meridian

ALABAMA
Birmingham
Montgomery
Columbus

GEORGIA
Macon
Savannah

Shreveport

LOUISIANA
Baton Rouge
Beaumont
New Orleans
Chandeleur Islands

Mobile

Tallahassee

Jacksonville

FLORIDA
Orlando
Cape Canaveral
Tampa
St. Petersburg
Lake Okeechobee

Fort Lauderdale
Hialeah
Miami

Cape Sable
Florida Keys

GULF OF MEXICO

THE BAHAMAS

CUBA

ATLANTIC OCEAN

⊗ National capital
★ State capitals
• Other cities

SCALE
0   250   500 Miles
0   250   500 Kilometers
Projection: Albers Equal Area

23

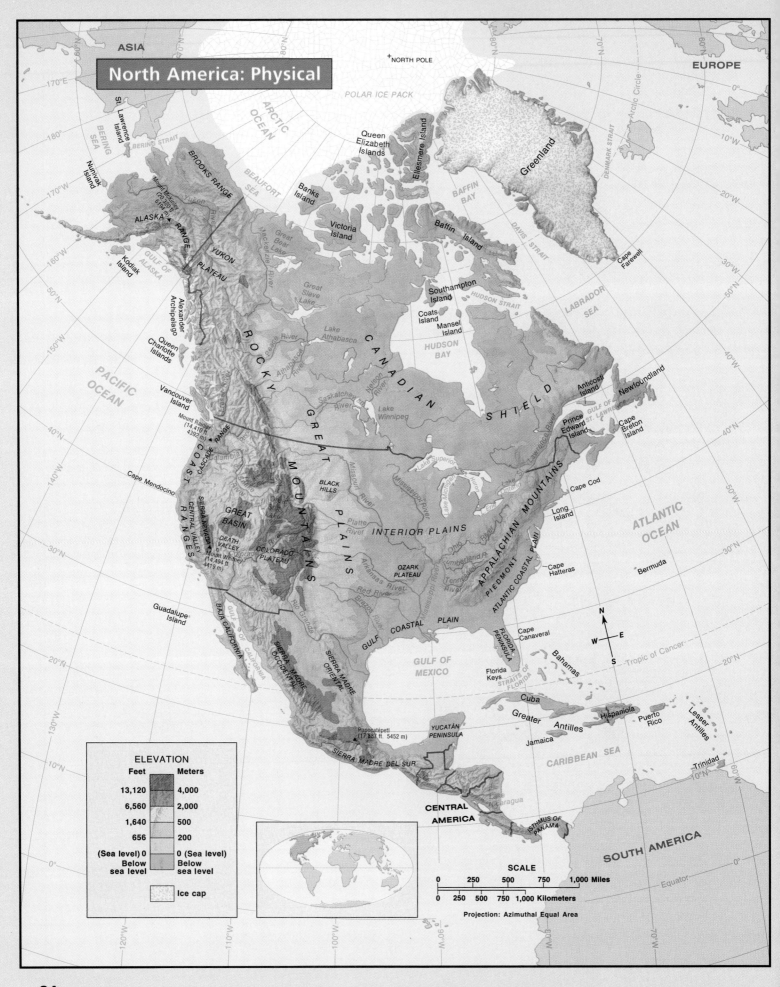

North America: Physical

ASIA

EUROPE

+ NORTH POLE

POLAR ICE PACK

ARCTIC OCEAN

BERING SEA

BERING STRAIT

BEAUFORT SEA

Queen Elizabeth Islands

Ellesmere Island

Greenland

DENMARK STRAIT

St. Lawrence Island

Nunivak Island

BROOKS RANGE

Banks Island

Victoria Island

Baffin Island

BAFFIN BAY

Arctic Circle

Cape Farewell

ALASKA RANGE

Mount McKinley (20,320 ft. 6194 m)

YUKON PLATEAU

GULF OF ALASKA

Kodiak Island

Alexander Archipelago

Queen Charlotte Islands

Vancouver Island

PACIFIC OCEAN

Cape Mendocino

DAVIS STRAIT

LABRADOR SEA

Great Bear Lake

Mackenzie River

Peace River

Great Slave Lake

Athabasca River

Lake Athabasca

Saskatchewan River

Nelson River

CANADIAN SHIELD

Southampton Island

Coats Island

Mansel Island

HUDSON STRAIT

HUDSON BAY

ROCKY MOUNTAINS

COAST RANGES

CASCADE RANGE

Mount Rainier (14,410 ft. 4392 m)

Columbia River

SIERRA NEVADA

GREAT BASIN

DEATH VALLEY

Mount Whitney (14,494 ft. 4419 m)

CENTRAL VALLEY

COLORADO PLATEAU

BLACK HILLS

GREAT PLAINS

Missouri River

Lake Winnipeg

Lake Superior

Lake Michigan

Lake Huron

Lake Ontario

Lake Erie

Anticosti Island

Prince Edward Island

GULF OF ST. LAWRENCE

St. Lawrence River

Newfoundland

Cape Breton Island

APPALACHIAN MOUNTAINS

Cape Cod

Long Island

ATLANTIC OCEAN

Platte River

INTERIOR PLAINS

OZARK PLATEAU

Arkansas River

Red River

Colorado River

Cumberland R.

Tennessee River

Ohio River

Mississippi River

PIEDMONT

ATLANTIC COASTAL PLAIN

Cape Hatteras

Bermuda

Guadalupe Island

BAJA CALIFORNIA

GULF OF CALIFORNIA

Rio Grande

Brazos River

GULF COASTAL PLAIN

FLORIDA PENINSULA

Cape Canaveral

Bahamas

SIERRA MADRE OCCIDENTAL

SIERRA MADRE ORIENTAL

GULF OF MEXICO

Florida Keys

STRAITS OF FLORIDA

Tropic of Cancer

Popocatépetl (17,887 ft. 5452 m)

YUCATÁN PENINSULA

Cuba

Greater Antilles

Jamaica

Hispaniola

Puerto Rico

Lesser Antilles

CARIBBEAN SEA

Trinidad

SIERRA MADRE DEL SUR

CENTRAL AMERICA

Lake Nicaragua

ISTHMUS OF PANAMA

SOUTH AMERICA

Equator

N
W   E
S

ELEVATION

Feet		Meters
13,120		4,000
6,560		2,000
1,640		500
656		200
(Sea level) 0		0 (Sea level)
Below sea level		Below sea level

Ice cap

SCALE

0   250   500   750   1,000 Miles

0   250   500   750   1,000 Kilometers

Projection: Azimuthal Equal Area

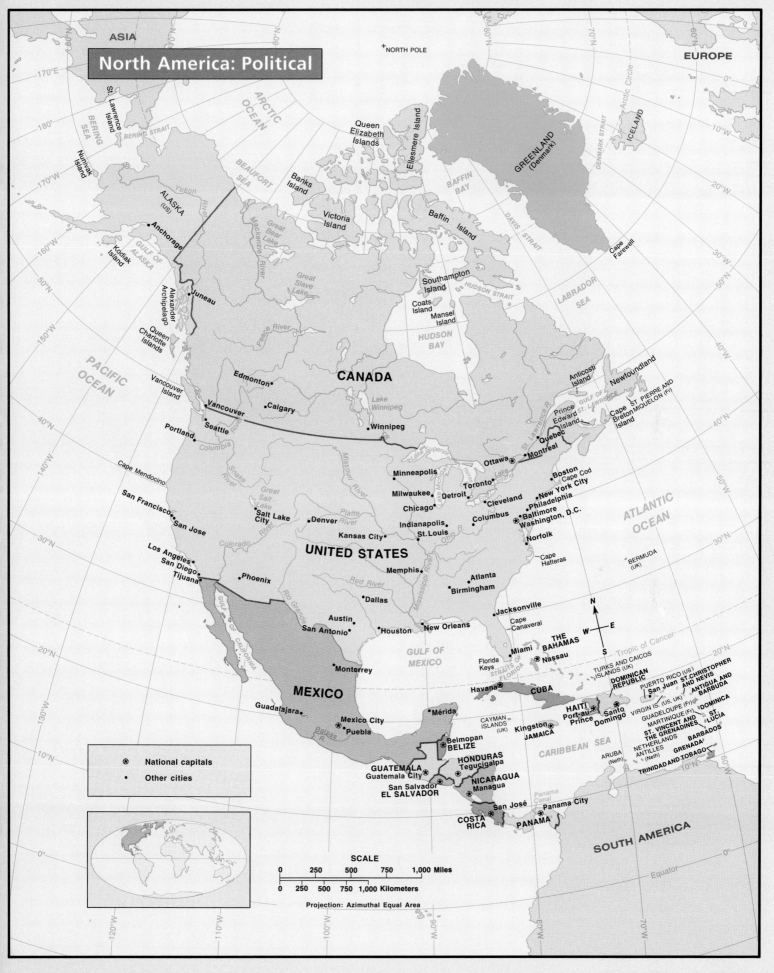

North America: Political

ASIA

NORTH POLE

EUROPE

ARCTIC OCEAN

St. Lawrence Island

BERING SEA

BERING STRAIT

Nunivak Island

ALASKA (US)

Yukon River

BEAUFORT SEA

Banks Island

Queen Elizabeth Islands

Ellesmere Island

GREENLAND (Denmark)

ICELAND

DENMARK STRAIT

BAFFIN BAY

DAVIS STRAIT

Kodiak Island

GULF OF ALASKA

Anchorage

Juneau

Alexander Archipelago

Queen Charlotte Islands

Great Bear Lake

Mackenzie River

Victoria Island

Baffin Island

Southampton Island

Coats Island

Mansel Island

HUDSON STRAIT

HUDSON BAY

Cape Farewell

LABRADOR SEA

PACIFIC OCEAN

Vancouver Island

Cape Mendocino

Peace River

Great Slave Lake

CANADA

Edmonton

Calgary

Vancouver

Seattle

Portland

Columbia

Lake Winnipeg

Winnipeg

Lake Superior

Anticosti Island

Prince Edward Island

Newfoundland

Cape Breton Island

ST. PIERRE AND MIQUELON (Fr)

St. Lawrence R.

GULF OF ST. LAWRENCE

Quebec

Montreal

ATLANTIC OCEAN

San Francisco

San Jose

Snake River

Great Salt Lake

Salt Lake City

Denver

Platte River

Colorado River

Missouri River

Minneapolis

Milwaukee

Chicago

Lake Michigan

Detroit

Cleveland

Toronto

Lake Huron

Lake Erie

Lake Ontario

Ottawa

Boston

Cape Cod

New York City

Philadelphia

Baltimore

Columbus

Washington, D.C.

UNITED STATES

Kansas City

Indianapolis

St. Louis

Norfolk

Los Angeles

San Diego

Tijuana

Phoenix

Dallas

Red River

Mississippi River

Memphis

Birmingham

Atlanta

Cape Hatteras

BERMUDA (UK)

Austin

San Antonio

Houston

New Orleans

Jacksonville

Cape Canaveral

GULF OF CALIFORNIA

GULF OF MEXICO

Miami

Florida Keys

STRAITS OF FLORIDA

THE BAHAMAS

Nassau

Tropic of Cancer

TURKS AND CAICOS ISLANDS (UK)

Monterrey

MEXICO

Guadalajara

Balsas R.

Mexico City

Puebla

Mérida

Havana

CUBA

CAYMAN ISLANDS (UK)

Kingston

JAMAICA

HAITI

Port-au-Prince

DOMINICAN REPUBLIC

Santo Domingo

PUERTO RICO (US)

San Juan

VIRGIN IS. (US, UK)

GUADELOUPE (Fr)

MARTINIQUE (Fr)

ST. VINCENT AND THE GRENADINES

NETHERLANDS ANTILLES (Neth)

ARUBA (Neth)

ST. CHRISTOPHER AND NEVIS

ANTIGUA AND BARBUDA

DOMINICA

ST. LUCIA

BARBADOS

GRENADA

TRINIDAD AND TOBAGO

CARIBBEAN SEA

Belmopan

BELIZE

GUATEMALA

Guatemala City

San Salvador

EL SALVADOR

HONDURAS

Tegucigalpa

NICARAGUA

Managua

COSTA RICA

San José

Panama Canal

PANAMA

Panama City

SOUTH AMERICA

Equator

N
W · E
S

⊛	National capitals
•	Other cities

SCALE

0   250   500   750   1,000 Miles

0   250   500   750   1,000 Kilometers

Projection: Azimuthal Equal Area

25

South America: Physical

CENTRAL AMERICA

CARIBBEAN SEA

Panama Canal

GULF OF PANAMA

Malpelo Island

Galápagos Islands

ATLANTIC OCEAN

Margarita Island   Tobago   Trinidad

Orinoco River Delta

LLANOS

Meta River

GUIANA HIGHLANDS

Angel Falls

Devil's Island
Cape Orange

Amazon River Delta

ANDES MOUNTAINS

Mount Tolima
(18,425 ft. 5616 m)

Mount Chimborazo
(20,561 ft. 6267 m)

Equator   0°

GULF OF GUAYAQUIL

Caquetá River

Japurá River

Amazon River

Negro River

AMAZON BASIN

Juruá River

Purus River

Madeira River

Tapajós River

Xingu River

Tocantins River

Mount Huascarán
(22,205 ft. 6768 m)

BRAZILIAN HIGHLANDS

MATO GROSSO PLATEAU

Ucayali River

Beni River

Ancohuma Peak
(20,958 ft. 6388 m)

PACIFIC OCEAN

ATACAMA DESERT

ANDES MOUNTAINS

CHACO

BRAZILIAN PLATEAU

Pilcomayo River

Paraguay River

Paraná River

São Francisco River

Tropic of Capricorn

San Ambrosio Island

San Félix Island

Mount Aconcagua
(22,834 ft. 6960 m)

Salado River

Uruguay River

N
W   E
S

Juan Fernández Islands

RÍO DE LA PLATA

PAMPAS

ATLANTIC OCEAN

GULF OF SAN MATÍAS

Chiloé Island

PATAGONIA

Chonos Archipelago

GULF OF SAN JORGE

Colorado River

Negro River

Cape Tres Puntas

BAHÍA GRANDE

STRAIT OF MAGELLAN

Falkland Islands

South Georgia Islands

Tierra del Fuego

Cape Horn

ELEVATION

Feet	Meters
13,120	4,000
6,560	2,000
1,640	500
656	200
(Sea level) 0	0 (Sea level)
Below sea level	Below sea level

SCALE

0   250   500   750   1,000 Miles

0   250   500   750   1,000 Kilometers

Projection: Azimuthal Equal Area

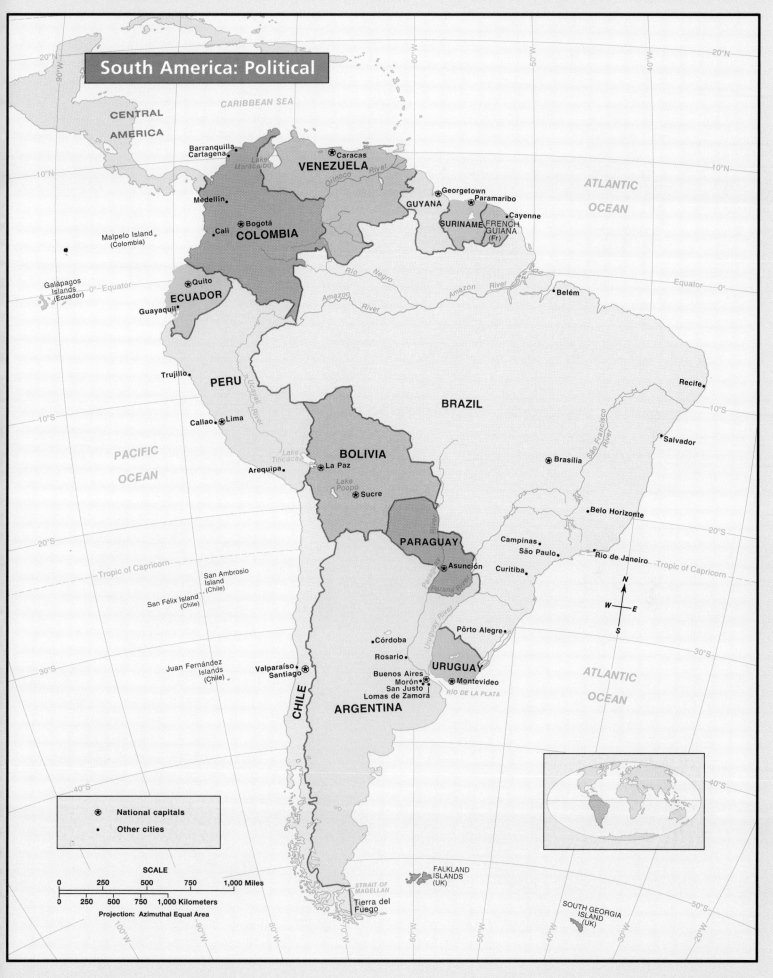

South America: Political

CENTRAL AMERICA

CARIBBEAN SEA

ATLANTIC OCEAN

Barranquilla
Cartagena
Lake Maracaibo
⊛ Caracas
VENEZUELA
Orinoco River
Medellín
⊛ Bogotá
GUYANA
⊛ Georgetown
Paramaribo ⊛
Cali
COLOMBIA
SURINAME
Cayenne
FRENCH GUIANA (Fr)

Malpelo Island (Colombia)

Galápagos Islands (Ecuador)
Equator
⊛ Quito
ECUADOR
Río Negro
Equator 0°
Amazon River
Amazon River
• Belém

Guayaquil

Trujillo
PERU
Ucayali River
Recife
BRAZIL
São Francisco River

Callao ⊛ Lima
10°S

PACIFIC OCEAN
Lake Titicaca
BOLIVIA
⊛ La Paz
• Brasília
Salvador

Arequipa
Lake Poopó
⊛ Sucre
Belo Horizonte

Campinas
São Paulo
PARAGUAY
Curitiba
Rio de Janeiro
Tropic of Capricorn

Tropic of Capricorn
San Ambrosio Island (Chile)
Paraguay River
⊛ Asunción
Paraná River

San Félix Island (Chile)

Juan Fernández Islands (Chile)
Uruguay River
Pôrto Alegre

Córdoba
Rosario
URUGUAY
Valparaíso
Santiago ⊛
Buenos Aires
Morón
San Justo
Lomas de Zamora
⊛ Montevideo
RÍO DE LA PLATA
ATLANTIC OCEAN

CHILE
ARGENTINA

N
W   E
S

⊛ National capitals
• Other cities

FALKLAND ISLANDS (UK)
STRAIT OF MAGELLAN
Tierra del Fuego
SOUTH GEORGIA ISLAND (UK)

SCALE
0   250   500   750   1,000 Miles
0   250   500   750   1,000 Kilometers
Projection: Azimuthal Equal Area

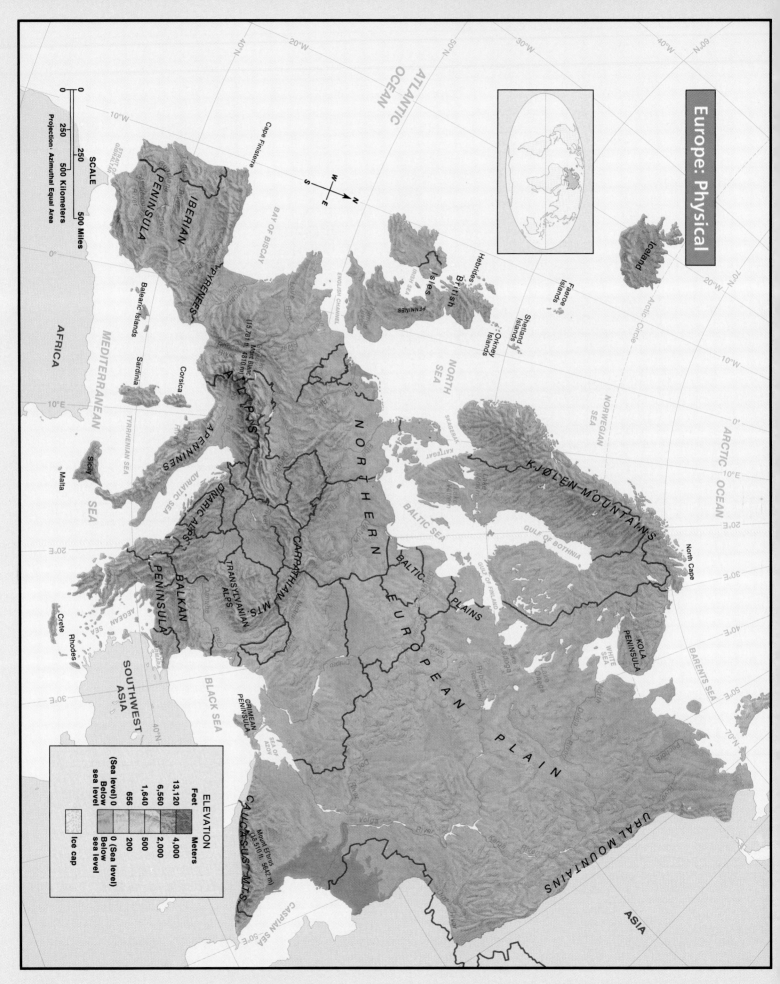

Europe: Physical

SCALE
0
250
250
500 Kilometers
0
250
250
500 Miles
Projection: Azimuthal Equal Area

ELEVATION
Feet   Meters
13,120   4,000
6,560   2,000
1,640   500
656   200
0 (Sea level)   0 (Sea level)
Below   Below
sea level   sea level

Ice cap

ATLANTIC OCEAN

ARCTIC OCEAN

NORWEGIAN SEA

BARENTS SEA

WHITE SEA

NORTH SEA

BALTIC SEA

GULF OF BOTHNIA

GULF OF FINLAND

MEDITERRANEAN SEA

TYRRHENIAN SEA

ADRIATIC SEA

AEGEAN SEA

BLACK SEA

SEA OF AZOV

CASPIAN SEA

BAY OF BISCAY

ENGLISH CHANNEL

IRISH SEA

SKAGERRAK

KATTEGAT

STRAIT OF GIBRALTAR

IBERIAN PENINSULA

PYRENEES

ALPS

APENNINES

DINARIC ALPS

BALKAN PENINSULA

TRANSYLVANIAN ALPS

CARPATHIAN MTS.

NORTHERN EUROPEAN PLAIN

BALTIC PLAINS

KJØLEN MOUNTAINS

URAL MOUNTAINS

CAUCASUS MTS.

CRIMEAN PENINSULA

KOLA PENINSULA

Iceland

Faeroe Islands

Shetland Islands

Orkney Islands

Hebrides

British Isles

PENNINES

Balearic Islands

Sardinia

Corsica

Sicily

Malta

Crete

Rhodes

Cape Finisterre

North Cape

Mont Blanc (15,781 ft. 4810 m)

Mount Elbrus (18,510 ft. 5642 m)

AFRICA

ASIA

SOUTHWEST ASIA

Arctic Circle

Volga River

Don River

Danube River

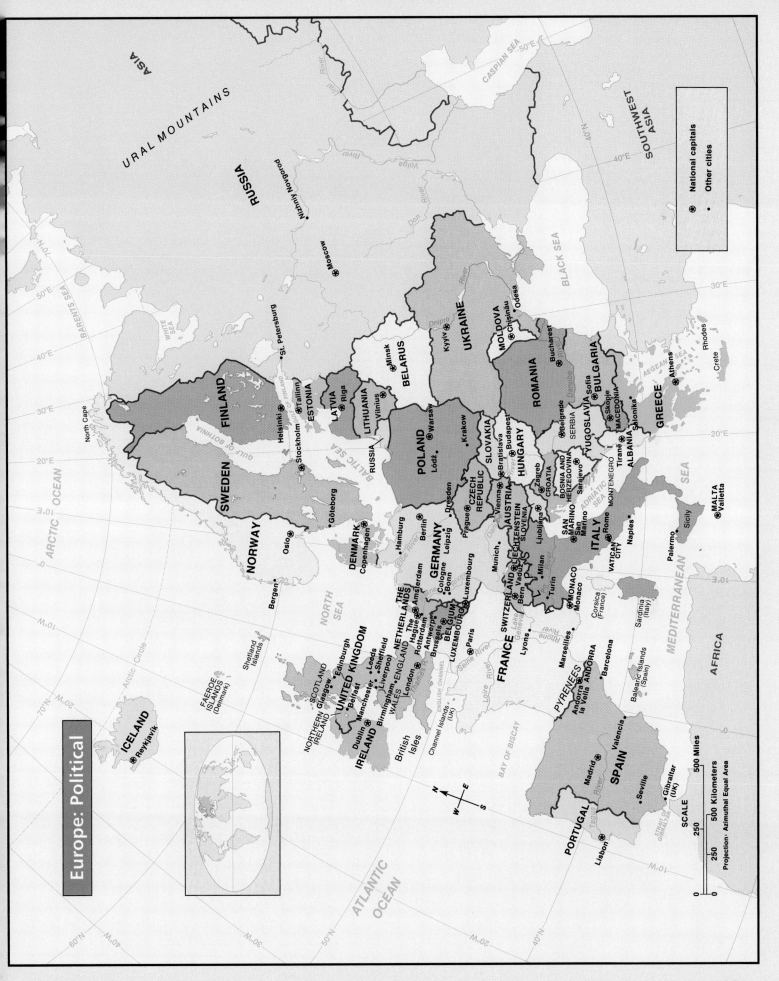

Europe: Political

Legend:
- ⊛ National capitals
- • Other cities

SCALE

500 Miles
250

500 Kilometers
250

Projection: Azimuthal Equal Area

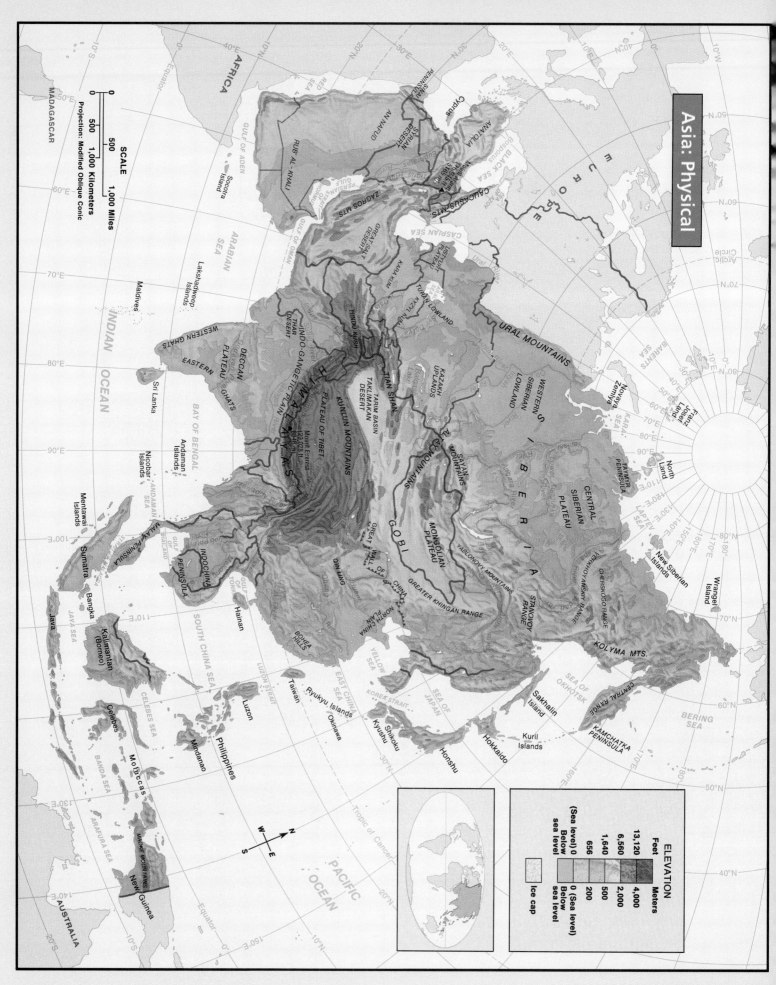

Asia: Physical

SCALE

Projection: Modified Oblique Conic

ELEVATION

Feet	Meters
13,120	4,000
6,560	2,000
1,640	500
656	200
0 (Sea level)	0 (Sea level)
Below sea level	Below sea level

Ice cap

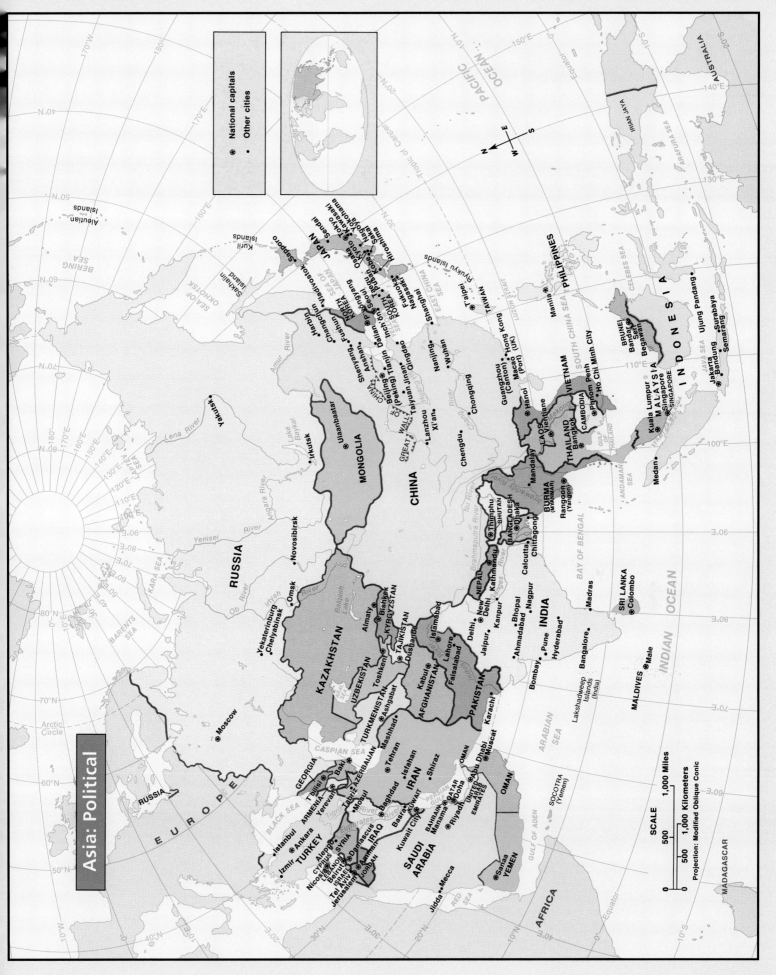

Asia: Political

Legend:
⊛ National capitals
● Other cities

SCALE

1,000 Miles
500

1,000 Kilometers
500

Projection: Modified Oblique Conic

Countries and regions:

RUSSIA
EUROPE
MONGOLIA
CHINA
KAZAKHSTAN
UZBEKISTAN
TURKMENISTAN
KYRGYZSTAN
TAJIKISTAN
AFGHANISTAN
PAKISTAN
INDIA
NEPAL
BHUTAN
BANGLADESH
BURMA (MYANMAR)
THAILAND
LAOS
VIETNAM
CAMBODIA
MALAYSIA
INDONESIA
PHILIPPINES
BRUNEI
SRI LANKA
MALDIVES
TURKEY
GEORGIA
ARMENIA
AZERBAIJAN
SYRIA
LEBANON
ISRAEL
JORDAN
IRAQ
IRAN
SAUDI ARABIA
KUWAIT
BAHRAIN
QATAR
UNITED ARAB EMIRATES
OMAN
YEMEN
CYPRUS
KOREA (NORTH KOREA, SOUTH KOREA)
JAPAN
TAIWAN
AUSTRALIA
IRIAN JAYA
AFRICA
MADAGASCAR

Cities:

Moscow
Yekaterinburg
Chelyabinsk
Omsk
Novosibirsk
Irkutsk
Yakutsk
Vladivostok
Khabarovsk
Ulaanbaatar
Harbin
Changchun
Shenyang
Anshan
Beijing (Peking)
Tianjin
Dalian
Jinan
Qingdao
Taiyuan
Lanzhou
Xi'an
Chengdu
Chongqing
Wuhan
Nanjing
Shanghai
Guangzhou (Canton)
Macao (Port.)
Hong Kong (UK)
T'aipei
Sapporo
Sendai
Tokyo
Yokohama
Kawasaki
Nagoya
Kyoto
Osaka
Kobe
Hiroshima
Fukuoka
Nagasaki
Seoul
Inch'on
Pyongyang
Hanoi
Vientiane
Bangkok
Phnom Penh
Ho Chi Minh City
Kuala Lumpur
Singapore
Bandar Seri Begawan
Manila
Medan
Jakarta
Bandung
Semarang
Surabaya
Ujung Pandang
Rangoon (Yangon)
Mandalay
Thimphu
Dhaka
Chittagong
Kathmandu
Calcutta
New Delhi
Delhi
Jaipur
Kanpur
Bhopal
Nagpur
Ahmadabad
Bombay
Pune
Hyderabad
Bangalore
Madras
Colombo
Male
Islamabad
Lahore
Faisalabad
Kabul
Karachi
Toshkent
Ashgabat
Dushanbe
Bishkek
Almaty
Mashhad
Tehran
Isfahan
Shiraz
Baghdad
Basra
Kuwait
Kuwait City
Manama
Doha
Abu Dhabi
Muscat
Riyadh
Mecca
Jidda
Sanaa
Istanbul
Ankara
Izmir
Nicosia
Aleppo
Damascus
Beirut
Tel Aviv
Jerusalem
Amman
Mosul
Tabriz
Baku
Yerevan
T'bilisi

Water bodies and features:

PACIFIC OCEAN
INDIAN OCEAN
ARCTIC
Arctic Circle
Tropic of Cancer
Equator
BERING SEA
SEA OF OKHOTSK
SEA OF JAPAN
EAST CHINA SEA
SOUTH CHINA SEA
YELLOW SEA
CELEBES SEA
JAVA SEA
ARAFURA SEA
ANDAMAN SEA
BAY OF BENGAL
ARABIAN SEA
GULF OF THAILAND
LUZON STRAIT
RED SEA
GULF OF ADEN
PERSIAN GULF
CASPIAN SEA
BLACK SEA
BARENTS SEA
KARA SEA
LAPTEV SEA
Aral Sea
Lake Baykal
Balqash Lake
Aleutian Islands
Kuril Islands
Sakhalin Island
Ryukyu Islands
Socotra (Yemen)
Lakshadweep Islands (India)
Amur River
Lena River
Yenisei River
Ob River
Irtysh River
Angara River
Huang He (Yellow River)
Chang River
Xi River
Mekong River
Irrawaddy River
Brahmaputra River
Ganges River
Indus River
Nu River
Tigris River
Euphrates River
GREAT WALL

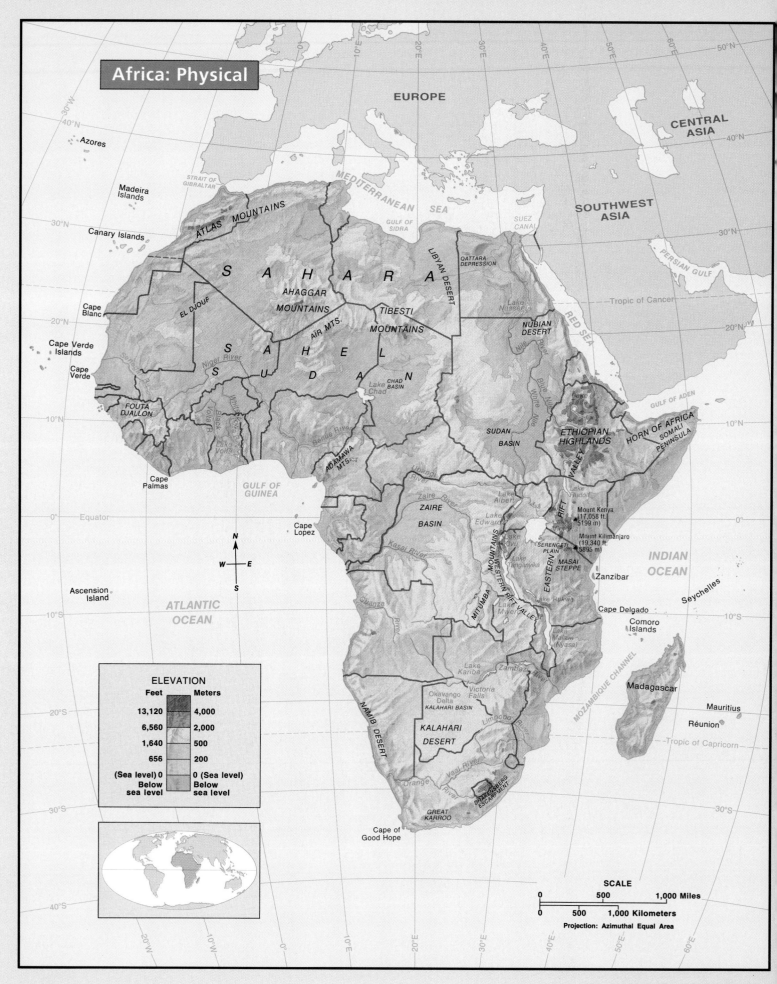

Africa: Physical

EUROPE

CENTRAL ASIA

SOUTHWEST ASIA

Azores

Madeira Islands

STRAIT OF GIBRALTAR

MEDITERRANEAN SEA

GULF OF SIDRA

SUEZ CANAL

PERSIAN GULF

Canary Islands

ATLAS MOUNTAINS

QATTARA DEPRESSION

LIBYAN DESERT

Tropic of Cancer

Cape Blanc

S A H A R A

AHAGGAR MOUNTAINS

AÏR MTS.

TIBESTI MOUNTAINS

NUBIAN DESERT

Lake Nasser

RED SEA

EL DJOUF

Cape Verde Islands

Cape Verde

S A H E L

S U D A N

Niger River

Senegal R.

Lake Chad

CHAD BASIN

Nile River

GULF OF ADEN

FOUTA DJALLON

White Volta

Black Volta

Lake Volta

Benue River

ADAMAWA MTS.

SUDAN BASIN

ETHIOPIAN HIGHLANDS

HORN OF AFRICA

SOMALI PENINSULA

Blue Nile

White Nile

Cape Palmas

GULF OF GUINEA

Ubangi River

ZAIRE BASIN

Zaire River

Kasai River

Lake Albert

Lake Edward

RIFT VALLEY

Lake Rudolf

EASTERN

Mount Kenya (17,058 ft. 5199 m)

Mount Kilimanjaro (19,340 ft. 5895 m)

INDIAN OCEAN

Equator

Cape Lopez

N W E S

Lake Kivu

MOUNTAINS

WESTERN RIFT VALLEY

SERENGETI PLAIN

MASAI STEPPE

Zanzibar

Seychelles

Ascension Island

ATLANTIC OCEAN

MITUMBA

Lake Tanganyika

Lake Rukwa

Cape Delgado

Comoro Islands

Cuanza River

Lake Mweru

Lake Malawi (Nyasa)

MOZAMBIQUE CHANNEL

Madagascar

Mauritius

Réunion

NAMIB DESERT

Okavango Delta

KALAHARI BASIN

Lake Kariba

Victoria Falls

Zambezi River

Limpopo River

Tropic of Capricorn

KALAHARI DESERT

Vaal River

ELEVATION

Feet		Meters
13,120		4,000
6,560		2,000
1,640		500
656		200
(Sea level) 0		0 (Sea level)
Below sea level		Below sea level

DRAKENSBERG ESCARPMENT

Orange River

GREAT KARROO

Cape of Good Hope

SCALE

0   500   1,000 Miles

0   500   1,000 Kilometers

Projection: Azimuthal Equal Area

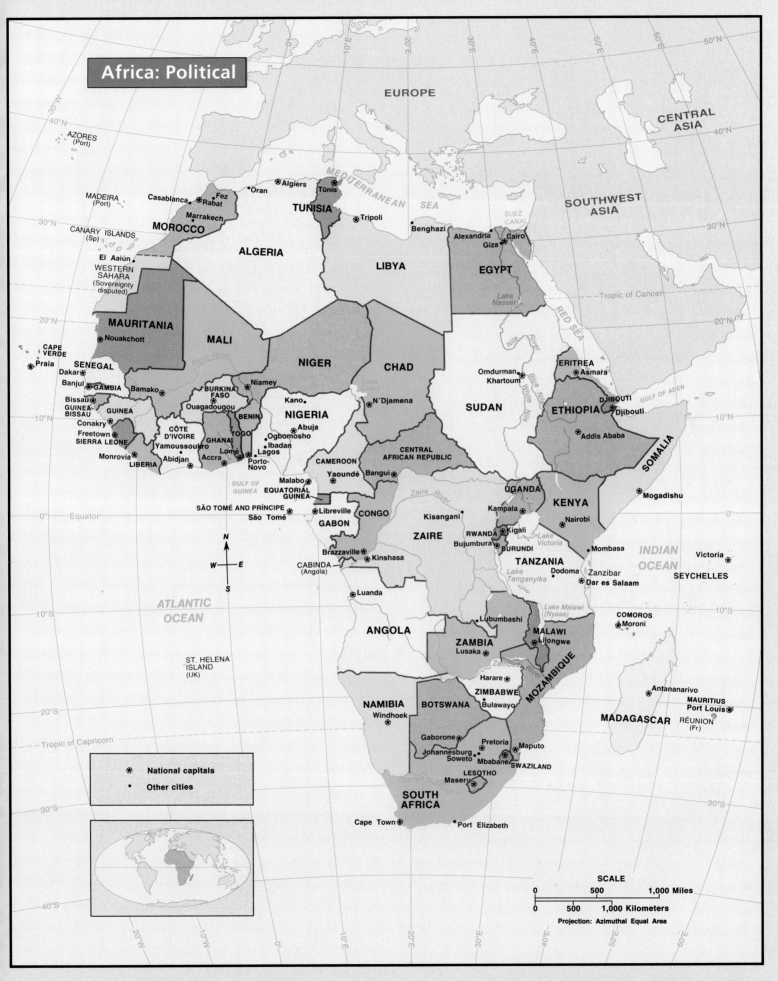

Africa: Political

EUROPE

CENTRAL ASIA

SOUTHWEST ASIA

MEDITERRANEAN SEA

AZORES (Port)

MADEIRA (Port)

CANARY ISLANDS (Sp)

● Oran ⊛ Algiers ⊛ Tūnis

TUNISIA

Casablanca ● Fez ⊛ ⊛ Tripoli
● Rabat
Marrakech ●

MOROCCO

ALGERIA

LIBYA

⊛ Benghazi

Alexandria ● ⊛ Cairo
Giza ●

EGYPT

SUEZ CANAL

El Aaiún ●

WESTERN SAHARA (Sovereignty disputed)

Tropic of Cancer

Lake Nasser

MAURITANIA

⊛ Nouakchott

MALI

NIGER

CHAD

RED SEA

Nile River

CAPE VERDE
⊛ Praia

SENEGAL
Dakar ⊛
Banjul ⊛ ⊛GAMBIA
Bissau ⊛
GUINEA-BISSAU

Bamako ⊛

Niamey ⊛

Kano ●

N'Djamena ●

Omdurman ● ⊛ Khartoum
White Nile
Blue Nile

ERITREA
⊛ Asmara

Lake Chad

SUDAN

DJIBOUTI
⊛ Djibouti

GULF OF ADEN

GUINEA
Conakry ⊛
Freetown ⊛
SIERRA LEONE

BURKINA FASO ⊛
Ouagadougou ⊛
BENIN

NIGERIA
● Abuja
Ogbomosho ●
Ibadan ●

ETHIOPIA
⊛ Addis Ababa

SOMALIA

CÔTE D'IVOIRE
Yamoussoukro ⊛
GHANA ⊛ TOGO
Lomé ⊛
Monrovia ⊛ Abidjan ● Accra ⊛ Porto-Novo
LIBERIA

Lagos ●

CAMEROON
Yaoundé ⊛

CENTRAL AFRICAN REPUBLIC
Bangui ⊛

⊛ Mogadishu

GULF OF GUINEA

Malabo ⊛
EQUATORIAL GUINEA

UGANDA
Kampala ⊛

KENYA
Nairobi ⊛

SÃO TOMÉ AND PRÍNCIPE
São Tomé ●

Libreville ⊛
GABON

CONGO

Kisangani ●

Zaire River

ZAIRE

RWANDA ⊛ Kigali
Bujumbura ⊛
BURUNDI

Lake Victoria

Mombasa ●

Equator

N
W—E
S

Brazzaville ⊛ ● Kinshasa

TANZANIA
Dodoma ⊛ ● Zanzibar
Dar es Salaam

Lake Tanganyika

Victoria ⊛
SEYCHELLES

INDIAN OCEAN

CABINDA (Angola)

⊛ Luanda

ATLANTIC OCEAN

ANGOLA

Lubumbashi ●

Lake Malawi (Nyasa)

COMOROS
⊛ Moroni

ST. HELENA ISLAND (UK)

ZAMBIA
Lusaka ⊛

MALAWI
⊛ Lilongwe

Zambezi River

Harare ⊛
ZIMBABWE
● Bulawayo

MOZAMBIQUE

Antananarivo ●
MADAGASCAR

MAURITIUS
Port Louis ●
RÉUNION (Fr)

Tropic of Capricorn

NAMIBIA
Windhoek ⊛

BOTSWANA

Orange River

⊛ Gaborone
Pretoria ⊛ Maputo ⊛
Johannesburg ●
Soweto ● Mbabane ⊛
SWAZILAND
LESOTHO
⊛ Maseru

SOUTH AFRICA

Cape Town ⊛ ● Port Elizabeth

⊛ **National capitals**
● **Other cities**

SCALE

0 — 500 — 1,000 Miles

0 — 500 — 1,000 Kilometers

Projection: Azimuthal Equal Area

33

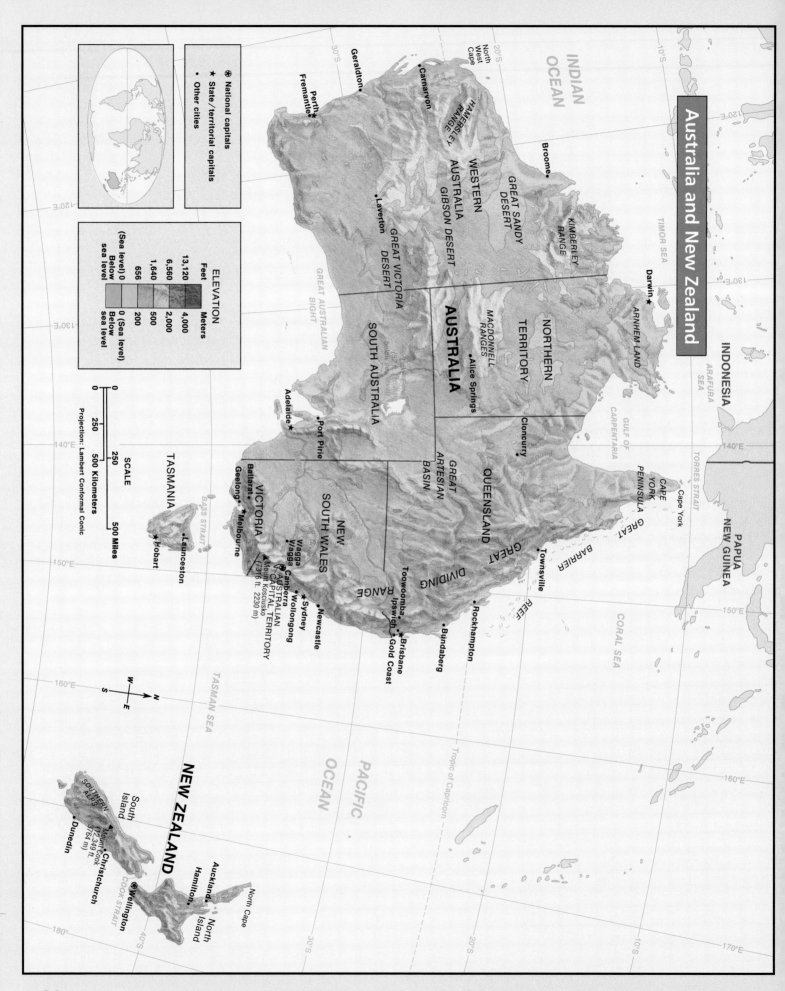

Australia and New Zealand

ELEVATION

Feet	Meters
13,120	4,000
6,560	2,000
1,640	500
656	200
0 (Sea level)	0 (Sea level)
Below sea level	Below sea level

National capitals ⊛
State/territorial capitals ★
Other cities •

SCALE

0   250   500 Kilometers
0   250   500 Miles

Projection: Lambert Conformal Conic

INDIAN OCEAN

North West Cape
Geraldton
Carnarvon
Perth ★
Fremantle
Broome
Laverton

HAMERSLEY RANGE
KIMBERLEY RANGE
GREAT SANDY DESERT
WESTERN AUSTRALIA
GIBSON DESERT
GREAT VICTORIA DESERT

TIMOR SEA
Darwin ★
ARNHEM LAND
NORTHERN TERRITORY
MACDONNELL RANGES
Alice Springs

INDONESIA
ARAFURA SEA
GULF OF CARPENTARIA
CAPE YORK PENINSULA
Cape York
TORRES STRAIT
PAPUA NEW GUINEA

AUSTRALIA

SOUTH AUSTRALIA
GREAT AUSTRALIAN BIGHT
Adelaide ★
Port Pirie

QUEENSLAND
GREAT ARTESIAN BASIN
Cloncurry
Townsville
Rockhampton
Bundaberg
GREAT DIVIDING RANGE
GREAT BARRIER REEF
CORAL SEA

Toowoomba
Ipswich ⊛ Brisbane
Gold Coast

NEW SOUTH WALES
Newcastle ★
Wagga Wagga
Wollongong
Sydney ★
Canberra ⊛
AUSTRALIAN CAPITAL TERRITORY
Mount Kościusko
(7316 ft. 2230 m)

VICTORIA
Ballarat
Geelong
Melbourne ★

TASMANIA
BASS STRAIT
Launceston
Hobart ★

TASMAN SEA

PACIFIC OCEAN

Tropic of Capricorn

NEW ZEALAND

South Island
SOUTHERN ALPS
Mount Cook (12,349 ft. 3764 m)
Dunedin
Christchurch •
Wellington ⊛
COOK STRAIT
North Island
Auckland
Hamilton
North Cape

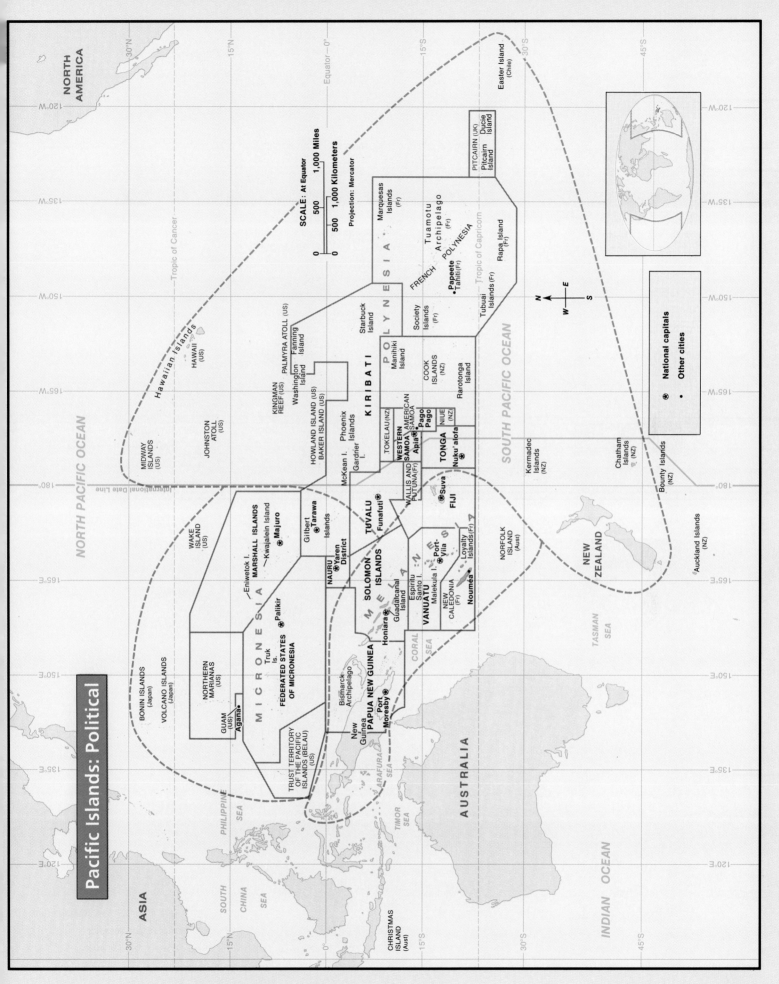

Pacific Islands: Political

NORTH AMERICA

ASIA

AUSTRALIA

NEW ZEALAND

NORTH PACIFIC OCEAN

SOUTH PACIFIC OCEAN

INDIAN OCEAN

SOUTH CHINA SEA

PHILIPPINE SEA

ARAFURA SEA

TIMOR SEA

CORAL SEA

TASMAN SEA

International Date Line

Tropic of Cancer

Tropic of Capricorn

Equator—0°

M I C R O N E S I A

M E L A N E S I A

P O L Y N E S I A

K I R I B A T I

BONIN ISLANDS (Japan)

VOLCANO ISLANDS (Japan)

NORTHERN MARIANAS (US)

GUAM (US) • Agana

TRUST TERRITORY OF THE PACIFIC ISLANDS (BELAU) (US)

Truk Is.

FEDERATED STATES OF MICRONESIA ⊛ Palikir

WAKE ISLAND (US)

— Eniwetok I.

MARSHALL ISLANDS — Kwajalein Island • Majuro

Gilbert Islands • Tarawa

NAURU ⊛ Yaren District

MIDWAY ISLANDS (US)

JOHNSTON ATOLL (US)

Hawaiian Islands

HAWAII (US)

KINGMAN REEF (US)

PALMYRA ATOLL (US)

Washington Island

Fanning Island

HOWLAND ISLAND (US)
BAKER ISLAND (US)

McKean I.
Gardner I.

Phoenix Islands

Starbuck Island

Manihiki Island

Marquesas Islands (Fr)

Tuamotu Archipelago (Fr)

FRENCH POLYNESIA

Society Islands (Fr)

• Papeete
Tahiti (Fr)

Tubuai Islands (Fr)

Rapa Island (Fr)

Easter Island (Chile)

PITCAIRN (UK)
Pitcairn Island
Ducie Island

COOK ISLANDS (NZ)

Rarotonga Island

TOKELAU (NZ)

WESTERN SAMOA Apia ⊛

WALLIS AND FUTUNA (Fr)

AMERICAN SAMOA
Pago Pago

NIUE (NZ)

TONGA
Nuku'alofa ⊛

• Suva
FIJI

TUVALU ⊛
Funafuti

SOLOMON ISLANDS

Bismarck Archipelago

PAPUA NEW GUINEA ⊛
Port Moresby

New Guinea

Guadalcanal Island

Honiara ⊛

Espiritu Santo I.

Malekula I.

VANUATU

Port-Vila •

Loyalty Islands (Fr)

NEW CALEDONIA

Nouméa •

NORFOLK ISLAND (Aust)

Kermadec Islands (NZ)

Chatham Islands (NZ)

Bounty Islands (NZ)

Auckland Islands (NZ)

CHRISTMAS ISLAND (Aust)

SCALE: At Equator

0   500   1,000 Miles

0   500   1,000 Kilometers

Projection: Mercator

N
W—E
S

⊛ National capitals

• Other cities

35

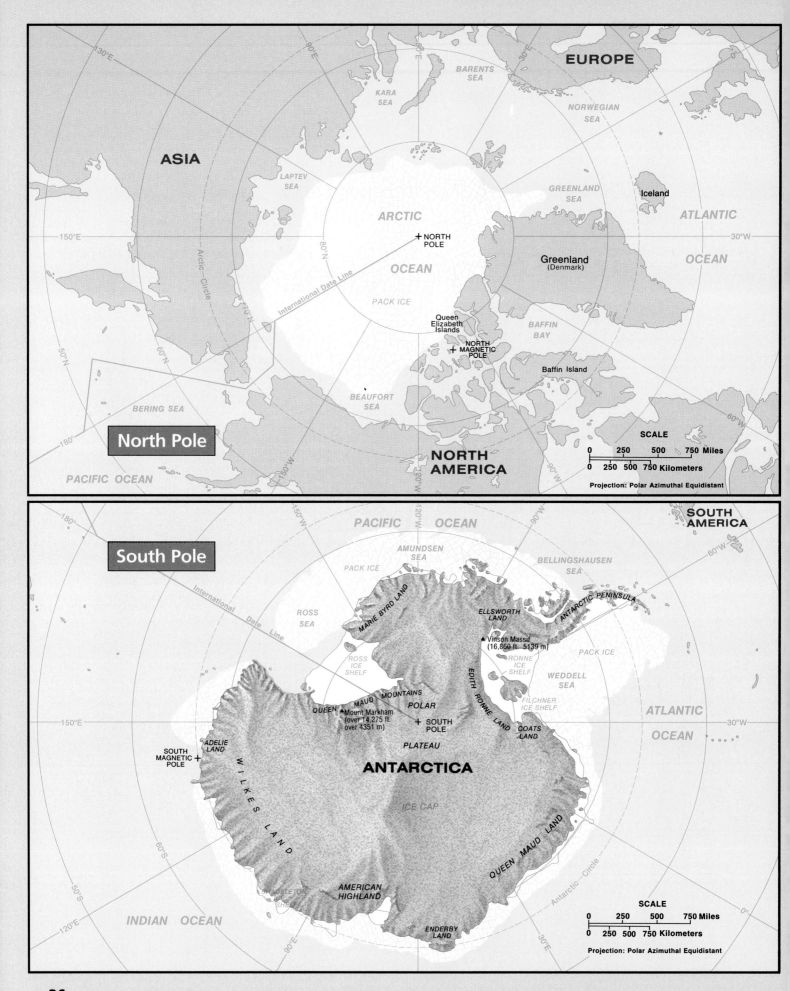

North Pole

ASIA

130°E

KARA
SEA

LAPTEV
SEA

150°E

80°N

Arctic Circle

International Date Line

70°N

BERING
SEA

180°

150°W

PACIFIC OCEAN

90°E

ARCTIC

OCEAN

PACK ICE

+ NORTH
POLE

Queen
Elizabeth
Islands

+ NORTH
MAGNETIC
POLE

BEAUFORT
SEA

120°W

90°W

NORTH
AMERICA

30°E

EUROPE

BARENTS
SEA

NORWEGIAN
SEA

GREENLAND
SEA

Iceland

ATLANTIC

30°W

Greenland
(Denmark)

OCEAN

BAFFIN
BAY

Baffin Island

60°W

SCALE

0   250   500   750 Miles

0 250 500 750 Kilometers

Projection: Polar Azimuthal Equidistant

South Pole

180°

International Date Line

150°E

120°E

INDIAN OCEAN

90°W

PACIFIC   OCEAN

120°W

AMUNDSEN
SEA

PACK ICE

ROSS
SEA

MARIE BYRD LAND

ROSS
ICE
SHELF

QUEEN   MAUD   MOUNTAINS

Mount Markham
(over 14,275 ft.
over 4351 m)

POLAR

+ SOUTH
POLE

PLATEAU

ANTARCTICA

ADELIE
LAND

SOUTH
MAGNETIC
POLE +

W I L K E S   L A N D

ICE CAP

SHACKLETON
ICE SHELF

AMERICAN
HIGHLAND

ENDERBY
LAND

ELLSWORTH
LAND

▲ Vinson Massif
(16,860 ft. 5139 m)

RONNE
ICE
SHELF

EDITH RONNE LAND

FILCHNER
ICE
SHELF

COATS
LAND

90°E

QUEEN MAUD LAND

Antarctic Circle

60°S

50°S

60°E

30°E

SOUTH
AMERICA

60°W

ANTARCTIC PENINSULA

BELLINGSHAUSEN
SEA

PACK ICE

WEDDELL
SEA

ATLANTIC

30°W

OCEAN

0°

SCALE

0   250   500   750 Miles

0 250 500 750 Kilometers

Projection: Polar Azimuthal Equidistant

36

WORLD GEOGRAPHY

World Religions

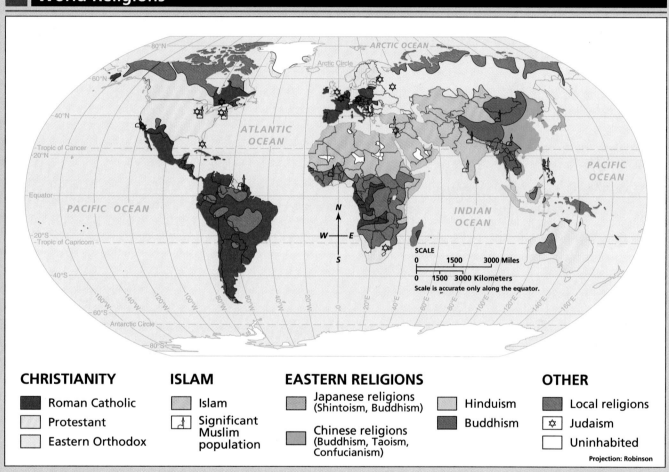

CHRISTIANITY
- Roman Catholic
- Protestant
- Eastern Orthodox

ISLAM
- Islam
- Significant Muslim population

EASTERN RELIGIONS
- Japanese religions (Shintoism, Buddhism)
- Chinese religions (Buddhism, Taoism, Confucianism)
- Hinduism
- Buddhism

OTHER
- Local religions
- Judaism
- Uninhabited

Projection: Robinson

The World's Climate Regions

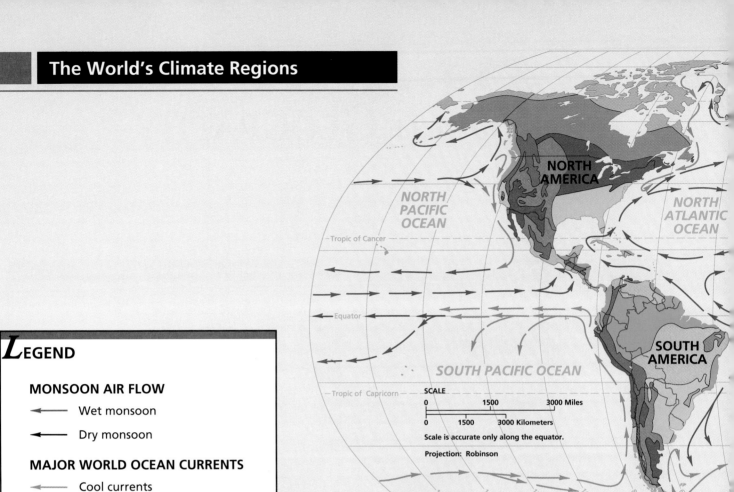

	Climate	Geographic Distribution	Major Weather Patterns	Vegetation
Low Latitudes	**HUMID TROPICAL**	along Equator; particularly equatorial South America, Zaire Basin in Africa, Southeast Asia	warm and rainy year-round, with rain totaling anywhere from 65 to more than 450 in. (165–1,143 cm) annually; typical temperatures are 90°–95°F (32°–35°C) during the day and 65°–70°F (18°–21°C) at night	tropical rain forest
	TROPICAL SAVANNA	between humid tropics and deserts; tropical regions of Africa, South and Central America, southern and Southeast Asia, Australia	warm all year; distinct rainy and dry seasons; precipitation during the summer of at least 20 in. (51 cm) and in some locations exceeding 150 in. (380 cm); summer temperatures average 90°F (32°C) during the day and 70°F (21°C) at night; typical winter temperatures are 75°–80°F (24°–27°C) during the day and 55°–60°F (13°–16°C) at night	tropical grassland with scattered trees
Dry/Semiarid	**DESERT**	centered along 30° latitude; some middle-latitude deserts in interior of large continents and along western coasts; particularly Saharan Africa, southwest Asia, central and western Australia, southwestern North America	arid; precipitation of less than 10 in. (25 cm) annually; sunny and hot in the tropics and sunny with great temperature ranges in middle latitudes; typical summer temperatures for lower-latitude deserts are 110°–115°F (43°–46°C) during the day and 60°–65°F (16°–18°C) at night, while winter temperatures average 80°F (27°C) during the day and 45°F (7°C) at night; in middle latitudes, the hottest month averages 70°F (24°C)	sparse drought-resistant plants; many barren, rocky, or sandy areas
	STEPPE	generally bordering deserts and interiors of large continents; particularly northern and southern Africa, interior western North America, central and interior Asia and Australia, southern South America	semiarid; about 10–20 in. (25–51 cm) of precipitation annually; hot summers and cooler winters with wide temperature ranges similar to desert temperatures	grassland; few trees
Middle Latitudes	**MEDITERRANEAN**	west coasts in middle latitudes; particularly southern Europe, part of southwest Asia, north-western Africa, California, southwestern Australia, central Chile, southwestern South Africa	dry, sunny, warm summers and mild, wetter winters; precipitation averages 15–20 in. (38–51 cm) annually; typical temperatures are 75°–80°F (24°–27°C) on summer days; the average winter temperature is 50°F (10°C)	scrub woodland and grassland
	HUMID SUBTROPICAL	east coasts in middle latitudes; particularly southeastern United States, eastern Asia, central southern Europe, southeastern parts of South America, South Africa, and Australia	hot, humid summers and mild, humid winters; precipitation year-round; coastal areas are in the paths of hurricanes and typhoons; precipitation averages 40 in. (102 cm) annually; typical temperatures are 75°–90°F (24°–32°C) in summer and 45°–50°F (7°–10°C) in winter	mixed forest

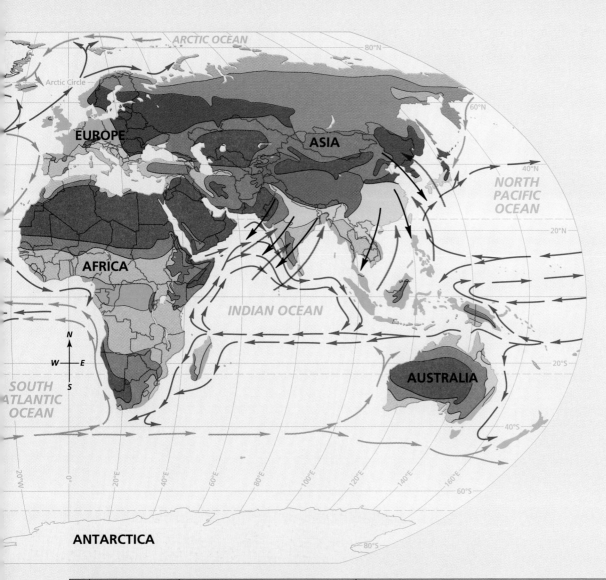

	Climate	Geographic Distribution	Major Weather Patterns	Vegetation
Middle Latitudes	**MARINE WEST COAST**	west coasts in upper-middle latitudes; particularly northwestern Europe and North America, southwestern South America, central southern South Africa, southeastern Australia, New Zealand	cloudy, mild summers and cool, rainy winters; strong ocean influence; precipitation averages 20–60 in. (51–152 cm) annually, with some coastal mountains receiving more than 200 in. (508 cm); average temperature in hottest month usually is between 60°F and 70°F (16°–21°C); average temperature in coolest month usually is above 32°F (0°C)	temperate evergreen forest
	HUMID CONTINENTAL	east coasts and interiors of upper-middle-latitude continents; particularly northeastern North America, northern and eastern Europe, northeastern Asia	four distinct seasons; long, cold winters and short, warm summers; precipitation amounts vary, usually 20–50 in. or more (51–127 cm) annually; average summer temperature is 75°F (24°C); average winter temperature is below freezing	mixed forest
High Latitudes	**SUBARCTIC**	higher latitudes of interior and east coasts of continents; particularly northern parts of North America, Europe, and Asia	extremes of temperature; long, cold winters and short, warm summers; low precipitation amounts all year; precipitation averages 5–15 in. (13–38 cm) in summer; temperatures in warmest month average 60°F (16°C), but can warm to 90°F (32°C); winter temperatures average below 0°F (–18°C)	northern evergreen forest
	TUNDRA	high-latitude coasts; particularly far northern parts of North America, Europe, and Asia, Antarctic Peninsula, subantarctic islands	cold all year; very long, cold winters and very short, cool summers; low precipitation amounts; precipitation average is 5–15 in. (13–38 cm) annually; warmest month averages 40°F (4°C); coolest month averages a little below 0°F (–18°C)	moss, lichens, low shrubs; permafrost bogs in summer
	ICE CAP	polar regions; particularly Antarctica, Greenland, Arctic Basin islands	freezing cold; snow and ice year-round; precipitation averages less than 10 in. (25 cm) annually; average temperatures in warmest month are not higher than freezing	no vegetation
	HIGHLAND	high mountain regions, particularly western parts of North and South America, eastern parts of Asia and Africa, southern and central Europe and Asia	greatly varied temperatures and precipitation amounts over short distances as elevation changes	forest to tundra vegetation, depending on altitude

The World's Basic Biomes

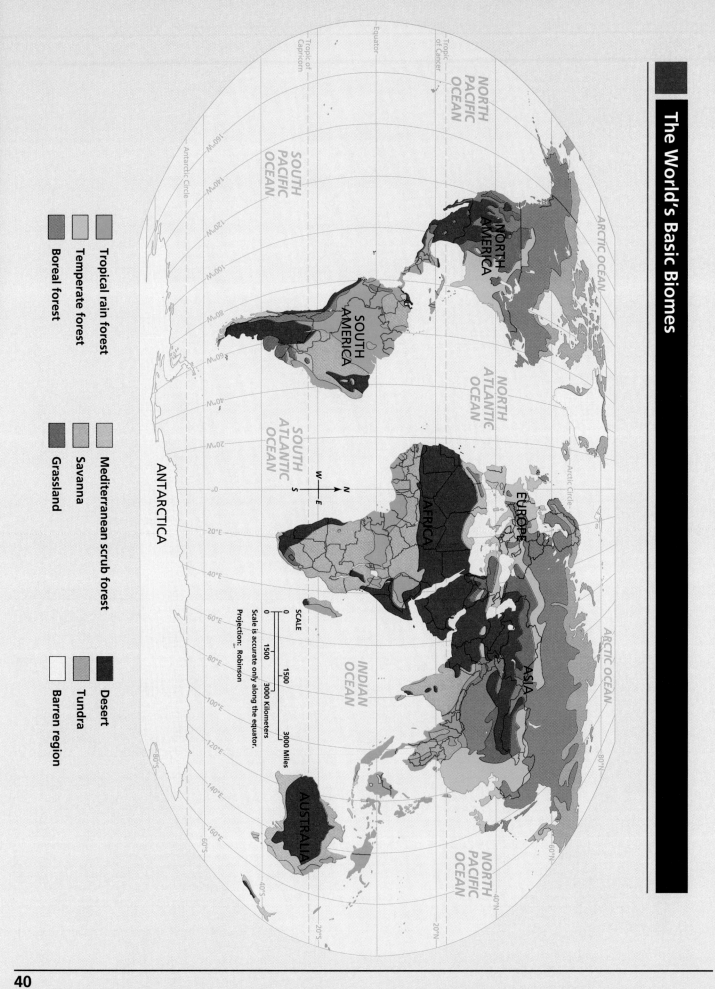

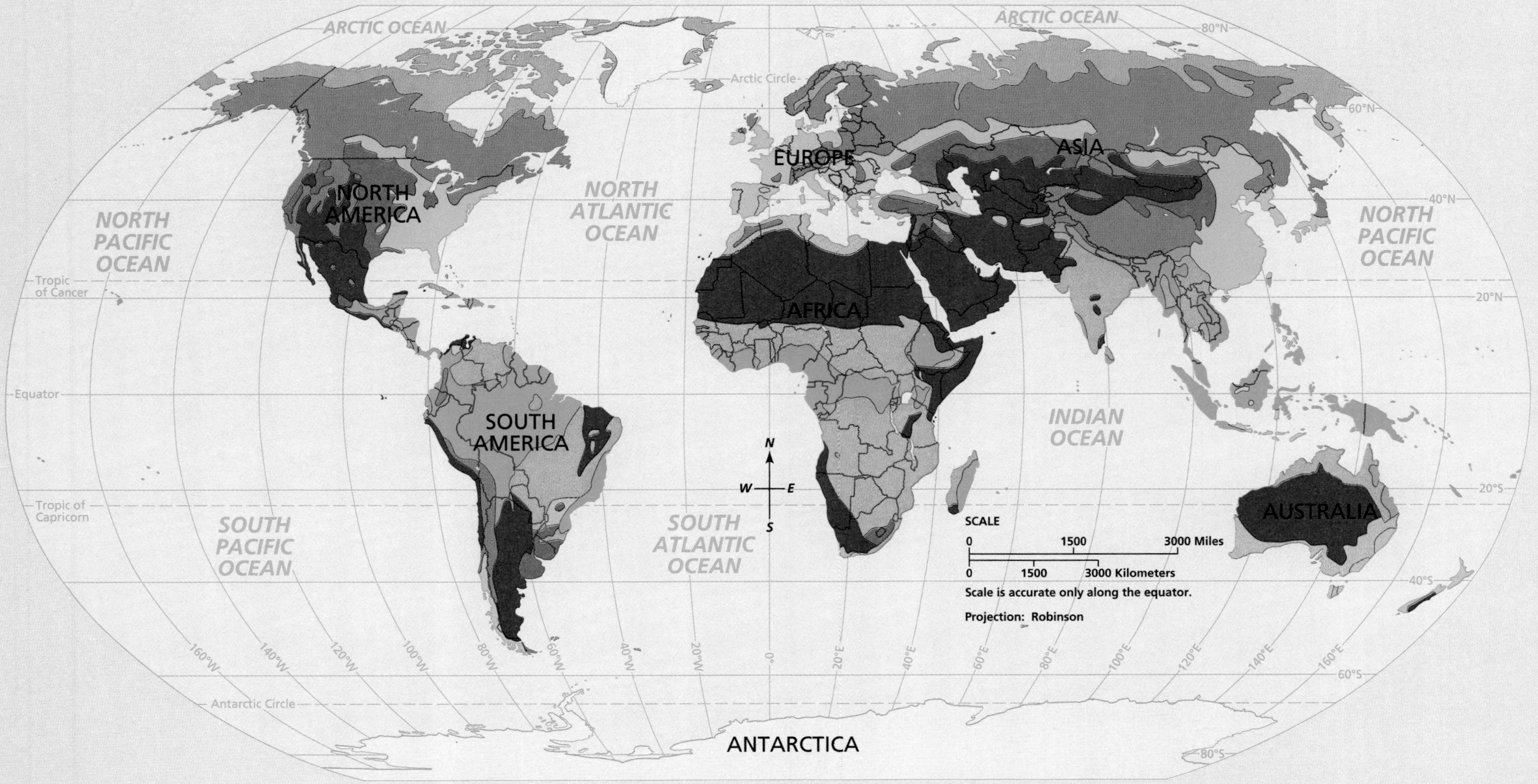
ARCTIC OCEAN
NORTH AMERICA
NORTH PACIFIC OCEAN
NORTH ATLANTIC OCEAN
EUROPE
ASIA
AFRICA
SOUTH AMERICA
SOUTH PACIFIC OCEAN
SOUTH ATLANTIC OCEAN
INDIAN OCEAN
AUSTRALIA
ANTARCTICA
Arctic Circle
Tropic of Cancer
Equator
Tropic of Capricorn
Antarctic Circle
80°N
60°N
40°N
20°N
20°S
40°S
60°S
80°S
160°W
140°W
120°W
100°W
80°W
60°W
40°W
20°W
0°
20°E
40°E
60°E
80°E
100°E
120°E
140°E
160°E
N
S
E
W
SCALE
0
1500
3000 Miles
0
1500
3000 Kilometers
Scale is accurate only along the equator.
Projection: Robinson

- Tropical rain forest
- Temperate forest
- Boreal forest
- Mediterranean scrub forest
- Savanna
- Grassland
- Desert
- Tundra
- Barren region

THE UNITED STATES AND CANADA

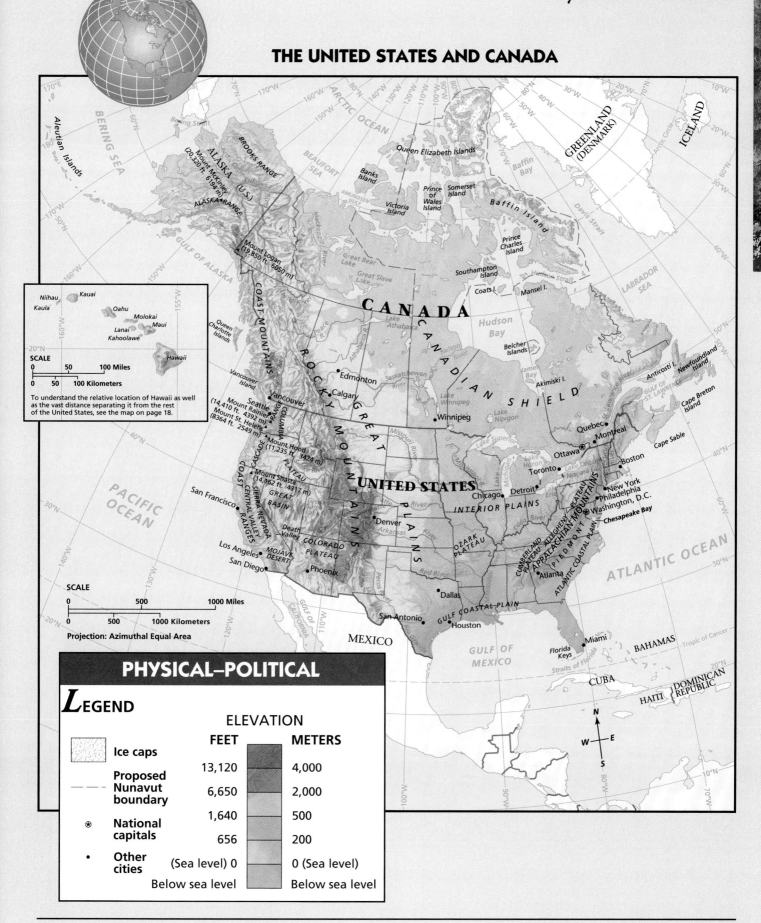

SCALE

0   50   100 Miles

0   50   100 Kilometers

To understand the relative location of Hawaii as well as the vast distance separating it from the rest of the United States, see the map on page 18.

SCALE

0   500   1000 Miles

0   500   1000 Kilometers

Projection: Azimuthal Equal Area

PHYSICAL–POLITICAL

*L*EGEND

	ELEVATION	
	FEET	METERS
Ice caps	13,120	4,000
Proposed Nunavut boundary	6,650	2,000
⊛ National capitals	1,640	500
• Other cities	656	200
	(Sea level) 0	0 (Sea level)
	Below sea level	Below sea level

Labels on map:

Aleutian Islands, BERING SEA, ARCTIC OCEAN, BROOKS RANGE, ALASKA (U.S.), Mount McKinley (20,320 ft. 6194 m), ALASKA RANGE, BEAUFORT SEA, AMUNDSEN GULF, Banks Island, Victoria Island, Prince of Wales Island, Somerset Island, Baffin Island, Baffin Bay, GREENLAND (DENMARK), ICELAND, Arctic Circle

GULF OF ALASKA, Mount Logan (19,850 ft. 6050 m), Mackenzie River, Great Bear Lake, Great Slave Lake, Southampton Island, Prince Charles Island, Hudson Strait, Coats I., Mansel I., LABRADOR SEA, Davis Strait

COAST MOUNTAINS, Queen Charlotte Islands, Peace R., Athabasca River, CANADA, CANADIAN SHIELD, Lake Athabasca, Nelson River, Hudson Bay, Belcher Islands, James Bay, Akimiski I., Anticosti I., Newfoundland Island, Cape Breton Island, GULF OF ST. LAWRENCE

Vancouver Island, Vancouver, Seattle, Mount Rainier (14,410 ft. 4392 m), Mount St. Helens (8364 ft. 2549 m), Mount Hood (11,235 ft. 3424 m), Edmonton, Calgary, ROCKY MOUNTAINS, Saskatchewan River, Lake Winnipeg, Lake Nipigon, Winnipeg, Lake Superior, Missouri River, Lake Huron, Lake Michigan, Quebec, Montreal, Ottawa, Toronto, Lake Erie, Lake Ontario, St. Lawrence River, Niagara Falls, Cape Sable, Boston, Cape Sable

COLUMBIA PLATEAU, Mount Shasta (14,162 ft. 4317 m), CASCADE RANGE, GREAT BASIN, UNITED STATES, GREAT PLAINS, INTERIOR PLAINS, Chicago, Detroit, New York, Philadelphia, Washington, D.C., Chesapeake Bay, ALLEGHENY PLATEAU, APPALACHIAN MOUNTAINS, PIEDMONT

San Francisco, COAST RANGES, CENTRAL VALLEY, SIERRA NEVADA, Death Valley, COLORADO PLATEAU, Denver, Arkansas River, Ohio River, OZARK PLATEAU, CUMBERLAND PLATEAU, Atlanta, ATLANTIC COASTAL PLAIN, ATLANTIC OCEAN

Los Angeles, San Diego, MOJAVE DESERT, Phoenix, Pecos River, Red River, Dallas, San Antonio, Houston, GULF COASTAL PLAIN, GULF OF MEXICO, MEXICO, GULF OF CALIFORNIA

PACIFIC OCEAN, Florida Keys, Miami, Straits of Florida, BAHAMAS, Tropic of Cancer, CUBA, HAITI, DOMINICAN REPUBLIC

Niihau, Kauai, Kaula, Oahu, Molokai, Maui, Lanai, Kahoolawe, Hawaii

Thematic Maps

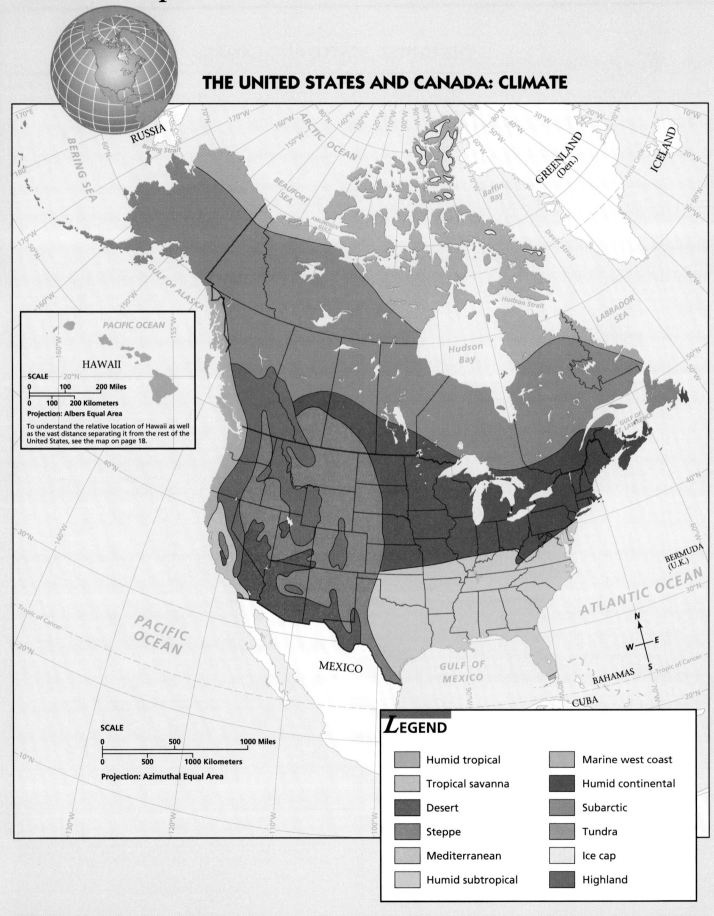

THE UNITED STATES AND CANADA: CLIMATE

HAWAII

SCALE

0   100   200 Miles

0   100   200 Kilometers

Projection: Albers Equal Area

To understand the relative location of Hawaii as well as the vast distance separating it from the rest of the United States, see the map on page 18.

SCALE

0   500   1000 Miles

0   500   1000 Kilometers

Projection: Azimuthal Equal Area

LEGEND

Humid tropical	Marine west coast
Tropical savanna	Humid continental
Desert	Subarctic
Steppe	Tundra
Mediterranean	Ice cap
Humid subtropical	Highland

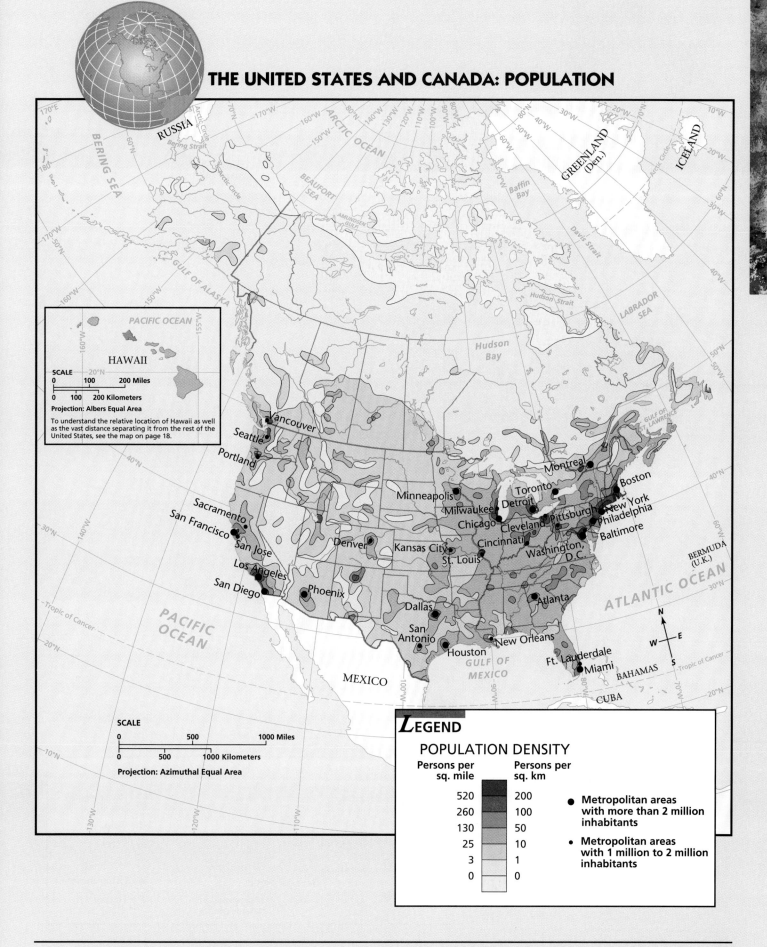

RUSSIA

BERING SEA

Bering Strait

Arctic Circle

ARCTIC OCEAN

BEAUFORT SEA

AMUNDSEN GULF

GULF OF ALASKA

GREENLAND (Den.)

ICELAND

Baffin Bay

Davis Strait

LABRADOR SEA

Hudson Strait

Hudson Bay

GULF OF ST. LAWRENCE

HAWAII

SCALE
0   100   200 Miles
0   100   200 Kilometers

Projection: Albers Equal Area

PACIFIC OCEAN

To understand the relative location of Hawaii as well as the vast distance separating it from the rest of the United States, see the map on page 18.

Vancouver
Seattle
Portland
Sacramento
San Francisco
San Jose
Los Angeles
San Diego
Phoenix
Denver
Kansas City
St. Louis
Minneapolis
Milwaukee
Chicago
Detroit
Cincinnati
Cleveland
Pittsburgh
Toronto
Montreal
Boston
New York
Philadelphia
Baltimore
Washington, D.C.
Dallas
San Antonio
Houston
New Orleans
Atlanta
Ft. Lauderdale
Miami

MEXICO

GULF OF MEXICO

BAHAMAS
CUBA

PACIFIC OCEAN

ATLANTIC OCEAN

BERMUDA (U.K.)

Tropic of Cancer

SCALE
0   500   1000 Miles
0   500   1000 Kilometers

Projection: Azimuthal Equal Area

LEGEND

POPULATION DENSITY

Persons per sq. mile	Persons per sq. km
520	200
260	100
130	50
25	10
3	1
0	0

● Metropolitan areas with more than 2 million inhabitants

• Metropolitan areas with 1 million to 2 million inhabitants

THE UNITED STATES AND CANADA: ECONOMY

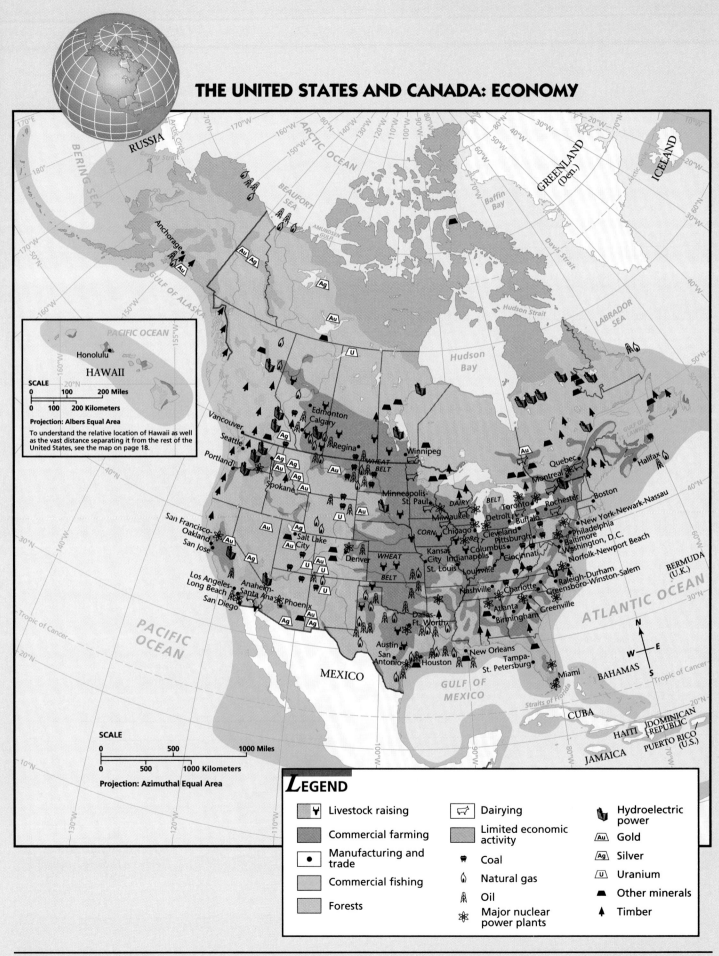

HAWAII

SCALE
0   100   200 Miles
0   100   200 Kilometers

Projection: Albers Equal Area

To understand the relative location of Hawaii as well as the vast distance separating it from the rest of the United States, see the map on page 18.

SCALE
0   500   1000 Miles
0   500   1000 Kilometers

Projection: Azimuthal Equal Area

LEGEND

Livestock raising	Dairying
Commercial farming	Limited economic activity
Manufacturing and trade	Coal
Commercial fishing	Natural gas
Forests	Oil
	Major nuclear power plants
Hydroelectric power	
Au Gold	
Ag Silver	
U Uranium	
Other minerals	
Timber	

MIDDLE AND SOUTH AMERICA

UNITED STATES

BERMUDA (U.K.)

ATLANTIC OCEAN

Tropic of Cancer

Tropic of Cancer

GULF OF MEXICO

Baja California

GULF OF CALIFORNIA

SIERRA MADRE OCCIDENTAL

SIERRA MADRE ORIENTAL

Rio Grande

Guadalajara • **MEXICO**
⊛ Mexico City

Yucatán Peninsula

BAHAMAS

Nassau ⊛

Havana ⊛

Greater Antilles

CUBA

CAYMAN ISLANDS (U.K.)

HAITI **DOMINICAN REPUBLIC**
Port-au-Prince ⊛ ⊛ Santo Domingo

BELIZE
⊛ Belmopan

JAMAICA
Kingston

Hispaniola

PUERTO RICO (U.S.)

ANTIGUA AND BARBUDA
DOMINICA
ST. LUCIA
ST. KITTS AND NEVIS
ST. VINCENT AND THE GRENADINES
BARBADOS
GRENADA
TRINIDAD AND TOBAGO
Port-of-Spain

Lesser Antilles

GULF OF HONDURAS

Guatemala City ⊛
GUATEMALA **HONDURAS**
San Salvador ⊛ Tegucigalpa
EL SALVADOR **NICARAGUA**
⊛ Managua
Lake Nicaragua

COSTA RICA
San José ⊛

CARIBBEAN SEA

Panama Canal

Panama City ⊛

Caracas ⊛

VENEZUELA

LLANOS

Orinoco River

Angel Falls

GUYANA
Georgetown ⊛
Paramaribo ⊛

SURINAME FRENCH GUIANA (Fr.)

PANAMA
Isthmus of Panama

⊛ Bogotá

COLOMBIA

Quito ⊛
ECUADOR

GALÁPAGOS ISLANDS (Ecuador)

Equator

ANDES MOUNTAINS

A M A Z O N

B A S I N

Rio Negro

Amazon River

GUIANA HIGHLANDS

Equator

PACIFIC OCEAN

PERU

Lima ⊛

N
W E
S

B R A Z I L

São Francisco River

BRAZILIAN HIGHLANDS

Brasília ⊛

⊛ La Paz
BOLIVIA
⊛ Sucre

BRAZILIAN PLATEAU

Paraná River

CHACO

PARAGUAY
Asunción ⊛

Rio de Janeiro •
São Paulo •

Iguaçu Falls

Peruvian (Humboldt) Current

ATACAMA DESERT

Tropic of Capricorn

CHILE

Mount Aconcagua (22,834 ft. 6960 m)

Paraguay River

ANDES MOUNTAINS

PAMPAS

Santiago ⊛

URUGUAY

Buenos Aires ⊛ ⊛ Montevideo

Rio de la Plata

ATLANTIC OCEAN

Tropic of Capricorn

ARGENTINA

PATAGONIA

FALKLAND ISLANDS (U.K.)

Tierra del Fuego

Cape Horn

SOUTH GEORGIA (U.K.)

PHYSICAL–POLITICAL

LEGEND

ELEVATION

FEET		METERS
13,120		4,000
6,560		2,000
1,640		500
656		200
(Sea level) 0		0 (Sea level)
Below sea level		Below sea level

⊛ **National capitals**

• **Other cities**

SCALE

0   500   1000 Miles

0   500   1000 Kilometers

Projection: Azimuthal Equal Area

Thematic Maps

MIDDLE AND SOUTH AMERICA: CLIMATE

UNITED STATES

ATLANTIC OCEAN

GULF OF MEXICO

GULF OF HONDURAS

CARIBBEAN SEA

PACIFIC OCEAN

ATLANTIC OCEAN

Rio de la Plata

SCALE

0   500   1000 Miles

0   500   1000 Kilometers

Projection: Azimuthal Equal Area

*L*EGEND

- Humid tropical
- Tropical savanna
- Desert
- Steppe
- Mediterranean
- Humid subtropical
- Marine west coast
- Subarctic
- Highland

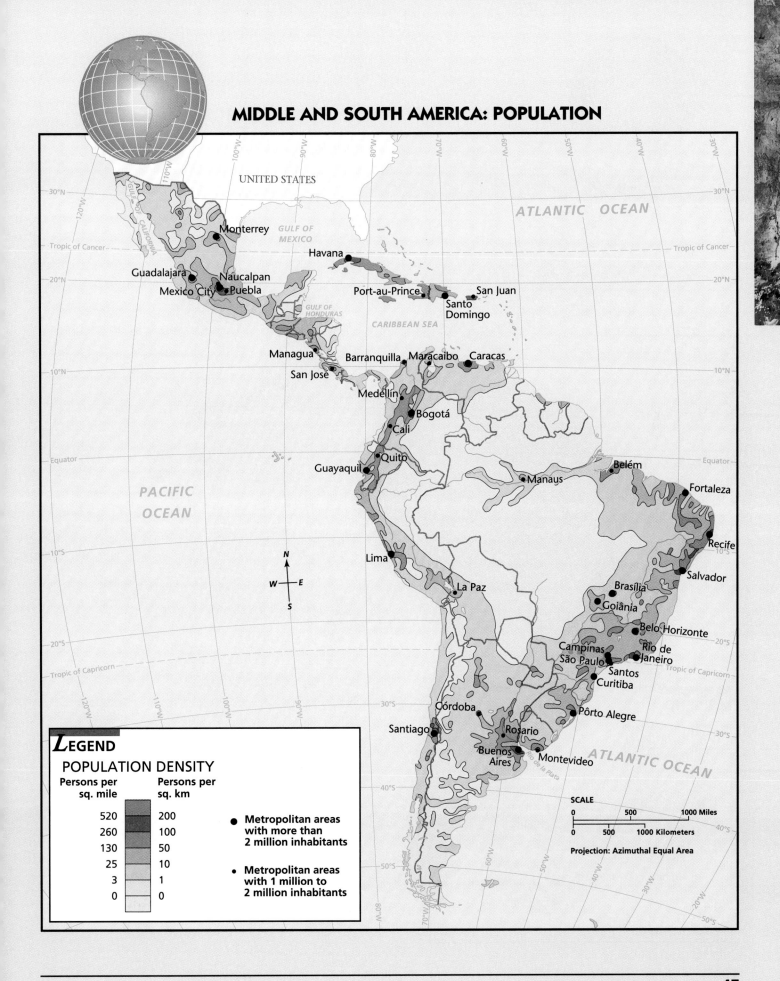

MIDDLE AND SOUTH AMERICA: POPULATION

UNITED STATES

ATLANTIC OCEAN

Tropic of Cancer

GULF OF MEXICO

Monterrey

Havana

Guadalajara

Naucalpan

Mexico City   Puebla

GULF OF HONDURAS

Port-au-Prince

San Juan

Santo Domingo

CARIBBEAN SEA

Managua

Barranquilla   Maracaibo   Caracas

San José

Medellín

Bogotá

Cali

Equator

Quito

Guayaquil

PACIFIC OCEAN

Manaus

Belém

Equator

Fortaleza

Lima

Recife

N
W   E
S

La Paz

Salvador

Brasília

Goiânia

Belo Horizonte

Campinas   Rio de Janeiro

São Paulo

Santos

Curitiba

Córdoba

Pôrto Alegre

Santiago

Rosario

Buenos Aires   Montevideo

Rio de la Plata

ATLANTIC OCEAN

LEGEND

POPULATION DENSITY

Persons per sq. mile	Persons per sq. km
520	200
260	100
130	50
25	10
3	1
0	0

● Metropolitan areas with more than 2 million inhabitants

• Metropolitan areas with 1 million to 2 million inhabitants

SCALE

0   500   1000 Miles

0   500   1000 Kilometers

Projection: Azimuthal Equal Area

MIDDLE AND SOUTH AMERICA: ECONOMY

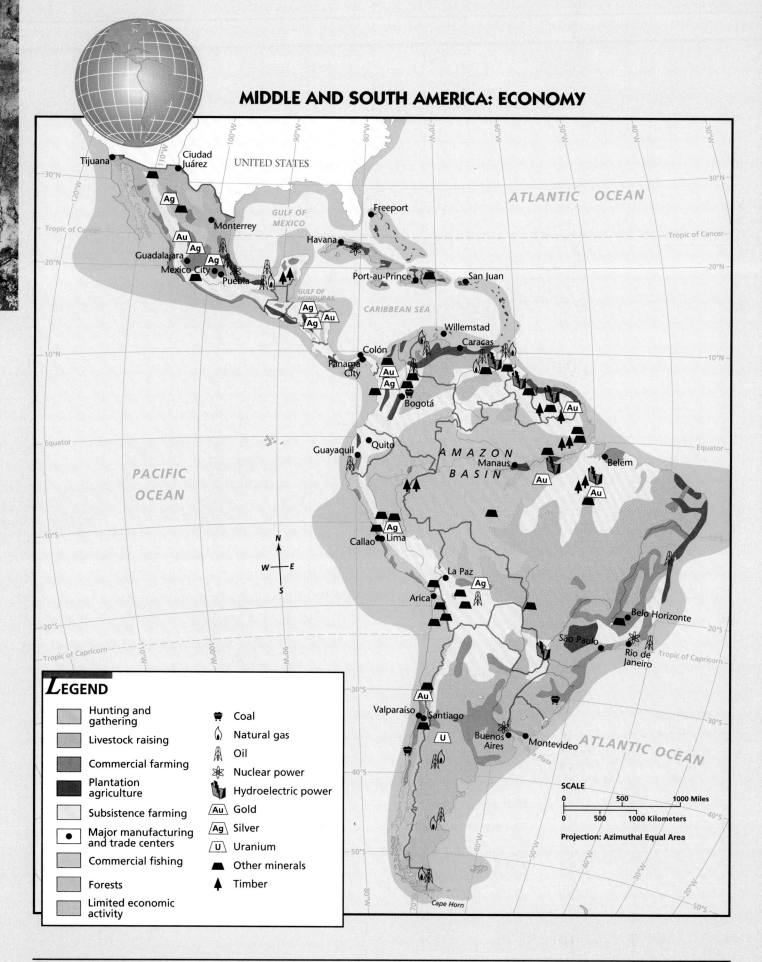

UNITED STATES

ATLANTIC OCEAN

Tijuana

Ciudad Juárez

Ag

Monterrey

GULF OF MEXICO

Freeport

Tropic of Cancer

Tropic of Cancer

Au
Ag

Guadalajara

Ag

Mexico City

Puebla

Havana

Port-au-Prince

San Juan

GULF OF HONDURAS

Ag **Au**

Ag

CARIBBEAN SEA

Willemstad

Caracas

Colón

Panama City

Au
Ag

Bogotá

Au

Guayaquil

Quito

Equator

A M A Z O N

B A S I N

Manaus

Belém

Au

Au

PACIFIC OCEAN

Callao

Ag

Lima

La Paz

Ag

Arica

Belo Horizonte

São Paulo

Rio de Janeiro

Tropic of Capricorn

Tropic of Capricorn

Au

Valparaíso

Santiago

Buenos Aires

U

Montevideo

ATLANTIC OCEAN

La Plata

SCALE

0   500   1000 Miles

0   500   1000 Kilometers

Projection: Azimuthal Equal Area

Cape Horn

N
W   E
S

LEGEND

Hunting and gathering	⛏ Coal
Livestock raising	🔥 Natural gas
Commercial farming	Oil
Plantation agriculture	✳ Nuclear power
Subsistence farming	Hydroelectric power
Major manufacturing and trade centers	**Au** Gold
Commercial fishing	**Ag** Silver
Forests	**U** Uranium
Limited economic activity	◣ Other minerals
	▲ Timber

48

AFRICA

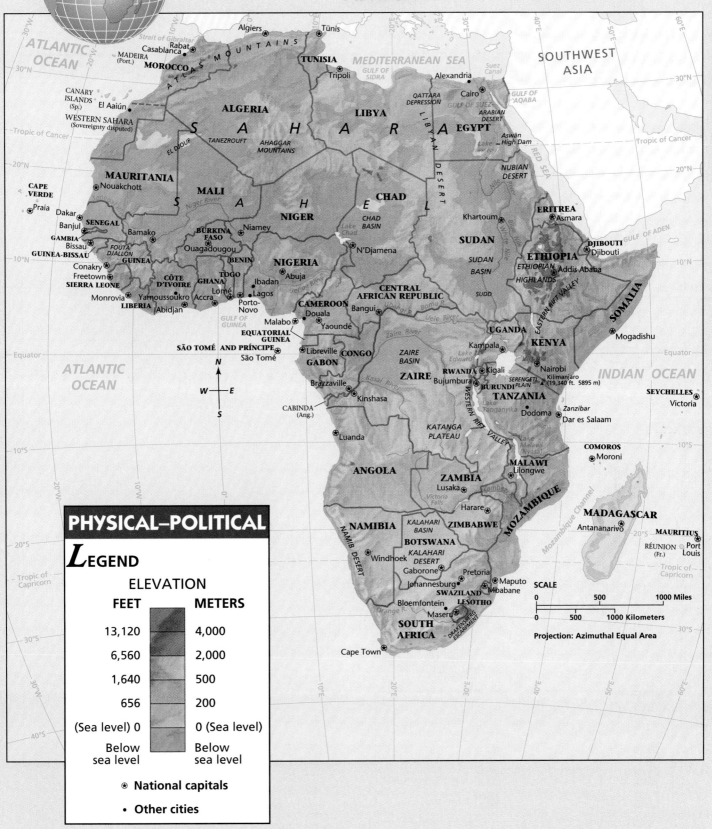

ATLANTIC OCEAN

Algiers
Tūnis
Strait of Gibraltar
Rabat
Casablanca
MADEIRA (Port.)
MOROCCO
ATLAS MOUNTAINS
TUNISIA
Tripoli
MEDITERRANEAN SEA
GULF OF SIDRA
Alexandria
Suez Canal
SOUTHWEST ASIA

CANARY ISLANDS (Sp.)
El Aaiún
WESTERN SAHARA (Sovereignty disputed)
ALGERIA
TANEZROUFT
AHAGGAR MOUNTAINS
LIBYA
QATTARA DEPRESSION
Cairo
GULF OF SUEZ
ARABIAN DESERT
EGYPT
GULF OF AQABA

S A H A R A

EL DJOUF
LIBYAN DESERT
Aswān High Dam
Lake Nasser
Nile River
NUBIAN DESERT
RED SEA

MAURITANIA
Nouakchott
MALI
Niger River
S A H E L
NIGER
CHAD
CHAD BASIN
Lake Chad
Khartoum
SUDAN
SUDAN BASIN
White Nile
Blue Nile
ERITREA
Asmara
GULF OF ADEN
DJIBOUTI
Djibouti

CAPE VERDE
Praia
Dakar
Banjul
SENEGAL
GAMBIA
Bissau
GUINEA-BISSAU
Conakry
Freetown
SIERRA LEONE
Monrovia
LIBERIA
Bamako
BURKINA FASO
Ouagadougou
FOUTA DJALLON
GUINEA
BENIN
TOGO
GHANA
CÔTE D'IVOIRE
Yamoussoukro
Accra
Lomé
Abidjan
Niamey
NIGERIA
Ibadan
Abuja
Lagos
Porto-Novo
N'Djamena
CENTRAL AFRICAN REPUBLIC
Bangui
SUDD
ETHIOPIA
ETHIOPIAN HIGHLANDS
Addis Ababa
SOMALIA

GULF OF GUINEA
Malabo
EQUATORIAL GUINEA
SÃO TOMÉ AND PRÍNCIPE
São Tomé
Libreville
GABON
CONGO
Douala
Yaoundé
CAMEROON
Benue River
Uele River
Ubangi River
Bomu
Zaire River
ZAIRE BASIN
Kasai River
UGANDA
Kampala
Lake Edward
KENYA
Nairobi
Mogadishu
EASTERN RIFT VALLEY
SERENGETI PLAIN
Kilimanjaro (19,340 ft. 5895 m)

ATLANTIC OCEAN
N
W E
S
Equator
INDIAN OCEAN
Equator

CABINDA (Ang.)
Brazzaville
Kinshasa
ZAIRE
RWANDA
Kigali
BURUNDI
Bujumbura
Lake Tanganyika
TANZANIA
Dodoma
Zanzibar
Dar es Salaam
WESTERN RIFT VALLEY
SEYCHELLES
Victoria

Luanda
KATANGA PLATEAU
Lake Malawi (Nyasa)
COMOROS
Moroni

ANGOLA
ZAMBIA
Lusaka
Victoria Falls
Zambezi
MALAWI
Lilongwe
Harare
MADAGASCAR
Antananarivo
MAURITIUS
RÉUNION (Fr.)
Port Louis

NAMIBIA
KALAHARI BASIN
ZIMBABWE
MOZAMBIQUE
Mozambique Channel

NAMIB DESERT
BOTSWANA
KALAHARI DESERT
Windhoek
Gaborone
Pretoria
Johannesburg
SWAZILAND
Maputo
Mbabane
Bloemfontein
LESOTHO
Maseru
DRAKENSBERG ESCARPMENT
Orange R.
Cape Town
SOUTH AFRICA

Tropic of Cancer
Tropic of Cancer
Tropic of Capricorn
Tropic of Capricorn

PHYSICAL–POLITICAL

*L*EGEND

ELEVATION

FEET		METERS
13,120		4,000
6,560		2,000
1,640		500
656		200
(Sea level) 0		0 (Sea level)
Below sea level		Below sea level

⊛ **National capitals**

• **Other cities**

SCALE

0	500	1000 Miles
0	500	1000 Kilometers

Projection: Azimuthal Equal Area

Thematic Maps

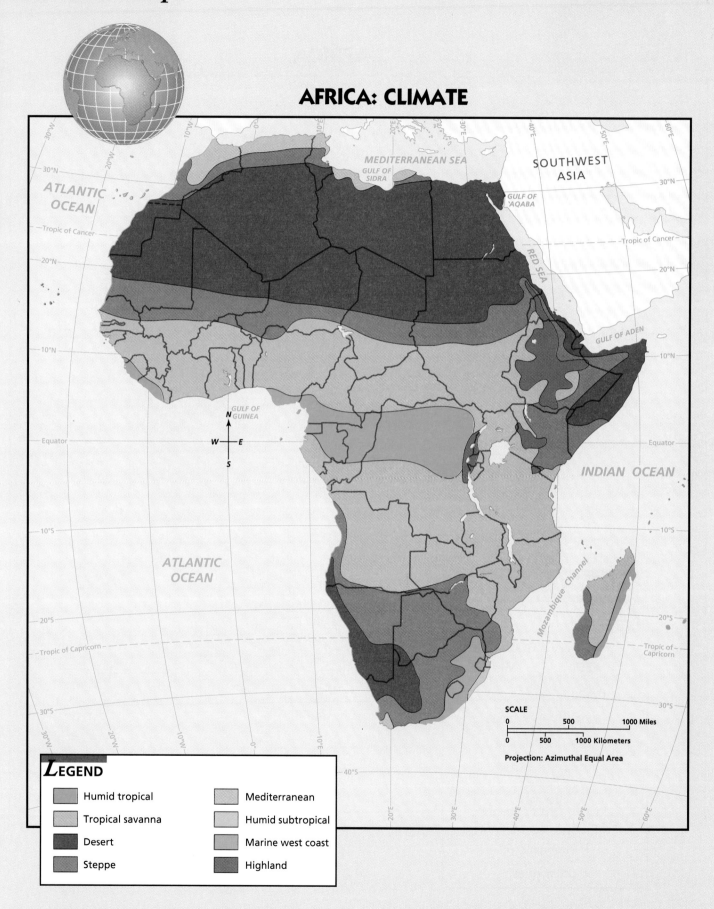

AFRICA: CLIMATE

ATLANTIC OCEAN

MEDITERRANEAN SEA

GULF OF SIDRA

SOUTHWEST ASIA

GULF OF 'AQABA

Tropic of Cancer

RED SEA

GULF OF ADEN

GULF OF GUINEA

Equator

INDIAN OCEAN

ATLANTIC OCEAN

Mozambique Channel

Tropic of Capricorn

SCALE

| 0 | 500 | 1000 Miles |
| 0 | 500 | 1000 Kilometers |

Projection: Azimuthal Equal Area

LEGEND

- Humid tropical
- Tropical savanna
- Desert
- Steppe
- Mediterranean
- Humid subtropical
- Marine west coast
- Highland

AFRICA: POPULATION

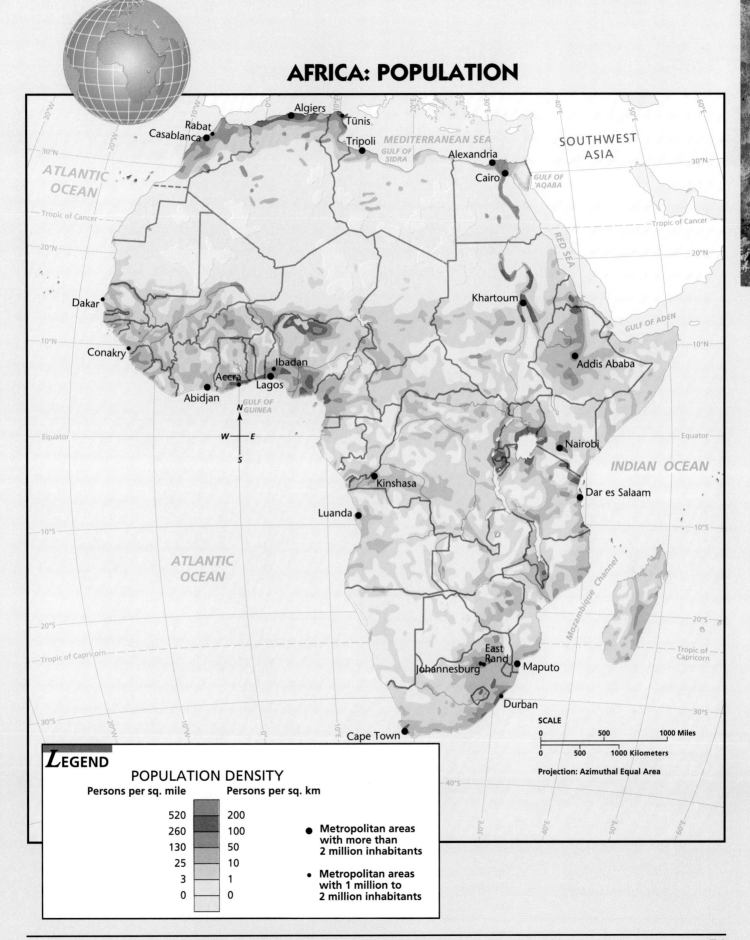

ATLANTIC OCEAN

MEDITERRANEAN SEA

GULF OF SIDRA

SOUTHWEST ASIA

GULF OF AQABA

RED SEA

GULF OF ADEN

Rabat
Casablanca
Algiers
Tūnis
Tripoli
Alexandria
Cairo

Tropic of Cancer

Dakar
Khartoum

Conakry
Addis Ababa

Accra
Ibadan
Abidjan
Lagos
GULF OF GUINEA

N
W E
S

Equator

Nairobi

INDIAN OCEAN

Kinshasa
Dar es Salaam

Luanda

ATLANTIC OCEAN

Mozambique Channel

Tropic of Capricorn

East Rand
Johannesburg
Maputo
Durban

Cape Town

SCALE
0   500   1000 Miles
0   500   1000 Kilometers

Projection: Azimuthal Equal Area

LEGEND

POPULATION DENSITY

Persons per sq. mile	Persons per sq. km
520	200
260	100
130	50
25	10
3	1
0	0

● Metropolitan areas with more than 2 million inhabitants

• Metropolitan areas with 1 million to 2 million inhabitants

AFRICA: ECONOMY

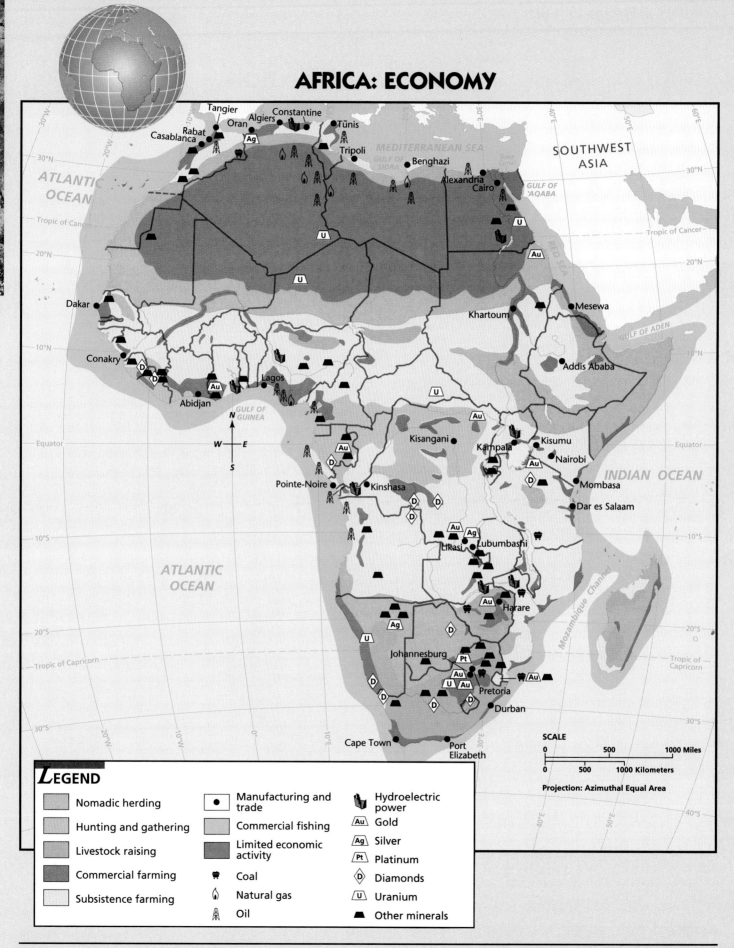

ATLANTIC OCEAN

MEDITERRANEAN SEA

SOUTHWEST ASIA

Tangier
Constantine
Algiers
Oran
Rabat
Casablanca
Tūnis
Tripoli
Benghazi
Alexandria
Cairo
GULF OF SIDRA
GULF OF AQABA

Tropic of Cancer

Dakar
Khartoum
Mesewa
GULF OF ADEN

Conakry
Addis Ababa

Lagos
Abidjan
GULF OF GUINEA

N
W   E
S

Equator

Kisangani
Kisumu
Kampala
Nairobi
INDIAN OCEAN
Mombasa

Pointe-Noire
Kinshasa
Dar es Salaam

ATLANTIC OCEAN

Likasi
Lubumbashi

Harare

Johannesburg
Pretoria
Durban

MOZAMBIQUE CHANNEL

Tropic of Capricorn

Cape Town
Port Elizabeth

SCALE

| 0 | 500 | 1000 Miles |
| 0 | 500 | 1000 Kilometers |

Projection: Azimuthal Equal Area

LEGEND

- Nomadic herding
- Hunting and gathering
- Livestock raising
- Commercial farming
- Subsistence farming
- Manufacturing and trade
- Commercial fishing
- Limited economic activity
- Coal
- Natural gas
- Oil
- Hydroelectric power
- Au Gold
- Ag Silver
- Pt Platinum
- D Diamonds
- U Uranium
- Other minerals

EUROPE

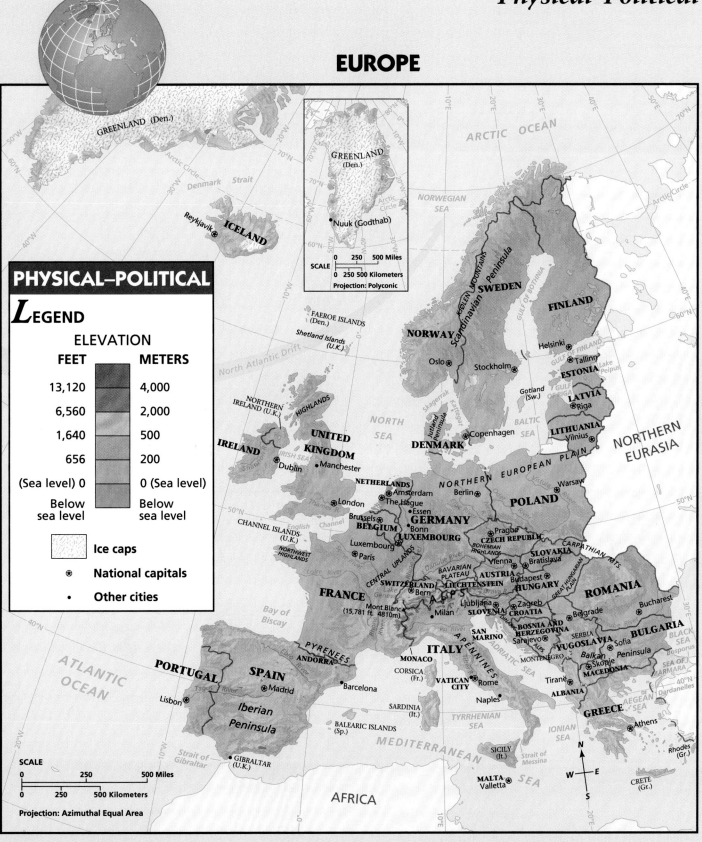

GREENLAND (Den.)

GREENLAND
(Den.)

• Nuuk (Godthab)

SCALE
0   250   500 Miles
0   250 500 Kilometers
Projection: Polyconic

ARCTIC OCEAN

NORWEGIAN SEA

Reykjavik ⊛ ICELAND

FAEROE ISLANDS
(Den.)

Shetland Islands
(U.K.)

North Atlantic Drift

PHYSICAL–POLITICAL

*L*EGEND

ELEVATION

FEET		METERS
13,120		4,000
6,560		2,000
1,640		500
656		200
(Sea level) 0		0 (Sea level)
Below sea level		Below sea level

Ice caps

⊛ National capitals

• Other cities

KÖLEN MOUNTAINS

Scandinavian Peninsula

SWEDEN

FINLAND

NORWAY

Helsinki ⊛
GULF OF FINLAND

Oslo ⊛
Stockholm ⊛   Tallinn ⊛
ESTONIA   Lake Peipus

Gotland
(Sw.)   GULF OF RIGA

LATVIA
⊛ Riga

GULF OF BOTHNIA

NORTHERN
IRELAND (U.K.)   HIGHLANDS

UNITED
KINGDOM

IRELAND
IRISH SEA

Shannon
⊛ Dublin   • Manchester

NETHERLANDS
⊛ Amsterdam
• The Hague   Berlin ⊛

• London

Thames

CHANNEL ISLANDS
(U.K.)

English Channel

Brussels ⊛
BELGIUM   • Essen
LUXEMBOURG
Luxembourg ⊛
Bonn ⊛   GERMANY

NORTHWEST
HIGHLANDS

⊛ Paris

NORTH
SEA

Jutland Peninsula

Skagerrak   Kattegat

DENMARK
• Copenhagen

BALTIC
SEA

LITHUANIA
⊛ Vilnius

NORTHERN EUROPEAN PLAIN

Vistula

Warsaw ⊛

POLAND

Prague ⊛
CZECH REPUBLIC
BOHEMIAN
HIGHLANDS

Vienna ⊛

SLOVAKIA
⊛ Bratislava

CARPATHIAN MTS.

NORTHERN
EURASIA

FRANCE

CENTRAL UPLANDS

Loire River

Seine

BAVARIAN
PLATEAU

SWITZERLAND
⊛ Bern

Lake Geneva

Danube River

A L P S

LIECHTENSTEIN

AUSTRIA

Budapest ⊛   HUNGARY

GREAT HUNGARIAN PLAIN

Drava River

Ljubljana ⊛   Zagreb ⊛

Mont Blanc
(15,781 ft. 4810m)   • Milan   SLOVENIA   CROATIA

Bay of
Biscay

Po River

DINARIC ALPS

ADRIATIC SEA

APENNINES

ROMANIA

Bucharest ⊛

Belgrade ⊛

BOSNIA AND
HERZEGOVINA
Sarajevo ⊛   SERBIA

YUGOSLAVIA   Sofia ⊛   BULGARIA

BLACK
SEA

Bosporus

SAN
MARINO

MONTENEGRO

Balkan Peninsula

Skopje ⊛
MACEDONIA

SEA OF
MARMARA

PYRENEES

ANDORRA ⊛

MONACO

CORSICA
(Fr.)

ITALY

VATICAN
CITY   Rome ⊛

Tiber

Tirane ⊛
ALBANIA

Dardanelles

PORTUGAL   SPAIN

Tagus River

⊛ Madrid   • Barcelona   • Naples

GREECE
⊛ Athens

AEGEAN
SEA

ATLANTIC
OCEAN

Lisbon ⊛

Ebro River

Iberian
Peninsula

SARDINIA
(It.)

BALEARIC ISLANDS
(Sp.)

TYRRHENIAN
SEA

MEDITERRANEAN

IONIAN
SEA

Rhodes
(Gr.)

SCALE
0   250   500 Miles
0   250   500 Kilometers
Projection: Azimuthal Equal Area

Strait of
Gibraltar
• GIBRALTAR
(U.K.)

SICILY
(It.)   Strait of
Messina

MALTA
Valletta ⊛   SEA

N
W   E
S

CRETE
(Gr.)

AFRICA

Thematic Maps

EUROPE

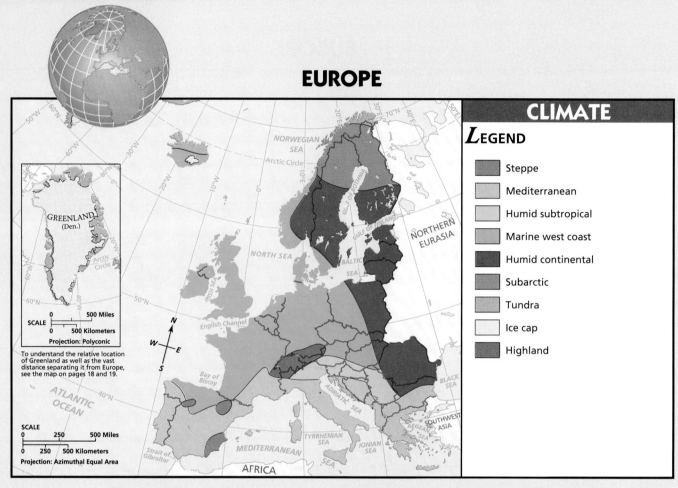

CLIMATE

LEGEND

- Steppe
- Mediterranean
- Humid subtropical
- Marine west coast
- Humid continental
- Subarctic
- Tundra
- Ice cap
- Highland

GREENLAND
(Den.)

SCALE
0 — 500 Miles
0 — 500 Kilometers
Projection: Polyconic

To understand the relative location of Greenland as well as the vast distance separating it from Europe, see the map on pages 18 and 19.

SCALE
0 — 250 — 500 Miles
0 — 250 — 500 Kilometers
Projection: Azimuthal Equal Area

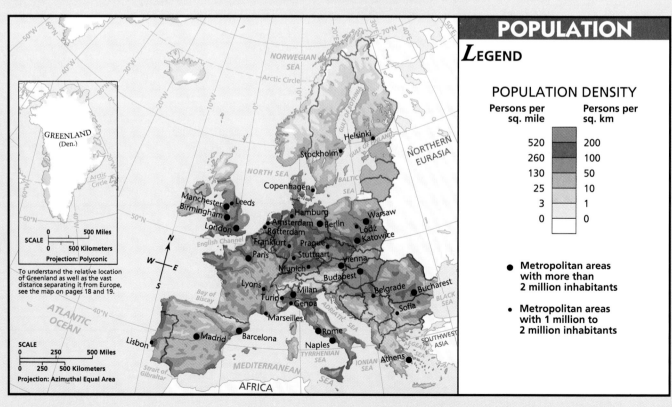

POPULATION

LEGEND

POPULATION DENSITY

Persons per sq. mile	Persons per sq. km
520	200
260	100
130	50
25	10
3	1
0	0

● Metropolitan areas with more than 2 million inhabitants

• Metropolitan areas with 1 million to 2 million inhabitants

GREENLAND
(Den.)

SCALE
0 — 500 Miles
0 — 500 Kilometers
Projection: Polyconic

To understand the relative location of Greenland as well as the vast distance separating it from Europe, see the map on pages 18 and 19.

SCALE
0 — 250 — 500 Miles
0 — 250 — 500 Kilometers
Projection: Azimuthal Equal Area

EUROPE

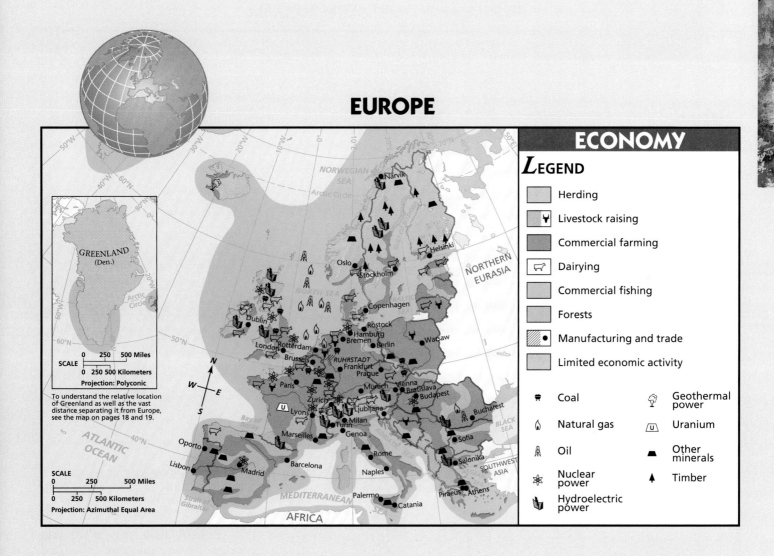

ECONOMY

LEGEND

- Herding
- Livestock raising
- Commercial farming
- Dairying
- Commercial fishing
- Forests
- Manufacturing and trade
- Limited economic activity

- Coal
- Natural gas
- Oil
- Nuclear power
- Hydroelectric power
- Geothermal power
- Uranium
- Other minerals
- Timber

GREENLAND (Den.)

SCALE
0   250   500 Miles
0   250 500 Kilometers
Projection: Polyconic

To understand the relative location of Greenland as well as the vast distance separating it from Europe, see the map on pages 18 and 19.

SCALE
0   250   500 Miles
0   250   500 Kilometers
Projection: Azimuthal Equal Area

RUSSIA AND NORTHERN EURASIA

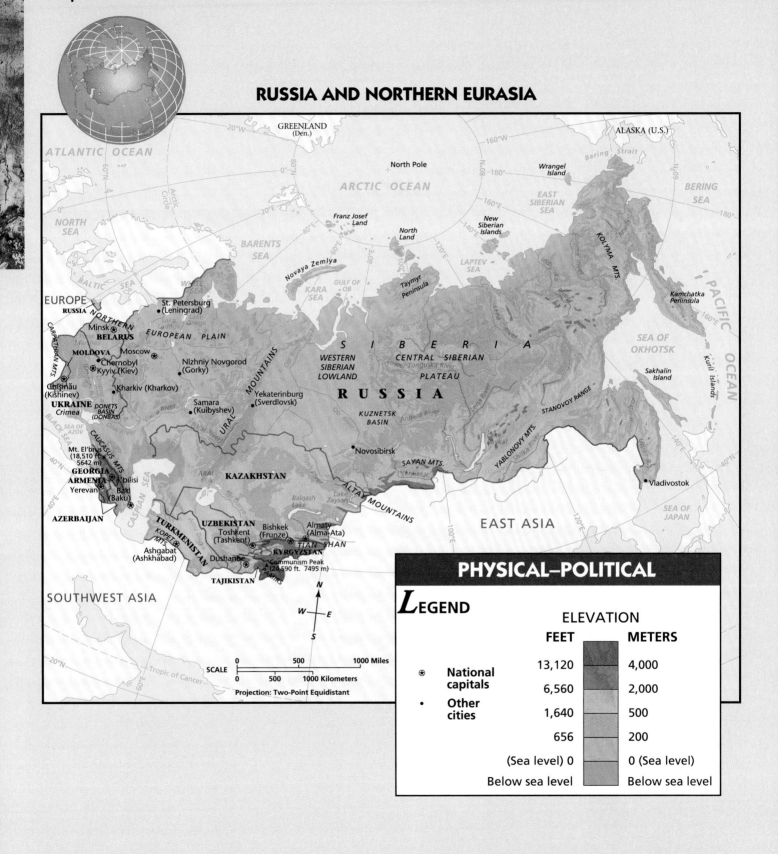

ATLANTIC OCEAN

GREENLAND
(Den.)

ALASKA (U.S.)

North Pole

ARCTIC OCEAN

Wrangel
Island

Bering Strait

BERING
SEA

NORTH
SEA

BARENTS
SEA

Franz Josef
Land

North
Land

New
Siberian
Islands

EAST
SIBERIAN
SEA

Novaya Zemlya

KARA
SEA

GULF OF
OB

Taymyr
Peninsula

LAPTEV
SEA

KOLYMA MTS.

Kamchatka
Peninsula

EUROPE

BALTIC SEA

RUSSIA

St. Petersburg
(Leningrad)

NORTHERN

EUROPEAN PLAIN

SEA OF
OKHOTSK

Minsk

BELARUS

Moscow

Nizhniy Novgorod
(Gorky)

S I B E R I A

WESTERN
SIBERIAN
LOWLAND

CENTRAL SIBERIAN
PLATEAU

Sakhalin
Island

Kuril Islands

MOLDOVA

CARPATHIAN MTS.

Chernobyl
Kyyiv (Kiev)

Kharkiv (Kharkov)

URAL MOUNTAINS

Yekaterinburg
(Sverdlovsk)

R U S S I A

PACIFIC OCEAN

Chişinău
(Kishinev)

Samara
(Kuibyshev)

KUZNETSK
BASIN

Lena River

Angara River

STANOVOY RANGE

Chişinău
(Kishinev)

UKRAINE

DONETS
BASIN
(DONBAS)

Crimea

SEA OF
AZOV

Volga River

Novosibirsk

SAYAN MTS.

YABLONOVY MTS.

Shilka River

Vladivostok

BLACK SEA

CAUCASUS MTS.

Mt. El'brus
(18,510 ft.
5642 m)

KAZAKHSTAN

Balqash
Lake

Lake
Zaysan

ALTAY MOUNTAINS

SEA OF
JAPAN

GEORGIA

Tbilisi

ARMENIA

Yerevan

Bakı
(Baku)

CASPIAN SEA

ARAL SEA

EAST ASIA

AZERBAIJAN

TURKMENISTAN

KOPET
MTS.

UZBEKISTAN

Toshkent
(Tashkent)

Bishkek
(Frunze)

Almaty
(Alma-Ata)

TIAN SHAN

Ashgabat
(Ashkhabad)

Dushanbe

KYRGYZSTAN

Communism Peak
(24,590 ft. 7495 m)

PAMIRS

SOUTHWEST ASIA

TAJIKISTAN

N
W — E
S

SCALE

0   500   1000 Miles
0   500   1000 Kilometers

Projection: Two-Point Equidistant

PHYSICAL–POLITICAL

*L*EGEND

ELEVATION

	FEET	METERS
⊛ **National capitals**	13,120	4,000
	6,560	2,000
• **Other cities**	1,640	500
	656	200
	(Sea level) 0	0 (Sea level)
	Below sea level	Below sea level

RUSSIA AND NORTHERN EURASIA

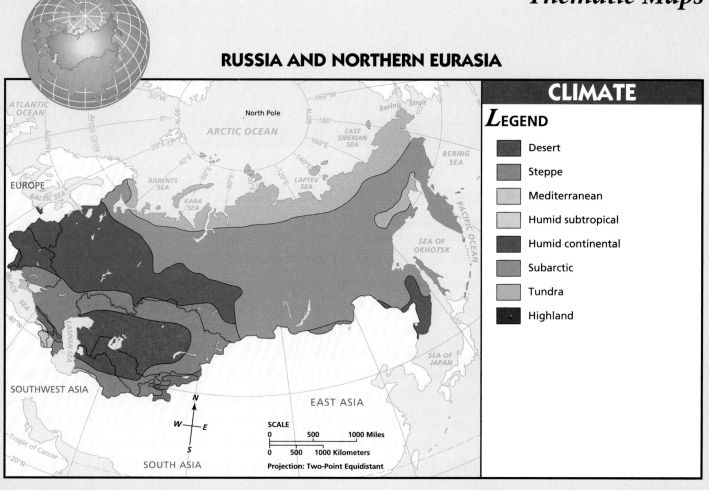

CLIMATE

*L*EGEND

- Desert
- Steppe
- Mediterranean
- Humid subtropical
- Humid continental
- Subarctic
- Tundra
- Highland

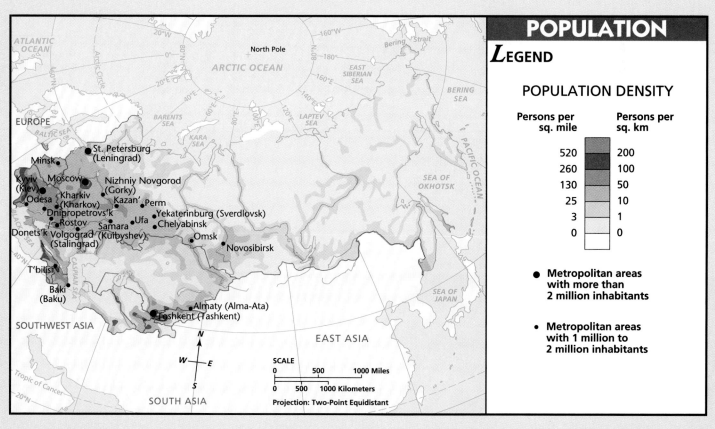

POPULATION

*L*EGEND

POPULATION DENSITY

Persons per sq. mile	Persons per sq. km
520	200
260	100
130	50
25	10
3	1
0	0

● **Metropolitan areas with more than 2 million inhabitants**

● **Metropolitan areas with 1 million to 2 million inhabitants**

RUSSIA AND NORTHERN EURASIA

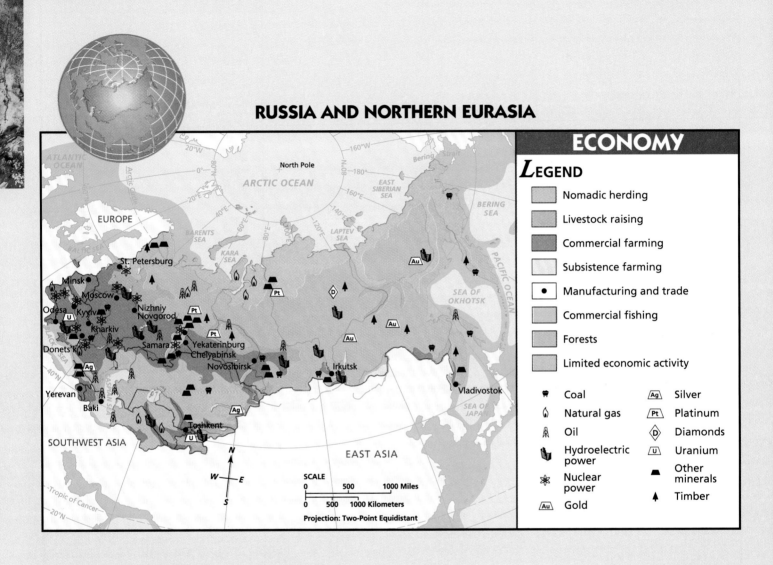

ECONOMY

LEGEND

- Nomadic herding
- Livestock raising
- Commercial farming
- Subsistence farming
- • Manufacturing and trade
- Commercial fishing
- Forests
- Limited economic activity

⚒	Coal	Ag	Silver
◊	Natural gas	Pt	Platinum
⚒	Oil	◊	Diamonds
⚒	Hydroelectric power	U	Uranium
✳	Nuclear power	⬣	Other minerals
Au	Gold	▲	Timber

ATLANTIC OCEAN
North Pole
ARCTIC OCEAN
EUROPE
St. Petersburg
Minsk
Moscow
Odesa Kyyiv Nizhniy Novgorod
Kharkiv
Donets'k Samara
Yekaterinburg
Chelyabinsk
Novosibirsk
Yerevan
Baki
Toshkent
SOUTHWEST ASIA
BARENTS SEA
KARA SEA
LAPTEV SEA
EAST SIBERIAN SEA
BERING SEA
PACIFIC OCEAN
SEA OF OKHOTSK
SEA OF JAPAN
Irkutsk
Vladivostok
EAST ASIA
Tropic of Cancer

SCALE
0   500   1000 Miles
0   500   1000 Kilometers
Projection: Two-Point Equidistant

N
W E
S

SOUTHWEST ASIA

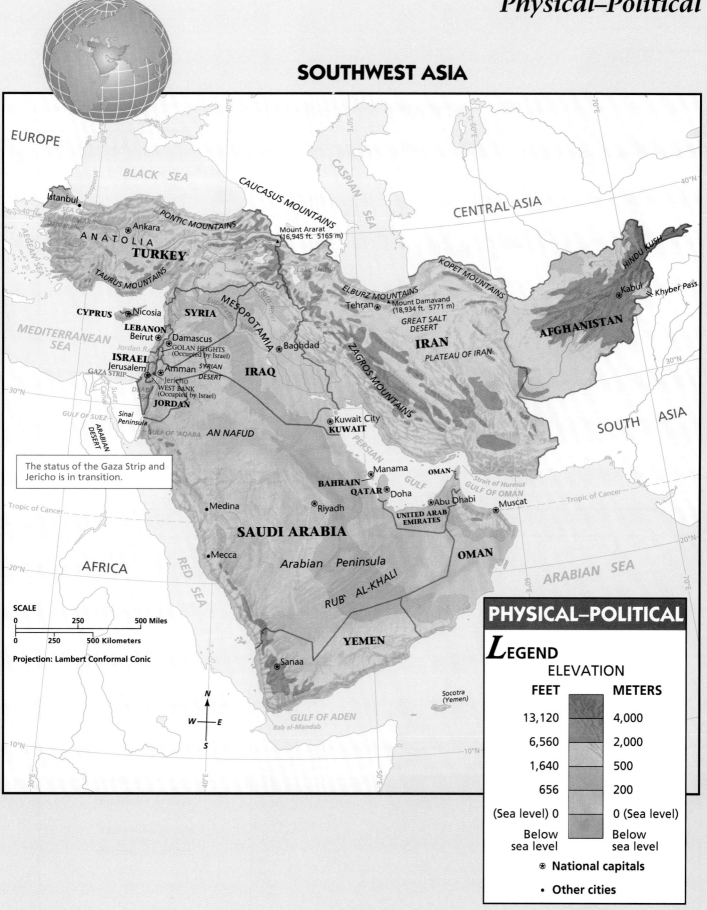

EUROPE

BLACK SEA

CAUCASUS MOUNTAINS

CASPIAN SEA

CENTRAL ASIA

SEA OF

Istanbul

Bosporus

Dardanelles

⊛ Ankara

PONTIC MOUNTAINS

Mount Ararat
(16,945 ft. 5165 m)

KOPET MOUNTAINS

HINDU KUSH

ANATOLIA

TURKEY

Lake Urmia

ELBURZ MOUNTAINS

Mount Damavand
(18,934 ft. 5771 m)

Kabul ⊛

Khyber Pass

AEGEAN SEA

TAURUS MOUNTAINS

Tehran ⊛

GREAT SALT
DESERT

AFGHANISTAN

CYPRUS ⊛ Nicosia

SYRIA

MESOPOTAMIA

Euphrates River

IRAN

PLATEAU OF IRAN

MEDITERRANEAN
SEA

LEBANON
Beirut ⊛ ⊛ Damascus
GOLAN HEIGHTS
(Occupied by Israel)

Jordan R.

Tigris River

ZAGROS MOUNTAINS

⊛ Baghdad

ISRAEL
Jerusalem ⊛ ⊛ Amman
GAZA STRIP ⊛ Jericho
WEST BANK
(Occupied by Israel)

SYRIAN
DESERT

IRAQ

Suez Canal

JORDAN

Dead Sea

Sinai
Peninsula

AN NAFUD

⊛ Kuwait City

KUWAIT

PERSIAN GULF

GULF OF SUEZ

GULF OF 'AQABA

ARABIAN
DESERT

The status of the Gaza Strip and
Jericho is in transition.

⊛ Manama

OMAN

Strait of Hormuz

GULF OF OMAN

BAHRAIN ⊛
QATAR ⊛ Doha

30°N

Tropic of Cancer

• Medina

⊛ Riyadh

UNITED ARAB
EMIRATES

⊛ Abu Dhabi

• Muscat

Tropic of Cancer

SAUDI ARABIA

OMAN

20°N

AFRICA

RED SEA

• Mecca

Arabian   Peninsula

ARABIAN   SEA

RUB' AL-KHALI

SCALE

| 0 | 250 | 500 Miles |

| 0 | 250 | 500 Kilometers |

Projection: Lambert Conformal Conic

N
W—E
S

YEMEN

• Sanaa

Socotra
(Yemen)

GULF OF ADEN
Bab al-Mandab

10°N

PHYSICAL–POLITICAL

LEGEND
ELEVATION

FEET		METERS
13,120		4,000
6,560		2,000
1,640		500
656		200
(Sea level) 0		0 (Sea level)
Below sea level		Below sea level

⊛ National capitals

• Other cities

Thematic Maps

SOUTHWEST ASIA

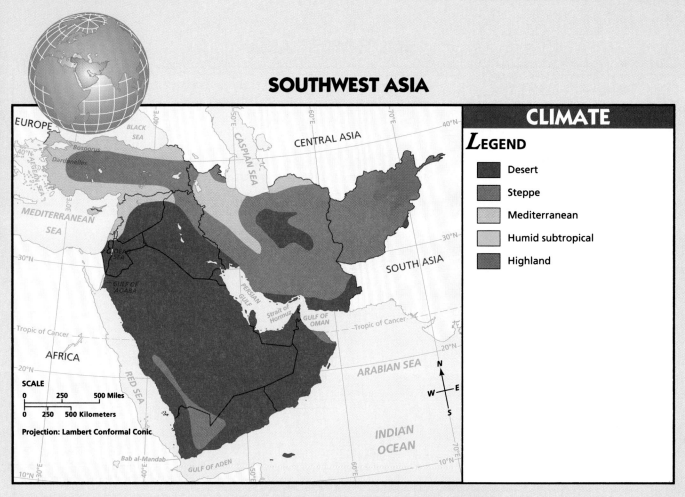

CLIMATE

*L*EGEND

- Desert
- Steppe
- Mediterranean
- Humid subtropical
- Highland

SCALE

0 — 250 — 500 Miles

0 — 250 — 500 Kilometers

Projection: Lambert Conformal Conic

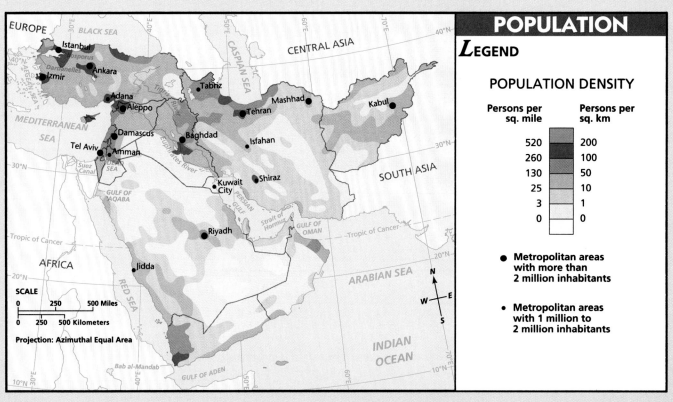

POPULATION

*L*EGEND

POPULATION DENSITY

Persons per sq. mile	Persons per sq. km
520	200
260	100
130	50
25	10
3	1
0	0

● Metropolitan areas with more than 2 million inhabitants

● Metropolitan areas with 1 million to 2 million inhabitants

SCALE

0 — 250 — 500 Miles

0 — 250 — 500 Kilometers

Projection: Azimuthal Equal Area

SOUTHWEST ASIA

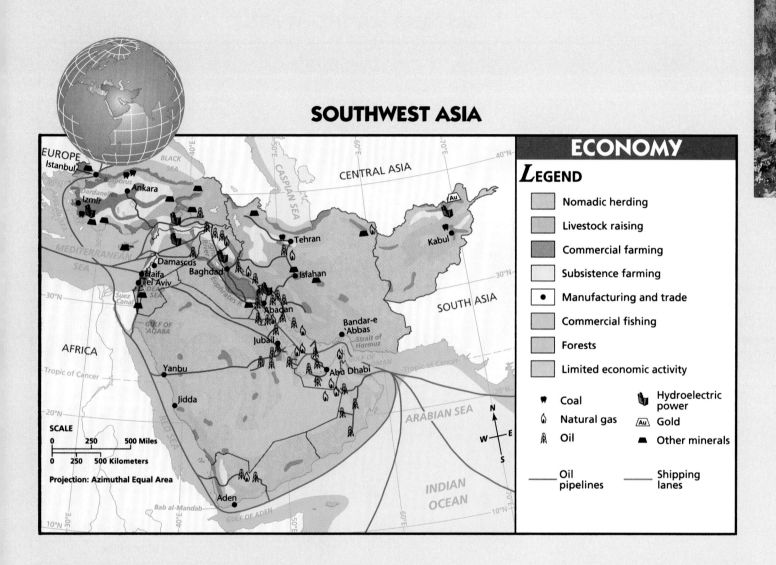

ECONOMY

LEGEND

- Nomadic herding
- Livestock raising
- Commercial farming
- Subsistence farming
- • Manufacturing and trade
- Commercial fishing
- Forests
- Limited economic activity

- ♦ Coal
- ◊ Natural gas
- ♠ Oil
- 🔋 Hydroelectric power
- Au Gold
- ◣ Other minerals

— Oil pipelines
— Shipping lanes

SCALE

0 250 500 Miles

0 250 500 Kilometers

Projection: Azimuthal Equal Area

EUROPE
Istanbul
BLACK SEA
Ankara
Izmir
Dardanelles
Bosporus
CENTRAL ASIA
CASPIAN SEA
Tehran
Isfahan
Damascus
Baghdad
Haifa
Tel Aviv
DEAD SEA
MEDITERRANEAN SEA
Suez Canal
GULF OF 'AQABA
AFRICA
Tropic of Cancer
RED SEA
Yanbu
Jidda
Abadan
Jubail
Bandar-e 'Abbas
Strait of Hormuz
GULF OF OMAN
Abu Dhabi
SOUTH ASIA
Kabul
Au
Tropic of Cancer
ARABIAN SEA
N
W E
S
Aden
Bab al-Mandab
GULF OF ADEN
INDIAN OCEAN
Euphrates R.
Tigris R.

Physical–Political

EAST AND SOUTHEAST ASIA

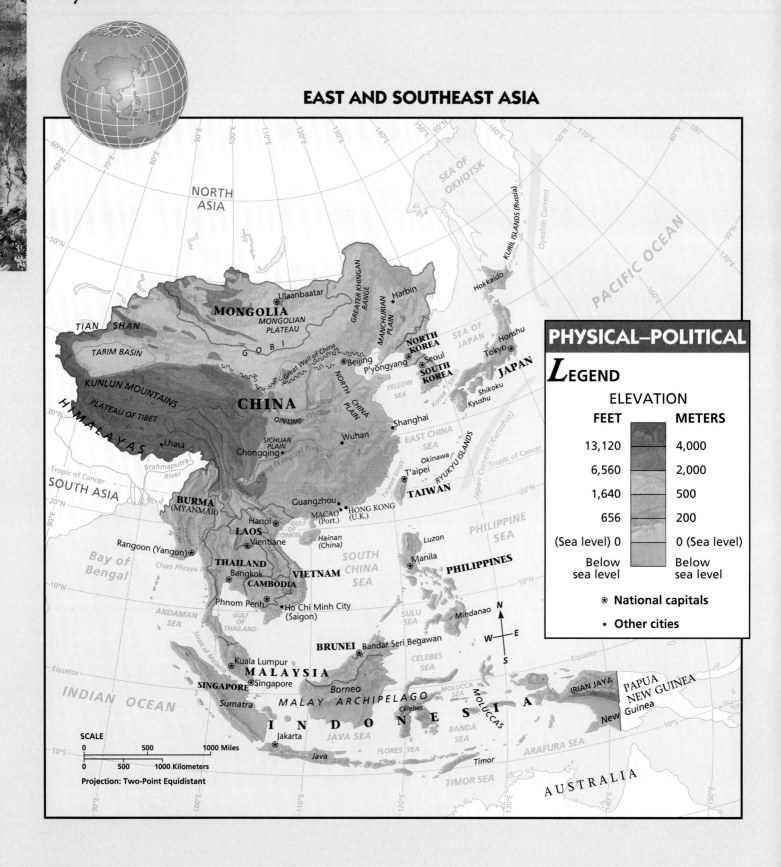

NORTH ASIA

NORTH
ASIA

MONGOLIA
MONGOLIAN
PLATEAU

Ulaanbaatar

GREATER KHINGAN RANGE

MANCHURIAN PLAIN

Harbin

Hokkaido

SEA OF OKHOTSK

KURIL ISLANDS (Russia)

Oyashio Current

PACIFIC OCEAN

TIAN SHAN

TARIM BASIN

GOBI

Great Wall of China

NORTH KOREA
P'yongyang
Beijing
SOUTH KOREA
Seoul

SEA OF JAPAN

Tokyo
Honshu

JAPAN

KUNLUN MOUNTAINS

PLATEAU OF TIBET

HIMALAYAS

CHINA

Huang He (Yellow R.)
QIN LING

NORTH CHINA PLAIN

YELLOW SEA

Korea Strait

Shikoku
Kyushu

Lhasa

Brahmaputra River

SICHUAN PLAIN
Chongqing

Chang (Yangtze) River

Wuhan

Shanghai

EAST CHINA SEA

Okinawa

RYUKYU ISLANDS

Japan Current (Kuroshio)

Tropic of Cancer

SOUTH ASIA

BURMA
(MYANMAR)

Hanoi
LAOS
Vientiane
GULF OF TONKIN

Guangzhou
MACAO (Port.)
HONG KONG (U.K.)

T'aipei
TAIWAN

Taiwan Strait

Irrawaddy River

Hainan (China)

Luzon

PHILIPPINE SEA

Rangoon (Yangon)

Bay of Bengal

Chao Phraya River

THAILAND
Bangkok
CAMBODIA

VIETNAM

Mekong River

SOUTH CHINA SEA

Manila

PHILIPPINES

Phnom Penh

Ho Chi Minh City (Saigon)

ANDAMAN SEA

GULF OF THAILAND

SULU SEA

Mindanao

N
W E
S

Strait of Malacca

BRUNEI   Bandar Seri Begawan

CELEBES SEA

Equator

Kuala Lumpur

MALAYSIA
SINGAPORE   Singapore

Borneo

MALAY ARCHIPELAGO

Sumatra

INDIAN OCEAN

MOLUCCA SEA

MOLUCCAS

Celebes

INDONESIA

BANDA SEA

IRIAN JAYA

New Guinea

PAPUA NEW GUINEA

Jakarta   JAVA SEA

Java

FLORES SEA

Timor

TIMOR SEA

ARAFURA SEA

AUSTRALIA

PHYSICAL–POLITICAL

*L*EGEND

ELEVATION

FEET		METERS
13,120		4,000
6,560		2,000
1,640		500
656		200
(Sea level) 0		0 (Sea level)
Below sea level		Below sea level

⊛ National capitals

• Other cities

SCALE

0   500   1000 Miles

0   500   1000 Kilometers

Projection: Two-Point Equidistant

Thematic Maps

EAST AND SOUTHEAST ASIA

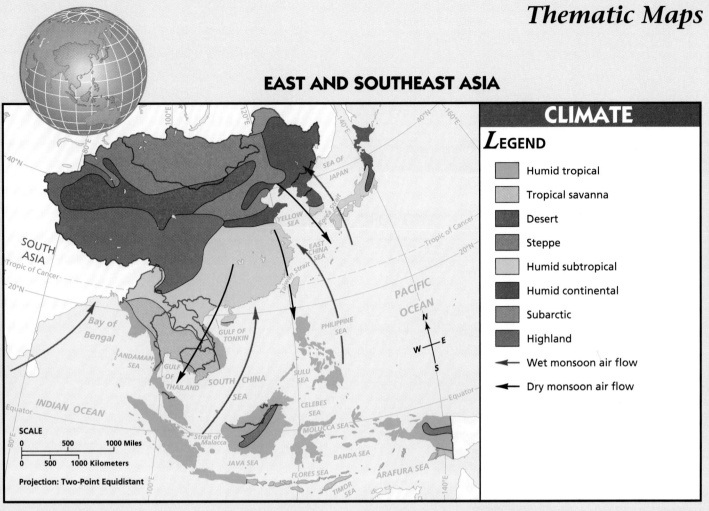

CLIMATE

LEGEND

- Humid tropical
- Tropical savanna
- Desert
- Steppe
- Humid subtropical
- Humid continental
- Subarctic
- Highland
- ← Wet monsoon air flow
- ← Dry monsoon air flow

SCALE
0   500   1000 Miles
0   500   1000 Kilometers

Projection: Two-Point Equidistant

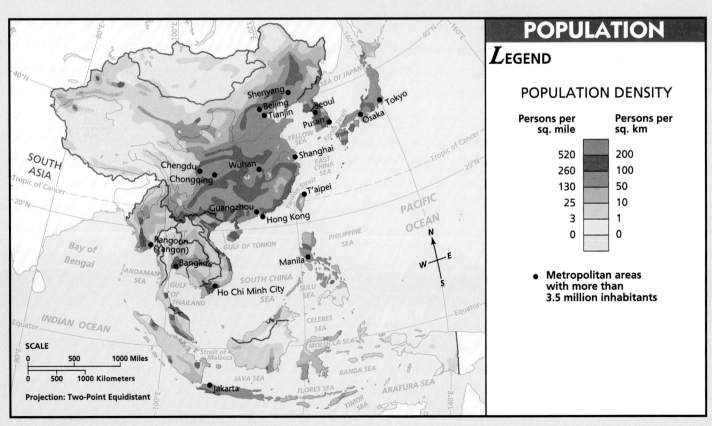

POPULATION

LEGEND

POPULATION DENSITY

Persons per sq. mile	Persons per sq. km
520	200
260	100
130	50
25	10
3	1
0	0

● Metropolitan areas with more than 3.5 million inhabitants

SCALE
0   500   1000 Miles
0   500   1000 Kilometers

Projection: Two-Point Equidistant

EAST AND SOUTHEAST ASIA

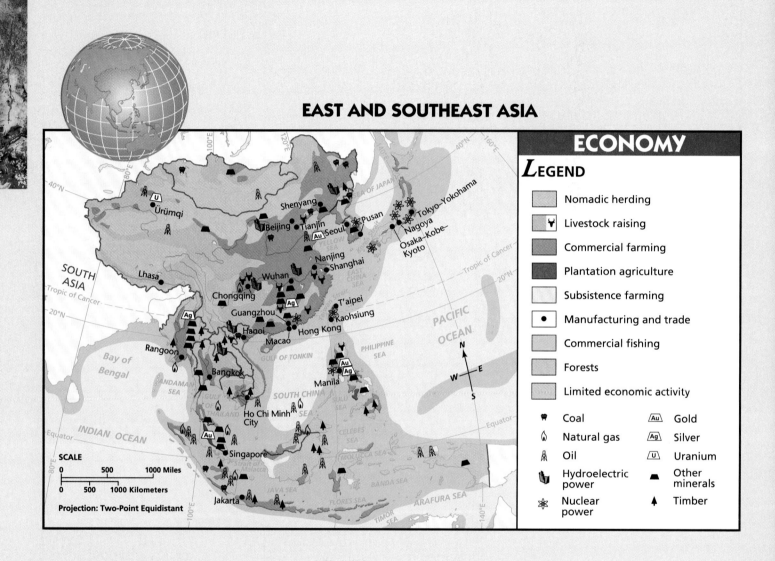

ECONOMY

LEGEND

	Nomadic herding
	Livestock raising
	Commercial farming
	Plantation agriculture
	Subsistence farming
●	Manufacturing and trade
	Commercial fishing
	Forests
	Limited economic activity

Coal		Au	Gold
Natural gas		Ag	Silver
Oil		U	Uranium
Hydroelectric power			Other minerals
Nuclear power			Timber

Map labels: Ürümqi, Shenyang, Beijing, Tianjin, Seoul, Pusan, Nagoya, Tokyo–Yokohama, Osaka–Kobe–Kyoto, Lhasa, Nanjing, Shanghai, Wuhan, Chongqing, Guangzhou, T'aipei, Kaohsiung, Hanoi, Hong Kong, Macao, Rangoon, Bangkok, Manila, Ho Chi Minh City, Singapore, Jakarta

SOUTH ASIA, Tropic of Cancer, Bay of Bengal, INDIAN OCEAN, ANDAMAN SEA, GULF OF THAILAND, SOUTH CHINA SEA, GULF OF TONKIN, YELLOW SEA, EAST CHINA SEA, SEA OF JAPAN, PACIFIC OCEAN, PHILIPPINE SEA, SULU SEA, CELEBES SEA, MOLUCCA SEA, BANDA SEA, JAVA SEA, FLORES SEA, TIMOR SEA, ARAFURA SEA, Strait of Malacca, Equator

SCALE

0 — 500 — 1000 Miles

0 — 500 — 1000 Kilometers

Projection: Two-Point Equidistant

SOUTH ASIA

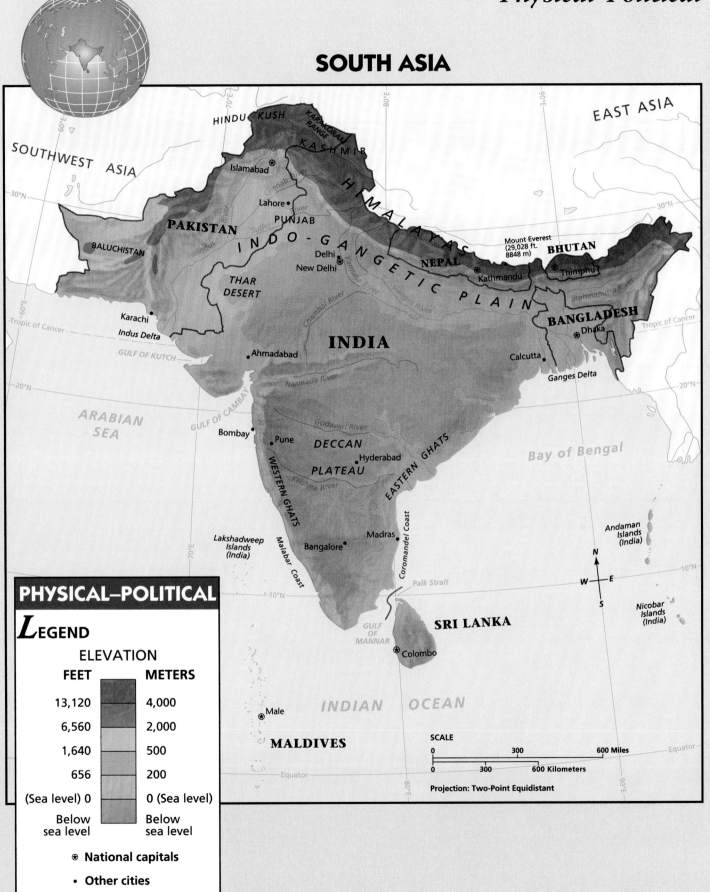

EAST ASIA

SOUTHWEST ASIA

HINDU KUSH
KARAKORAM RANGE
KASHMIR

Islamabad ⊛

30°N

Lahore •

PAKISTAN
PUNJAB

INDO-GANGETIC PLAIN

HIMALAYAS

Mount Everest
(29,028 ft.
8848 m)

BHUTAN

NEPAL
Kathmandu ⊛
Thimphu ⊛

BALUCHISTAN

Delhi
New Delhi ⊛

THAR
DESERT

Chambal River

Yamuna River
Ganges River

Brahmaputra River

BANGLADESH
⊛ Dhaka

Karachi •
Indus Delta

Tropic of Cancer

Tropic of Cancer

INDIA

Ahmadabad •

Narmada River

Calcutta •
Ganges Delta

20°N

20°N

ARABIAN
SEA

GULF OF CAMBAY

GULF OF KUTCH

Godavari River

Bombay •
Pune •

DECCAN
PLATEAU

Hyderabad •

Krishna River

WESTERN GHATS

EASTERN GHATS

Bay of Bengal

Andaman
Islands
(India)

N
W   E
S

Lakshadweep
Islands
(India)

Bangalore •

Madras •

Coromandel Coast

Nicobar
Islands
(India)

Malabar Coast

Palk Strait

10°N

SRI LANKA

GULF OF MANNAR

⊛ Colombo

• Male

INDIAN   OCEAN

MALDIVES

Equator

Equator

PHYSICAL–POLITICAL

*L*EGEND

ELEVATION

FEET		METERS
13,120		4,000
6,560		2,000
1,640		500
656		200
(Sea level) 0		0 (Sea level)
Below sea level		Below sea level

⊛ **National capitals**

• **Other cities**

SCALE

0   300   600 Miles

0   300   600 Kilometers

Projection: Two-Point Equidistant

Thematic Maps

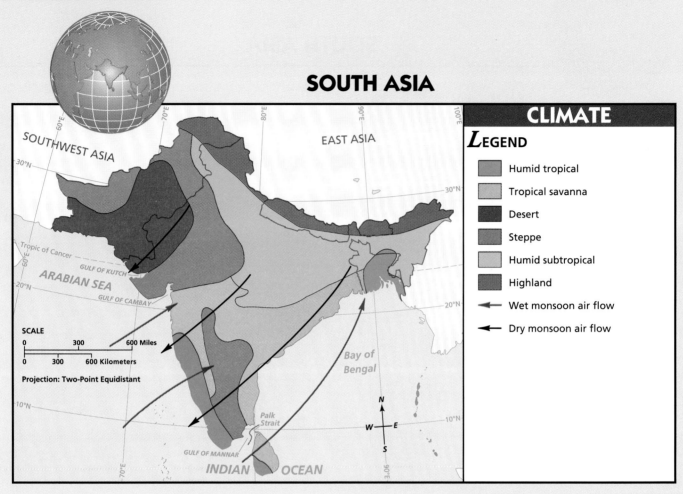

SOUTH ASIA

CLIMATE

LEGEND

- Humid tropical
- Tropical savanna
- Desert
- Steppe
- Humid subtropical
- Highland
- ← Wet monsoon air flow
- ← Dry monsoon air flow

SOUTHWEST ASIA

EAST ASIA

30°N

Tropic of Cancer

GULF OF KUTCH

ARABIAN SEA

GULF OF CAMBAY

20°N

Bay of Bengal

10°N

Palk Strait

GULF OF MANNAR

INDIAN OCEAN

SCALE

0 — 300 — 600 Miles

0 — 300 — 600 Kilometers

Projection: Two-Point Equidistant

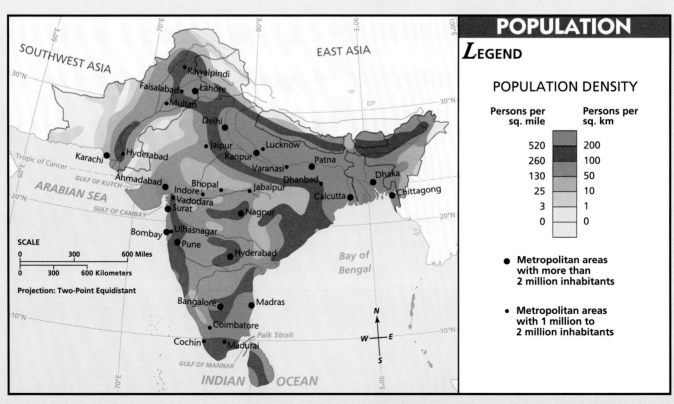

POPULATION

LEGEND

POPULATION DENSITY

Persons per sq. mile	Persons per sq. km
520	200
260	100
130	50
25	10
3	1
0	0

● Metropolitan areas with more than 2 million inhabitants

• Metropolitan areas with 1 million to 2 million inhabitants

SOUTHWEST ASIA

EAST ASIA

30°N

Rawalpindi

Faisalabad
Lahore

Multan

Delhi

Jaipur

Lucknow

Karachi

Hyderabad

Kanpur

Patna

Tropic of Cancer

Varanasi

Dhaka

GULF OF KUTCH

Ahmadabad

Bhopal

Dhanbad

Chittagong

Indore

Jabalpur

Calcutta

20°N

Vadodara

GULF OF CAMBAY

Surat

Nagpur

Bombay

Ulhasnagar

Pune

Hyderabad

Bay of Bengal

Bangalore

Madras

10°N

Coimbatore

Palk Strait

Cochin

Madurai

GULF OF MANNAR

INDIAN OCEAN

SCALE

0 — 300 — 600 Miles

0 — 300 — 600 Kilometers

Projection: Two-Point Equidistant

SOUTH ASIA

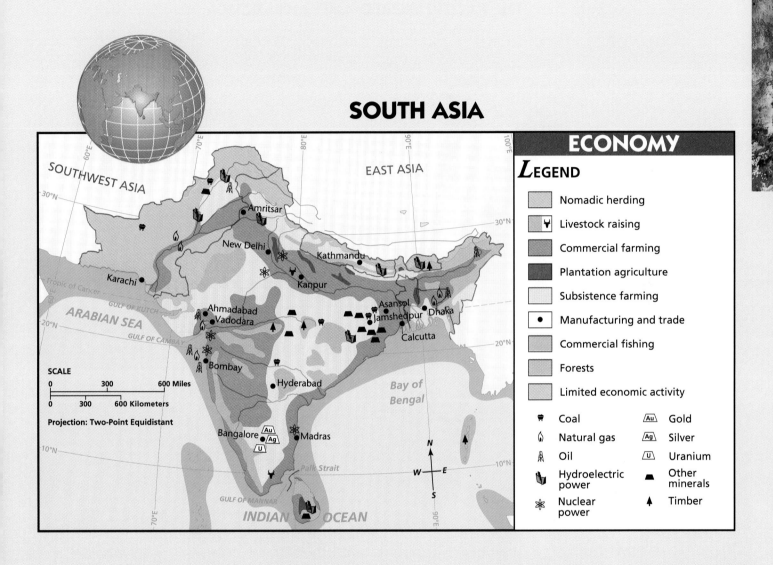

ECONOMY

LEGEND

- Nomadic herding
- Livestock raising
- Commercial farming
- Plantation agriculture
- Subsistence farming
- • Manufacturing and trade
- Commercial fishing
- Forests
- Limited economic activity

☗ Coal	Au Gold
⌕ Natural gas	Ag Silver
⚒ Oil	U Uranium
Hydroelectric power	Other minerals
✳ Nuclear power	▲ Timber

SOUTHWEST ASIA

EAST ASIA

30°N

30°N

Amritsar

New Delhi

Kathmandu

Karachi

Kanpur

Tropic of Cancer

GULF OF KUTCH

ARABIAN SEA

Ahmadabad

Vadodara

Asansol

Dhaka

20°N

Jamshedpur

Calcutta

GULF OF CAMBAY

20°N

Bombay

Hyderabad

Bay of Bengal

SCALE

0	300	600 Miles
0	300	600 Kilometers

Projection: Two-Point Equidistant

Bangalore

Au
Ag

Madras

U

N

10°N

Palk Strait

W — E

10°N

S

GULF OF MANNAR

INDIAN OCEAN

70°E

90°E

Physical–Political

THE PACIFIC WORLD AND ANTARCTICA

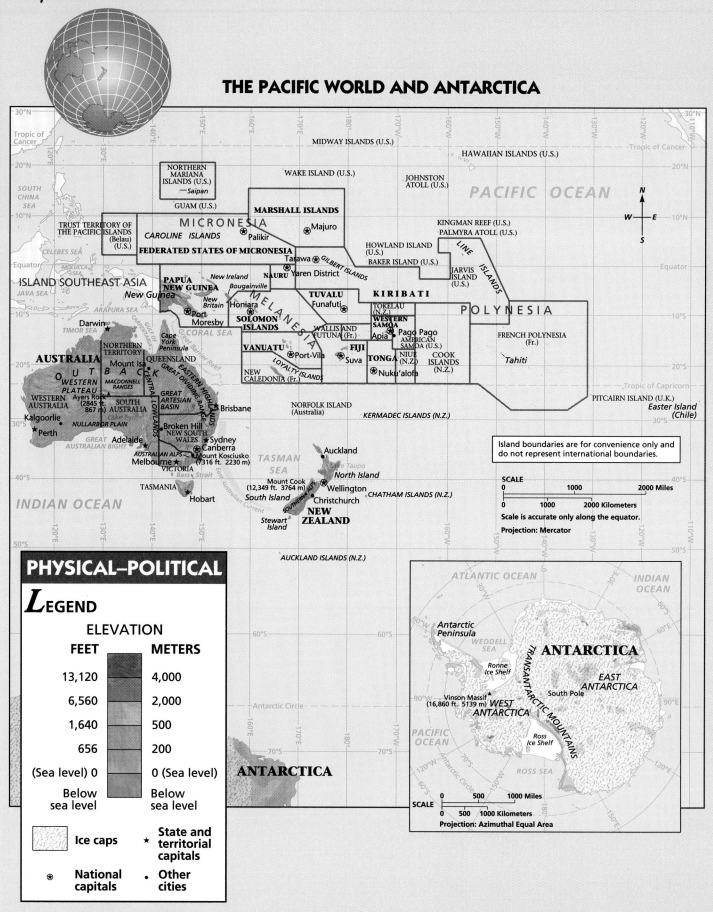

30°N Tropic of Cancer

MIDWAY ISLANDS (U.S.)

HAWAIIAN ISLANDS (U.S.)

Tropic of Cancer

20°N **WAKE ISLAND (U.S.)** **JOHNSTON ATOLL (U.S.)** **PACIFIC OCEAN** 20°N

SOUTH CHINA SEA

NORTHERN MARIANA ISLANDS (U.S.) —Saipan

GUAM (U.S.)

MARSHALL ISLANDS ⊛ Majuro

N
W — E
S

TRUST TERRITORY OF THE PACIFIC ISLANDS (Belau) (U.S.)

MICRONESIA

KINGMAN REEF (U.S.)
PALMYRA ATOLL (U.S.)

10°N

CELEBES SEA

CAROLINE   ISLANDS ⊛ Palikir

FEDERATED STATES OF MICRONESIA

HOWLAND ISLAND (U.S.)
BAKER ISLAND (U.S.)

LINE

Equator MOLUCCA SEA JAVA SEA

Tarawa ⊛

NAURU Yaren District

KIRIBATI

JARVIS ISLAND (U.S.) ISLANDS Equator

ISLAND SOUTHEAST ASIA

ARAFURA SEA

PAPUA NEW GUINEA New Ireland Bougainville **NAURU** Yaren District

GILBERT ISLANDS

KIRIBATI

10°S New Guinea New Britain Honiara **TUVALU** Funafuti ⊛

POLYNESIA

MELANESIA

Darwin ★ TIMOR SEA

Cape York Peninsula ⊛ Port Moresby

SOLOMON ISLANDS

TOKELAU (N.Z.)
WESTERN SAMOA ⊛ Apia

WALLIS AND FUTUNA (Fr.)

Pago Pago
AMERICAN SAMOA (U.S.)

FRENCH POLYNESIA (Fr.)

AUSTRALIA NORTHERN TERRITORY Mount Isa ★ QUEENSLAND

VANUATU ⊛ Port-Vila **FIJI** ⊛ Suva **TONGA** NIUE (N.Z.) COOK ISLANDS (N.Z.) Tahiti

20°S O U T B A C K WESTERN PLATEAU MACDONNELL RANGES GREAT ARTESIAN BASIN

NEW CALEDONIA (Fr.) LOYALTY ISLANDS ⊛ Nuku'alofa

Tropic of Capricorn

WESTERN AUSTRALIA Ayers Rock (2845 ft. 867 m) SOUTH AUSTRALIA

NORFOLK ISLAND (Australia)

KERMADEC ISLANDS (N.Z.)

PITCAIRN ISLAND (U.K.)
Easter Island (Chile)

Kalgoorlie ★ NULLARBOR PLAIN Lake Eyre Brisbane

30°S

★ Perth GREAT AUSTRALIAN BIGHT Adelaide ★ Broken Hill NEW SOUTH WALES Sydney

Island boundaries are for convenience only and do not represent international boundaries.

AUSTRALIAN ALPS Mount Kosciusko (7316 ft. 2230 m) ⊛ Canberra

TASMAN SEA Auckland

SCALE
0   1000   2000 Miles
0   1000   2000 Kilometers

Melbourne ★ VICTORIA

North Island Lake Taupo

Scale is accurate only along the equator.

40°S TASMANIA ★ Hobart

Mount Cook (12,349 ft. 3764 m) Wellington ⊛
South Island Christchurch CHATHAM ISLANDS (N.Z.)

Projection: Mercator

INDIAN OCEAN Bass Strait

SOUTHERN ALPS Stewart Island **NEW ZEALAND**

50°S AUCKLAND ISLANDS (N.Z.)

PHYSICAL–POLITICAL

LEGEND

ELEVATION

FEET	METERS
13,120	4,000
6,560	2,000
1,640	500
656	200
(Sea level) 0	0 (Sea level)
Below sea level	Below sea level

Ice caps   ★ State and territorial capitals

⊛ National capitals   • Other cities

ANTARCTICA

ATLANTIC OCEAN INDIAN OCEAN

Antarctic Peninsula WEDDELL SEA

Ronne Ice Shelf

ANTARCTICA

TRANSANTARCTIC MOUNTAINS

EAST ANTARCTICA

South Pole

Vinson Massif (16,860 ft. 5139 m) *WEST ANTARCTICA*

PACIFIC OCEAN

Ross Ice Shelf

ROSS SEA

Antarctic Circle

SCALE
0   500   1000 Miles
0   500   1000 Kilometers

Projection: Azimuthal Equal Area

ANTARCTICA

THE PACIFIC WORLD AND ANTARCTICA

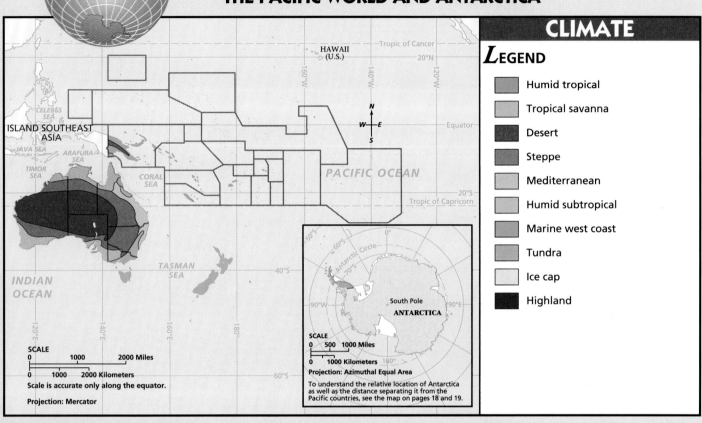

CLIMATE

LEGEND

- Humid tropical
- Tropical savanna
- Desert
- Steppe
- Mediterranean
- Humid subtropical
- Marine west coast
- Tundra
- Ice cap
- Highland

HAWAII (U.S.)

20°N

Tropic of Cancer

CELEBES SEA

ISLAND SOUTHEAST ASIA

JAVA SEA

ARAFURA SEA

TIMOR SEA

CORAL SEA

Equator

PACIFIC OCEAN

20°S

Tropic of Capricorn

TASMAN SEA

INDIAN OCEAN

SCALE
0   1000   2000 Miles
0 1000 2000 Kilometers
Scale is accurate only along the equator.

Projection: Mercator

SCALE
0   500 1000 Miles
0   1000 Kilometers
Projection: Azimuthal Equal Area

South Pole
ANTARCTICA

Antarctic Circle

To understand the relative location of Antarctica as well as the distance separating it from the Pacific countries, see the map on pages 18 and 19.

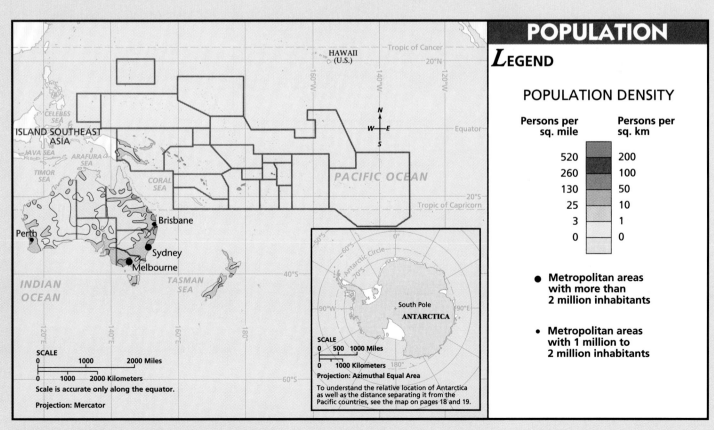

POPULATION

LEGEND

POPULATION DENSITY

Persons per sq. mile	Persons per sq. km
520	200
260	100
130	50
25	10
3	1
0	0

- Metropolitan areas with more than 2 million inhabitants
- Metropolitan areas with 1 million to 2 million inhabitants

HAWAII (U.S.)

20°N

Tropic of Cancer

CELEBES SEA

ISLAND SOUTHEAST ASIA

JAVA SEA

ARAFURA SEA

TIMOR SEA

CORAL SEA

Equator

PACIFIC OCEAN

20°S

Tropic of Capricorn

Perth

Brisbane

Sydney

Melbourne

TASMAN SEA

INDIAN OCEAN

SCALE
0   1000   2000 Miles
0 1000 2000 Kilometers
Scale is accurate only along the equator.

Projection: Mercator

SCALE
0   500 1000 Miles
0   1000 Kilometers
Projection: Azimuthal Equal Area

South Pole
ANTARCTICA

Antarctic Circle

To understand the relative location of Antarctica as well as the distance separating it from the Pacific countries, see the map on pages 18 and 19.

THE PACIFIC WORLD AND ANTARCTICA

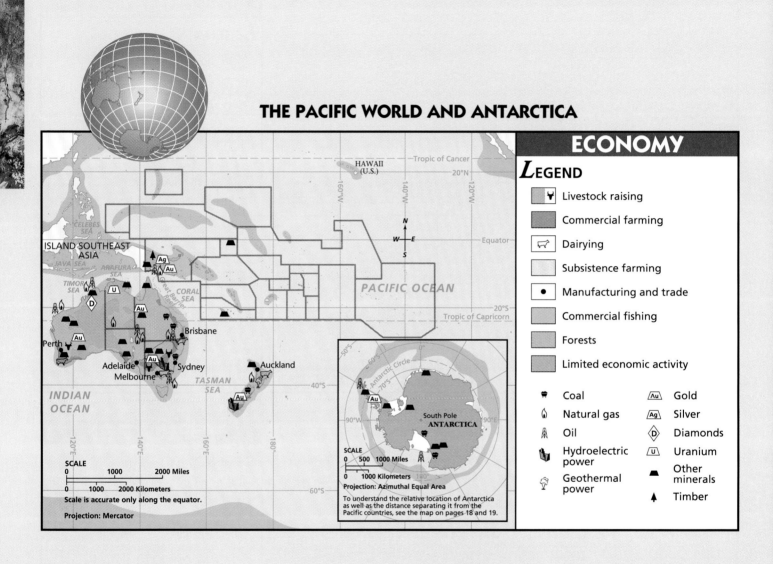

ECONOMY

LEGEND

- Livestock raising
- Commercial farming
- Dairying
- Subsistence farming
- Manufacturing and trade
- Commercial fishing
- Forests
- Limited economic activity

- Coal
- Natural gas
- Oil
- Hydroelectric power
- Geothermal power

- Au Gold
- Ag Silver
- D Diamonds
- U Uranium
- Other minerals
- Timber

HAWAII
(U.S.)

Tropic of Cancer
20°N

ISLAND SOUTHEAST ASIA

PACIFIC OCEAN

Equator

20°S
Tropic of Capricorn

CELEBES SEA
JAVA SEA
TIMOR SEA
ARAFURA SEA
CORAL SEA

Great Barrier Reef

Brisbane

Perth

Adelaide
Melbourne
Sydney

Auckland

INDIAN OCEAN

TASMAN SEA

40°S

60°S

SCALE
0   1000   2000 Miles
0   1000   2000 Kilometers
Scale is accurate only along the equator.

Projection: Mercator

ANTARCTICA

South Pole
ANTARCTICA

Antarctic Circle

SCALE
0   500   1000 Miles
0   1000 Kilometers
Projection: Azimuthal Equal Area

To understand the relative location of Antarctica as well as the distance separating it from the Pacific countries, see the map on pages 18 and 19.

70

WORLD HISTORY

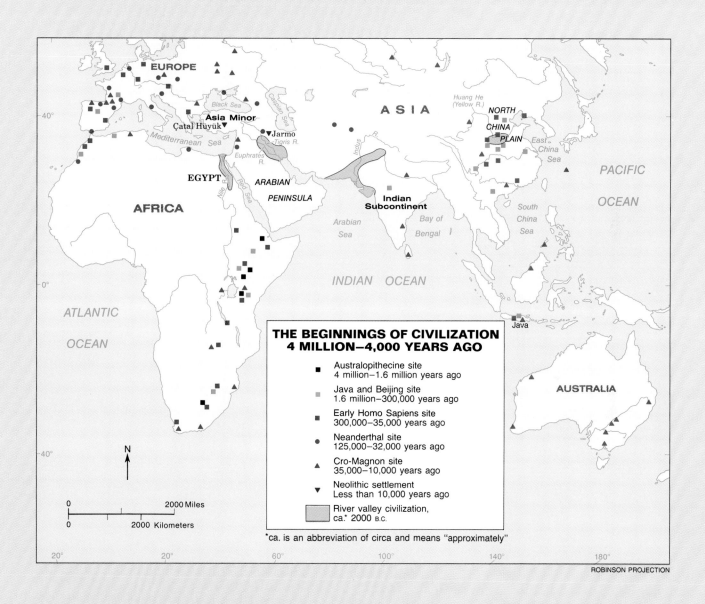

EUROPE

ASIA

Black Sea

Caspian Sea

Huang He
(Yellow R.)

NORTH
CHINA
PLAIN

East
China
Sea

Asia Minor

Çatal Hüyük

Jarmo

Tigris R.

Mediterranean Sea

Euphrates R.

EGYPT

ARABIAN
PENINSULA

Nile

Red Sea

Indus R.

Indian
Subcontinent

AFRICA

Arabian
Sea

Bay of
Bengal

South
China
Sea

PACIFIC

OCEAN

INDIAN OCEAN

ATLANTIC

OCEAN

Java

AUSTRALIA

N

THE BEGINNINGS OF CIVILIZATION
4 MILLION–4,000 YEARS AGO

- ■ Australopithecine site
  4 million–1.6 million years ago
- ■ Java and Beijing site
  1.6 million–300,000 years ago
- ■ Early Homo Sapiens site
  300,000–35,000 years ago
- ● Neanderthal site
  125,000–32,000 years ago
- ▲ Cro-Magnon site
  35,000–10,000 years ago
- ▼ Neolithic settlement
  Less than 10,000 years ago
- River valley civilization,
  ca.* 2000 B.C.

*ca. is an abbreviation of circa and means "approximately"

0   2000 Miles

0   2000 Kilometers

ROBINSON PROJECTION

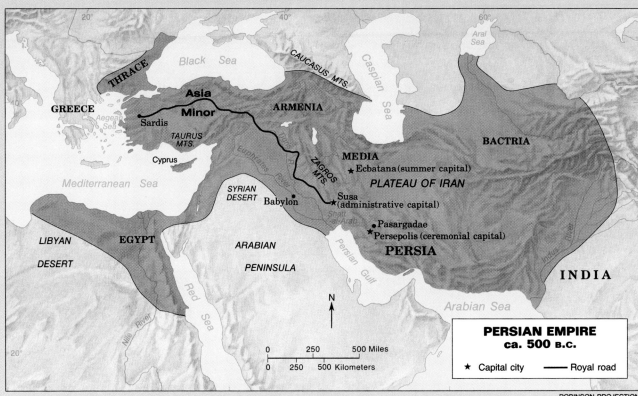

PERSIAN EMPIRE
ca. 500 B.C.

★ Capital city   —— Royal road

ROBINSON PROJECTION

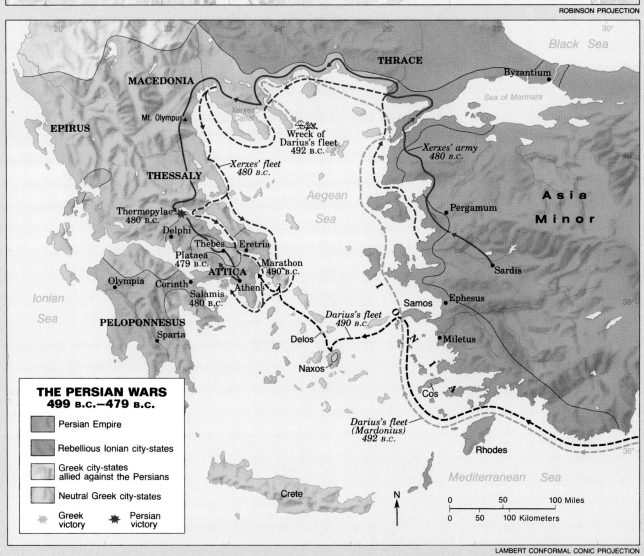

THE PERSIAN WARS
499 B.C.–479 B.C.

    Persian Empire

    Rebellious Ionian city-states

    Greek city-states allied against the Persians

    Neutral Greek city-states

    Greek victory   Persian victory

LAMBERT CONFORMAL CONIC PROJECTION

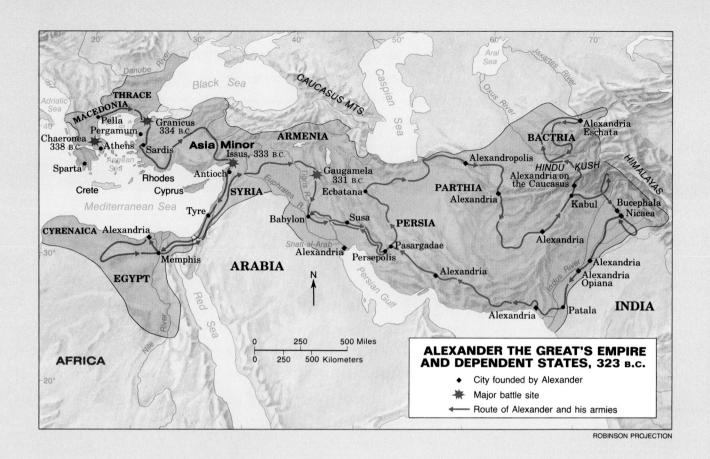

ALEXANDER THE GREAT'S EMPIRE AND DEPENDENT STATES, 323 B.C.

- ◆ City founded by Alexander
- ✦ Major battle site
- ← Route of Alexander and his armies

0 250 500 Miles
0 250 500 Kilometers

ROBINSON PROJECTION

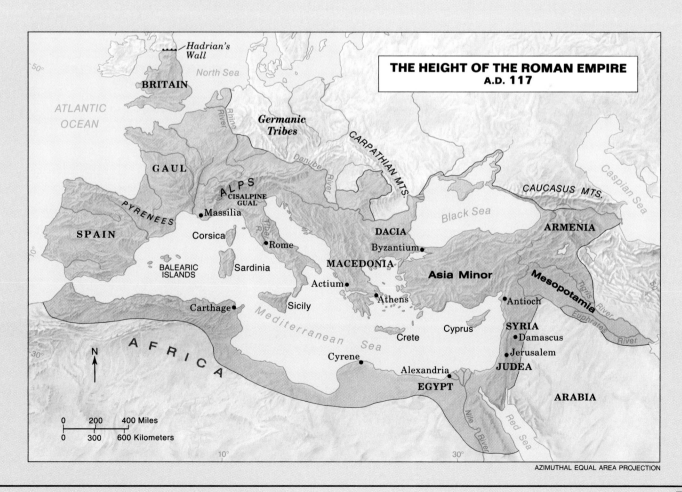

THE HEIGHT OF THE ROMAN EMPIRE
A.D. 117

0 200 400 Miles
0 300 600 Kilometers

AZIMUTHAL EQUAL AREA PROJECTION

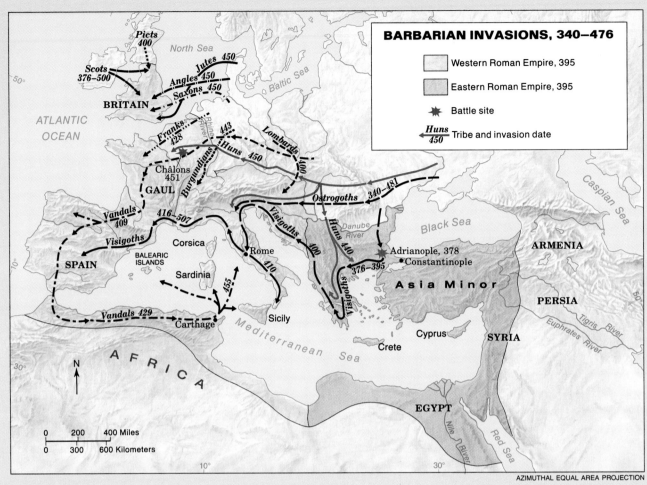

BARBARIAN INVASIONS, 340–476

Western Roman Empire, 395

Eastern Roman Empire, 395

★ Battle site

Huns 450 → Tribe and invasion date

Picts 400

Scots 376–500

Jutes 450

Angles 450

Saxons 450

BRITAIN

ATLANTIC OCEAN

North Sea

Baltic Sea

Franks 428

Rhine River

443

Lombards 400

Huns 450

Châlons 451

GAUL

Burgundians

Ostrogoths 340–481

Huns 440

Danube River

Black Sea

Vandals 409

416–507

Visigoths

Corsica

Rome 410

Visigoths 400

Visigoths 376–395

Adrianople, 378

Constantinople

ARMENIA

Caspian Sea

SPAIN

BALEARIC ISLANDS

Sardinia

455

Sicily

PERSIA

Tigris River

Euphrates River

Vandals 429

Carthage

Mediterranean Sea

Crete

Cyprus

SYRIA

Asia Minor

A F R I C A

N

EGYPT

Nile River

Red Sea

| 0 | 200 | 400 Miles |
| 0 | 300 | 600 Kilometers |

AZIMUTHAL EQUAL AREA PROJECTION

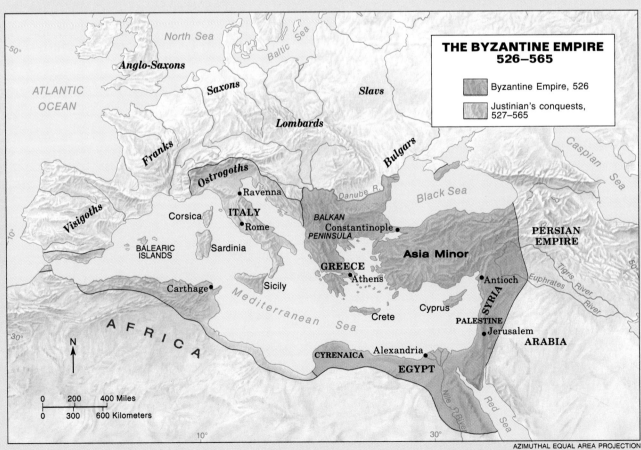

THE BYZANTINE EMPIRE 526–565

Byzantine Empire, 526

Justinian's conquests, 527–565

North Sea

Baltic Sea

Anglo-Saxons

Saxons

Slavs

ATLANTIC OCEAN

Lombards

Franks

Bulgars

Ostrogoths

Ravenna

ITALY

Rome

Danube R.

Black Sea

BALKAN PENINSULA

Constantinople

Caspian Sea

Visigoths

Corsica

BALEARIC ISLANDS

Sardinia

GREECE

Athens

Asia Minor

PERSIAN EMPIRE

Carthage

Sicily

Mediterranean Sea

Crete

Cyprus

Antioch

SYRIA

PALESTINE

Jerusalem

Tigris River

Euphrates River

A F R I C A

N

CYRENAICA

Alexandria

EGYPT

PALESTINE

ARABIA

Nile River

Red Sea

| 0 | 200 | 400 Miles |
| 0 | 300 | 600 Kilometers |

AZIMUTHAL EQUAL AREA PROJECTION

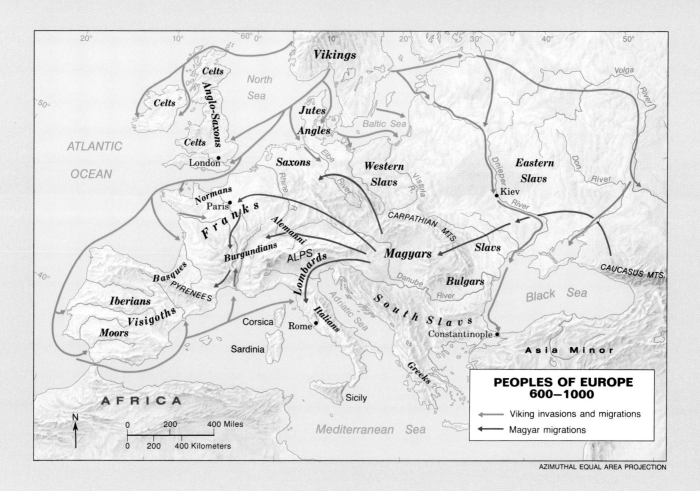

PEOPLES OF EUROPE 600–1000

→ Viking invasions and migrations
→ Magyar migrations

AZIMUTHAL EQUAL AREA PROJECTION

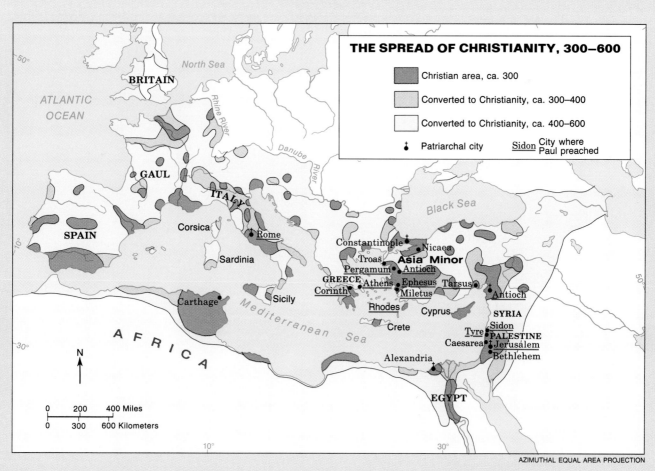

THE SPREAD OF CHRISTIANITY, 300–600

Christian area, ca. 300

Converted to Christianity, ca. 300–400

Converted to Christianity, ca. 400–600

✝ Patriarchal city   <u>Sidon</u> City where Paul preached

AZIMUTHAL EQUAL AREA PROJECTION

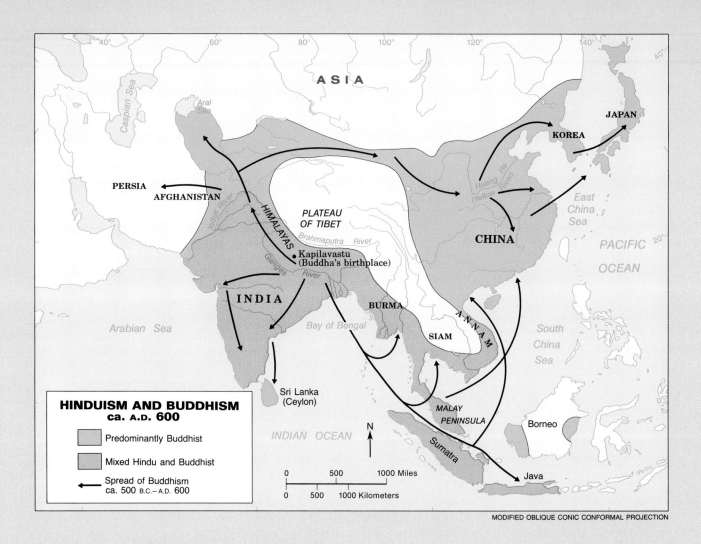

HINDUISM AND BUDDHISM
ca. A.D. 600

Predominantly Buddhist

Mixed Hindu and Buddhist

← Spread of Buddhism
ca. 500 B.C.–A.D. 600

ASIA

Aral Sea

Caspian Sea

PERSIA

AFGHANISTAN

HIMALAYAS

Indus River

Ganges River

PLATEAU OF TIBET

Brahmaputra River

Kapilavastu (Buddha's birthplace)

INDIA

Arabian Sea

Bay of Bengal

BURMA

SIAM

A-N-N-A-M

CHINA

Huang He (Yellow River)

KOREA

JAPAN

East China Sea

PACIFIC OCEAN

South China Sea

Sri Lanka (Ceylon)

INDIAN OCEAN

MALAY PENINSULA

Sumatra

Borneo

Java

N

0   500   1000 Miles

0   500   1000 Kilometers

MODIFIED OBLIQUE CONIC CONFORMAL PROJECTION

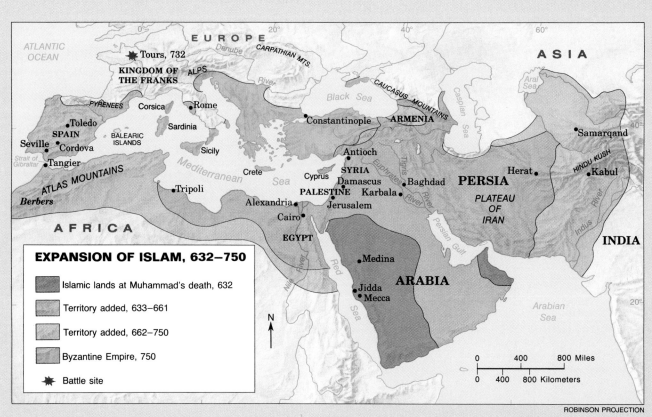

EXPANSION OF ISLAM, 632–750

Islamic lands at Muhammad's death, 632

Territory added, 633–661

Territory added, 662–750

Byzantine Empire, 750

★ Battle site

EUROPE

ATLANTIC OCEAN

Tours, 732

KINGDOM OF THE FRANKS

ALPS

Danube

CARPATHIAN MTS.

River

PYRENEES

Corsica

Rome

SPAIN

Toledo

BALEARIC ISLANDS

Sardinia

Seville

Cordova

Strait of Gibraltar

Tangier

ATLAS MOUNTAINS

Berbers

Tripoli

Sicily

Mediterranean

Crete

Sea

Cyprus

Black Sea

Constantinople

ARMENIA

CAUCASUS MOUNTAINS

ASIA

Aral Sea

Caspian Sea

Antioch

SYRIA

Damascus

Euphrates River

Tigris River

Baghdad

Karbala

PALESTINE

Jerusalem

Alexandria

Cairo

EGYPT

Nile River

Red Sea

ARABIA

Medina

Jidda

Mecca

PERSIA

PLATEAU OF IRAN

Herat

Persian Gulf

Samarqand

HINDU KUSH

Kabul

Indus River

INDIA

Arabian Sea

AFRICA

N

0   400   800 Miles

0   400   800 Kilometers

ROBINSON PROJECTION

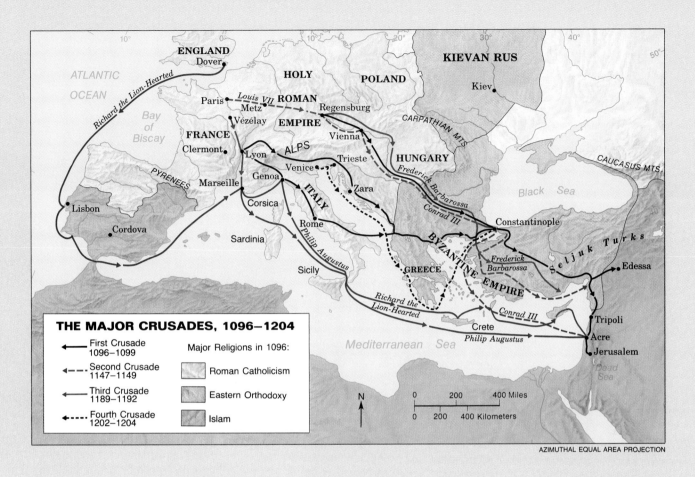

THE MAJOR CRUSADES, 1096–1204

→ First Crusade 1096–1099

◄--► Second Crusade 1147–1149

← Third Crusade 1189–1192

◄---► Fourth Crusade 1202–1204

Major Religions in 1096:

Roman Catholicism

Eastern Orthodoxy

Islam

0   200   400 Miles

0   200   400 Kilometers

N

AZIMUTHAL EQUAL AREA PROJECTION

EUROPE, ca. 1500

- - - - Boundary of the Holy Roman Empire

0   200   400 Miles

0   200   400 Kilometers

N

AZIMUTHAL EQUAL AREA PROJECTION

EUROPEAN RELIGIONS, 1600

- Lutheran
- Calvinist
- Anglican
- Roman Catholic with Protestant minorities
- Roman Catholic
- Orthodox
- Muslim

ICELAND

ATLANTIC OCEAN

SWEDEN

NORWAY

RUSSIA

SCOTLAND
Edinburgh

North Sea

DENMARK
Copenhagen

COURLAND

Baltic Sea

PRUSSIA

POLAND AND LITHUANIA
Warsaw

IRELAND
Dublin

ENGLAND
London

SPANISH NETHERLANDS

NETHERLANDS

HOLY
POMERANIA
MECKLENBURG
BRANDENBURG

HESSE
SAXONY
Wittenburg

English Channel

Worms
ROMAN
PALATINATE
ANSBACH
Prague
BOHEMIA

Paris

WÜRTTEMBERG

FRANCE

Nantes

Zurich
SWITZERLAND
EMPIRE
BAVARIA
TIROL

AUSTRIA

TRANSYLVANIA

HUNGARY

OTTOMAN EMPIRE

Black Sea

La Rochelle

Geneva
Milan
VENICE
Trent

PORTUGAL

PAPAL
STATES

Adriatic Sea

Lisbon

SPAIN
Madrid

Corsica
Rome

NAPLES
Naples

Sardinia

Mediterranean Sea

Sicily

0   250   500 Miles
0   250   500 Kilometers

N

AFRICA

AZIMUTHAL EQUAL AREA PROJECTION

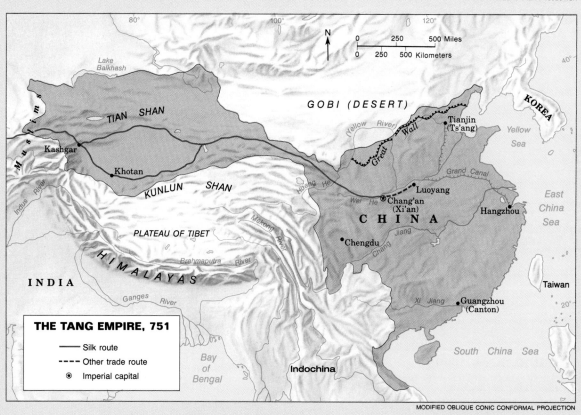

THE TANG EMPIRE, 751

—— Silk route
---- Other trade route
⊛ Imperial capital

Lake Balkhash

M u s l i m s

TIAN SHAN

Kashgar

Khotan

KUNLUN SHAN

Indus River

PLATEAU OF TIBET

HIMALAYAS

Brahmaputra River

INDIA

Ganges River

Bay of Bengal

GOBI (DESERT)

Yellow River

Great Wall

Tianjin (Ts'ang)

KOREA

Yellow Sea

Grand Canal

Huang He

Luoyang

Wei He
Chang'an (Xi'an)

CHINA

Chengdu

Mekong River

Chang Jiang

Hangzhou

East China Sea

Taiwan

Xi Jiang
Guangzhou (Canton)

South China Sea

Indochina

0   250   500 Miles
0   250   500 Kilometers

N

MODIFIED OBLIQUE CONIC CONFORMAL PROJECTION

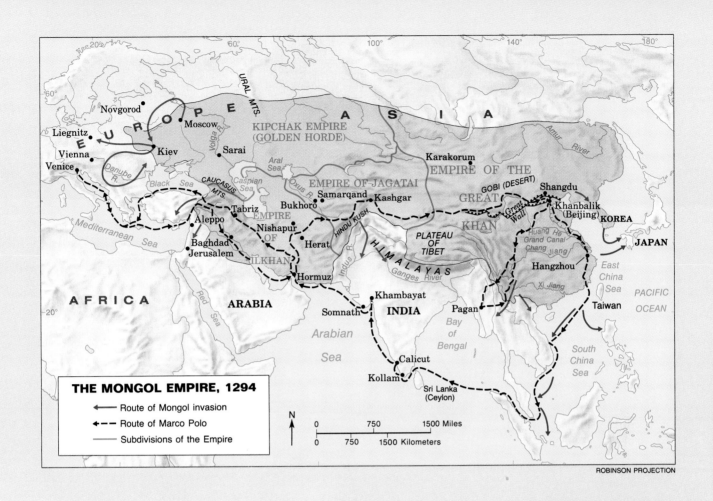

THE MONGOL EMPIRE, 1294

Route of Mongol invasion
Route of Marco Polo
Subdivisions of the Empire

EUROPE — ASIA — AFRICA

Novgorod · Moscow · Liegnitz · Vienna · Kiev · Sarai · Venice · Danube R. · Volga · Black Sea · CAUCASUS MTS. · Caspian Sea · Aral Sea · Oxus R.

KIPCHAK EMPIRE (GOLDEN HORDE)

URAL MTS.

EMPIRE OF JAGATAI · Bukhoro · Samarqand · Kashgar

Karakorum · EMPIRE OF THE GREAT KHAN · Shangdu · Khanbalik (Beijing) · KOREA · JAPAN

Great Wall · Amur River

Tabriz · Nishapur · EMPIRE OF ILKHAN · Aleppo · Baghdad · Jerusalem · Herat · Hormuz · HINDU KUSH · Indus R. · HIMALAYAS · Ganges River · PLATEAU OF TIBET

Huang He · Grand Canal · Chang Jiang · Hangzhou · Xi Jiang · East China Sea · PACIFIC OCEAN

ARABIA · Red Sea · Mediterranean Sea

Khambayat · INDIA · Somnath · Pagan · Taiwan

Arabian Sea · Bay of Bengal · South China Sea

Calicut · Kollam · Sri Lanka (Ceylon)

N

0   750   1500 Miles
0   750   1500 Kilometers

ROBINSON PROJECTION

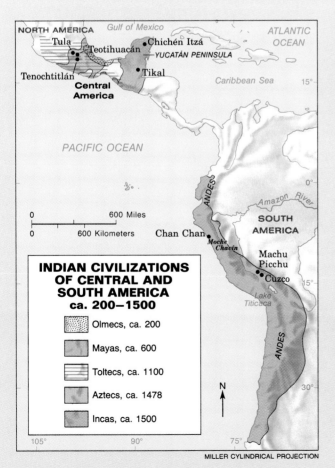

INDIAN CIVILIZATIONS OF CENTRAL AND SOUTH AMERICA ca. 200–1500

NORTH AMERICA · Gulf of Mexico · ATLANTIC OCEAN
Tula · Teotihuacán · Chichén Itzá · YUCATÁN PENINSULA
Tenochtitlán · Tikal · Central America · Caribbean Sea

PACIFIC OCEAN

Chan Chan · Moche · Chavín · Machu Picchu · Cuzco · Lake Titicaca · ANDES · SOUTH AMERICA · Amazon River

0   600 Miles
0   600 Kilometers

Olmecs, ca. 200
Mayas, ca. 600
Toltecs, ca. 1100
Aztecs, ca. 1478
Incas, ca. 1500

N

MILLER CYLINDRICAL PROJECTION

Early African Kingdoms

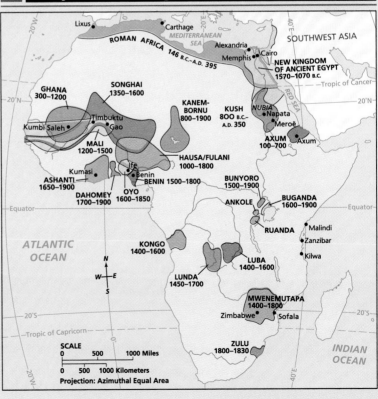

Lixus · Carthage · MEDITERRANEAN SEA · Alexandria · Memphis · Cairo · SOUTHWEST ASIA
ROMAN AFRICA 146 B.C.–A.D. 395
NEW KINGDOM OF ANCIENT EGYPT 1570–1070 B.C.
Tropic of Cancer

GHANA 300–1200 · SONGHAI 1350–1600 · KANEM-BORNU 800–1900 · KUSH 800 B.C.–A.D. 350 · NUBIA · Napata · Meroë · AXUM 100–700 · Axum · RED SEA

Kumbi Saleh · Timbuktu · Gao · MALI 1200–1500 · Kumasi · Ife · Benin · HAUSA/FULANI 1000–1800 · BENIN 1500–1800 · BUNYORO 1500–1900 · Malindi

ASHANTI 1650–1900 · DAHOMEY 1700–1900 · OYO 1600–1850 · ANKOLE · BUGANDA 1600–1900 · Zanzibar · RUANDA · Kilwa

ATLANTIC OCEAN · Equator

KONGO 1400–1600 · LUBA 1400–1600 · LUNDA 1450–1700 · MWENEMUTAPA 1400–1800 · Zimbabwe · Sofala · ZULU 1800–1830 · INDIAN OCEAN

N W E S

SCALE
0   500   1000 Miles
0   500   1000 Kilometers
Projection: Azimuthal Equal Area

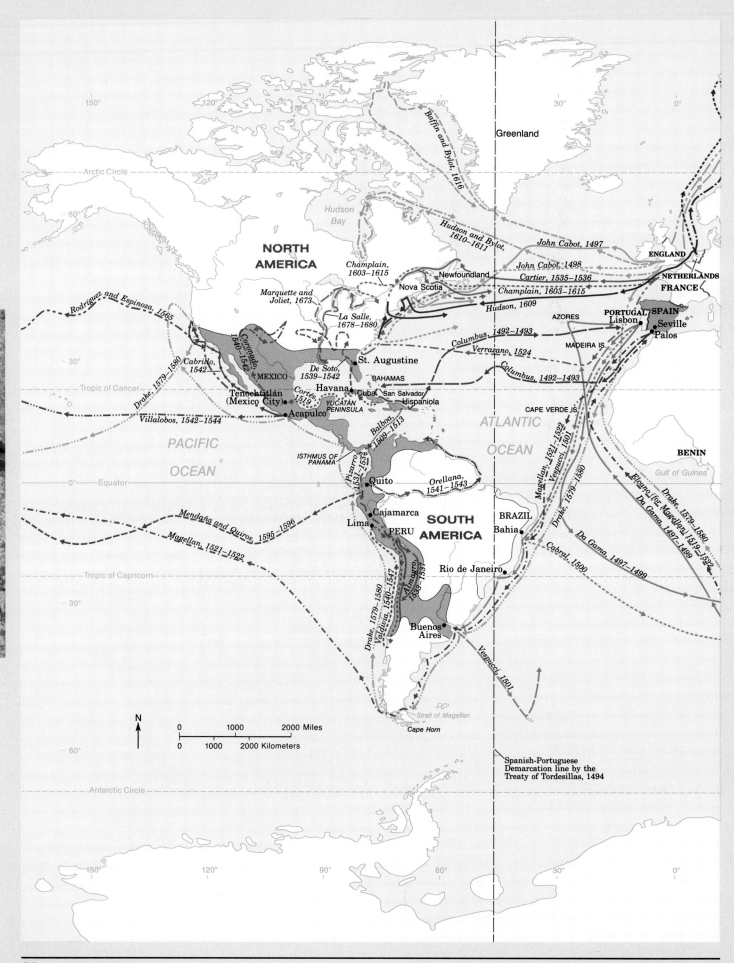

NORTH AMERICA

SOUTH AMERICA

PACIFIC OCEAN

ATLANTIC OCEAN

Greenland

Baffin and Bylot, 1616

Hudson and Bylot, 1610–1611

John Cabot, 1497

John Cabot, 1498

Cartier, 1535–1536

ENGLAND

NETHERLANDS

FRANCE

Hudson Bay

Champlain, 1603–1615

Newfoundland

Nova Scotia

Champlain, 1603–1615

Hudson, 1609

Marquette and Joliet, 1673

La Salle, 1678–1680

PORTUGAL Lisbon

SPAIN Seville Palos

AZORES

Columbus, 1492–1493

Verrazano, 1524

MADEIRA IS.

Rodriguez and Espinoza, 1565

Coronado, 1540–1542

Cabrillo, 1542

Drake, 1579–1580

St. Augustine

De Soto, 1539–1542

MEXICO

BAHAMAS

Columbus, 1492–1493

Tropic of Cancer

Havana

Cortés, 1519

Cuba San Salvador

Tenochtitlán (Mexico City)

Acapulco

YUCATÁN PENINSULA

Hispaniola

CAPE VERDE IS.

Villalobos, 1542–1544

BENIN

Gulf of Guinea

ISTHMUS OF PANAMA

Balboa, 1509–1513

Magellan, 1521–1522

Vespucci, 1501

Drake, 1579–1580

Elcano (for Magellan) 1519–1522

Da Gama, 1492–1499

Equator

Pizarro, 1531–1532

Quito

Orellana, 1541–1543

Mendaña and Quiros, 1595–1596

Cajamarca

Lima

PERU

BRAZIL

Bahia

Da Gama, 1497–1499

Magellan, 1521–1522

Cabral, 1500

Rio de Janeiro

Tropic of Capricorn

Drake, 1579–1580

Valdivia, 1540–1547

Almagro, 1535–1537

Buenos Aires

Vespucci, 1501

Strait of Magellan

Cape Horn

Spanish-Portuguese
Demarcation line by the
Treaty of Tordesillas, 1494

N

| 0 | 1000 | 2000 Miles |
| 0 | 1000 | 2000 Kilometers |

Arctic Circle

Antarctic Circle

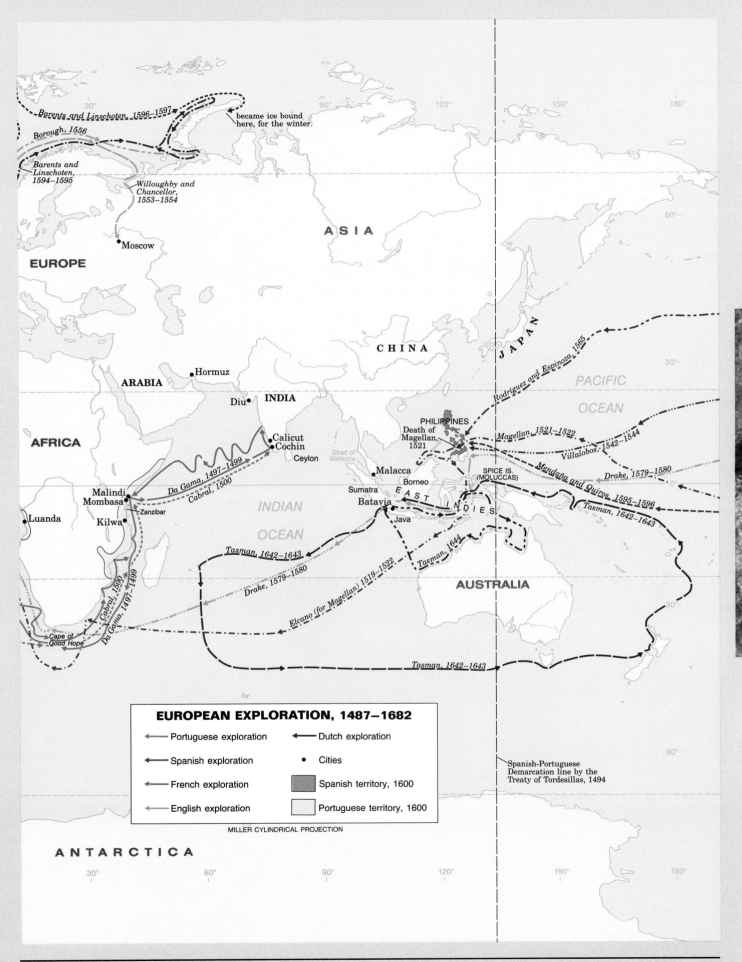

Barents and Linschoten, 1596–1597

became ice bound
here, for the winter.

Borough, 1556

Barents and
Linschoten,
1594–1595

Willoughby and
Chancellor,
1553–1554

• Moscow

EUROPE

ASIA

AFRICA

ARABIA

INDIA

CHINA

JAPAN

PACIFIC

OCEAN

• Hormuz

Diu •

Calicut
Cochin

Ceylon

Strait of
Malacca

PHILIPPINES
Death of
Magellan,
1521

Rodríguez and Espinoza, 1565

Magellan, 1521–1522

Villalobos, 1542–1544

Malindi
Mombasa
← Zanzibar

• Luanda

Kilwa

Malacca •

Borneo

SPICE IS.
(MOLUCCAS)

Mendaña and Quiros, 1595–1596

Drake, 1579–1580

Sumatra

Batavia •

E A S T

I N D I E S

Tasman, 1642–1643

Da Gama, 1497–1499

Cabral, 1500

Java

INDIAN

OCEAN

Tasman, 1642–1643

Drake, 1579–1580

Tasman, 1644

Cabral, 1500

Da Gama, 1497–1499

Elcano (for Magellan) 1519–1522

AUSTRALIA

Cape of
Good Hope

Tasman, 1642–1643

EUROPEAN EXPLORATION, 1487–1682

← Portuguese exploration   ← Dutch exploration

← Spanish exploration   • Cities

← French exploration   ▨ Spanish territory, 1600

← English exploration   ☐ Portuguese territory, 1600

MILLER CYLINDRICAL PROJECTION

Spanish-Portuguese
Demarcation line by the
Treaty of Tordesillas, 1494

ANTARCTICA

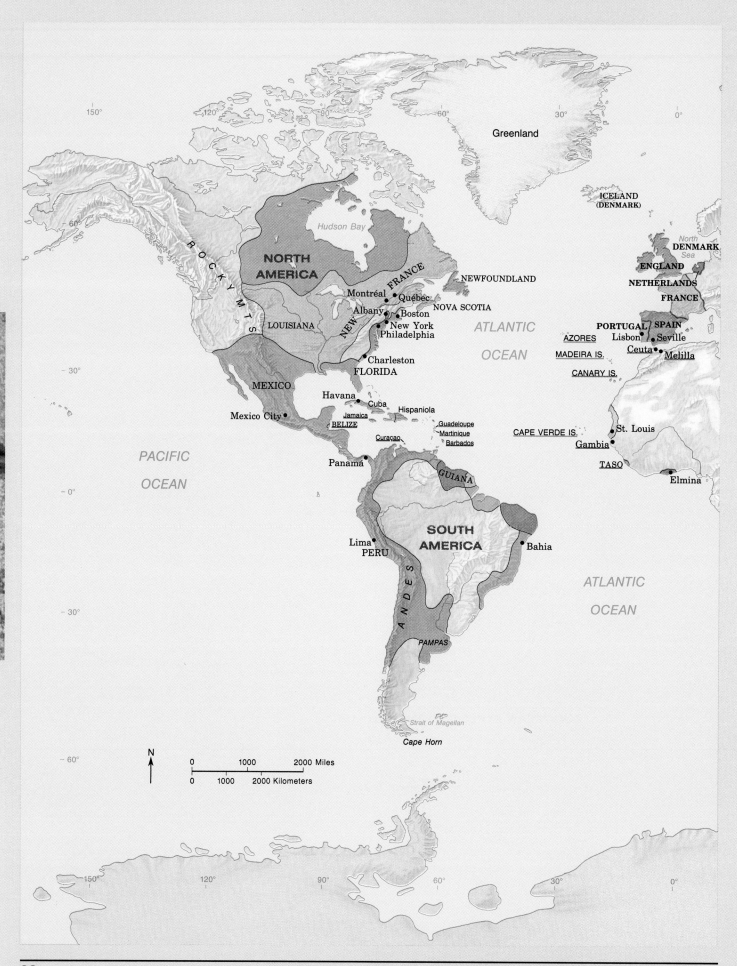

Greenland

North
America

Hudson Bay

ROCKY MTS

NORTH
AMERICA

NEWFOUNDLAND

FRANCE

Montréal
Québec

NOVA SCOTIA

Albany
Boston

NEW

LOUISIANA

New York
Philadelphia

ATLANTIC

OCEAN

Charleston

FLORIDA

MEXICO

Havana

Cuba

Hispaniola

Mexico City

Jamaica

BELIZE

Guadeloupe

Martinique

Curacao

Barbados

Panamá

GUIANA

PACIFIC

OCEAN

Lima
PERU

SOUTH
AMERICA

Bahia

ANDES

ATLANTIC

OCEAN

PAMPAS

Strait of Magellan

Cape Horn

ICELAND
(DENMARK)

North
Sea

DENMARK

ENGLAND

NETHERLANDS

FRANCE

PORTUGAL SPAIN

AZORES

Lisbon
Seville

Ceuta
Melilla

MADEIRA IS.

CANARY IS.

CAPE VERDE IS.

St. Louis

Gambia

TASO

Elmina

N

0	1000	2000 Miles
0	1000	2000 Kilometers

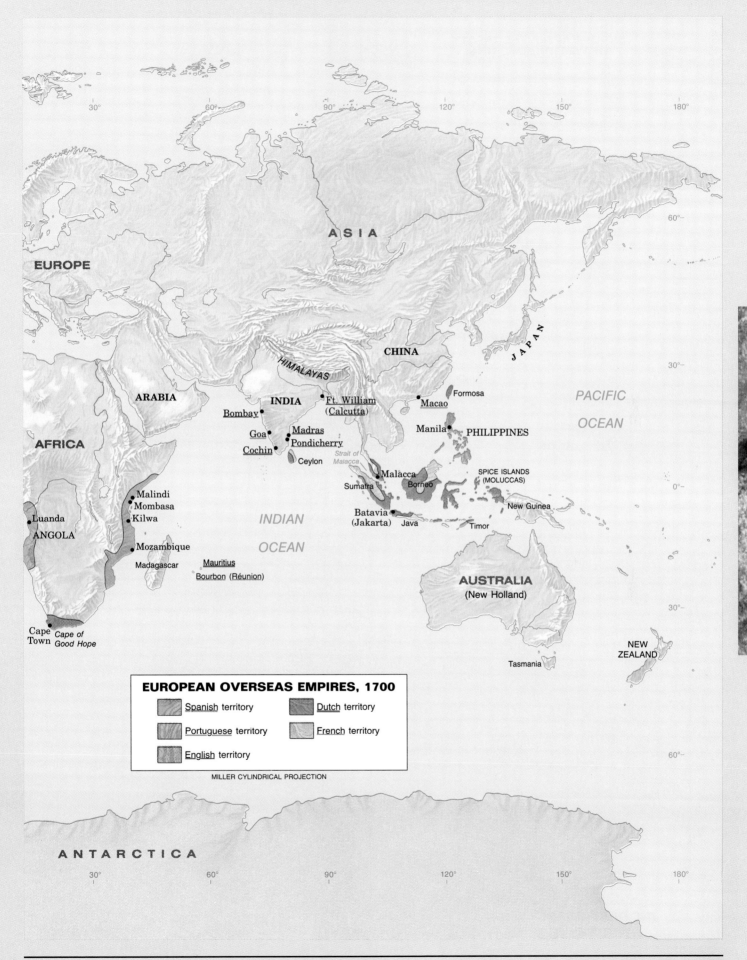

ASIA

EUROPE

CHINA

HIMALAYAS

JAPAN

ARABIA

INDIA

Ft. William
(Calcutta)

Bombay

Formosa

Macao

AFRICA

Goa
Cochin

Madras
Pondicherry

Ceylon

Strait of
Malacca

Manila

PHILIPPINES

Malindi
Mombasa
Kilwa

Luanda
ANGOLA

Mozambique

Madagascar

INDIAN

OCEAN

Mauritius

Bourbon (Réunion)

Malacca

Sumatra

Borneo

SPICE ISLANDS
(MOLUCCAS)

New Guinea

Batavia
(Jakarta)   Java

Timor

PACIFIC

OCEAN

AUSTRALIA
(New Holland)

Cape
Town

Cape of
Good Hope

Tasmania

NEW
ZEALAND

30°   60°   90°   120°   150°   180°

60°

30°

0°

30°

60°

EUROPEAN OVERSEAS EMPIRES, 1700

Spanish territory   Dutch territory

Portuguese territory   French territory

English territory

MILLER CYLINDRICAL PROJECTION

ANTARCTICA

30°   60°   90°   120°   150°   180°

EUROPE AFTER THE TREATY OF WESTPHALIA, 1648

Possessions of the Spanish Hapsburgs

Possessions of the Austrian Hapsburgs

Possessions of the Hohenzollerns

RUSSIA

Moscow

Stockholm

SWEDEN

KINGDOM
OF
DENMARK
AND
NORWAY

Baltic Sea

EAST PRUSSIA

POLAND

SCOTLAND

North Sea

IRELAND

POMERANIA

Berlin

Warsaw

ENGLAND

London

UNITED NETHERLANDS

BRANDENBURG PRUSSIA

SAXONY

ATLANTIC OCEAN

English Channel

SPANISH NETHERLANDS

Rhine

HOLY

BOHEMIA

Prague

ROMAN EMPIRE

Paris

ALSACE

BAVARIA

Vienna

Buda Pest

Bay of Biscay

FRANCE

FRANCHE COMTÉ

SWITZERLAND

AUSTRIA

HUNGARY

Black Sea

SAVOY

PIEDMONT

MILAN

REPUBLIC OF VENICE

Danube River

Avignon

GENOA

TUSCANY

Adriatic Sea

OTTOMAN

Constantinople

Corsica

PAPAL STATES

Rome

PORTUGAL

Madrid

SPAIN

NAPLES

EMPIRE

Aegean Sea

BALEARIC ISLANDS

Sardinia

N

Mediterranean Sea

Sicily

Crete

AFRICA

| 0 | 150 | 300 Miles |
| 0 | 150 | 300 Kilometers |

AZIMUTHAL EQUAL AREA PROJECTION

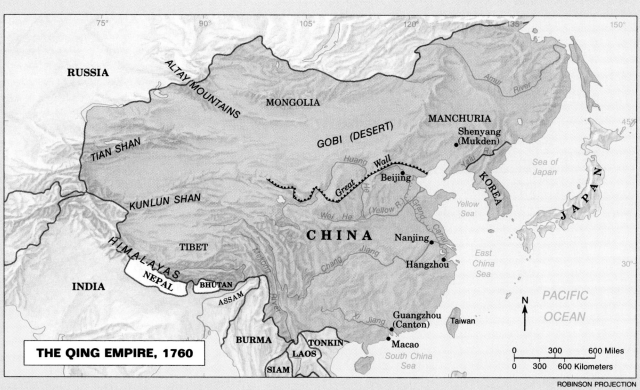

THE QING EMPIRE, 1760

RUSSIA

ALTAY MOUNTAINS

MONGOLIA

GOBI (DESERT)

MANCHURIA

Shenyang (Mukden)

Amur River

TIAN SHAN

Great Wall

Huang He

Beijing

Yalu

Sea of Japan

KUNLUN SHAN

Wei He

(Yellow R.)

Grand Canal

Yellow Sea

KOREA

JAPAN

TIBET

CHINA

Nanjing

HIMALAYAS

NEPAL

BHUTAN

Chang Jiang

Hangzhou

East China Sea

INDIA

ASSAM

Mekong River

PACIFIC OCEAN

BURMA

LAOS

TONKIN

Xi Jiang

Guangzhou (Canton)

Taiwan

Macao

SIAM

South China Sea

N

| 0 | 300 | 600 Miles |
| 0 | 300 | 600 Kilometers |

ROBINSON PROJECTION

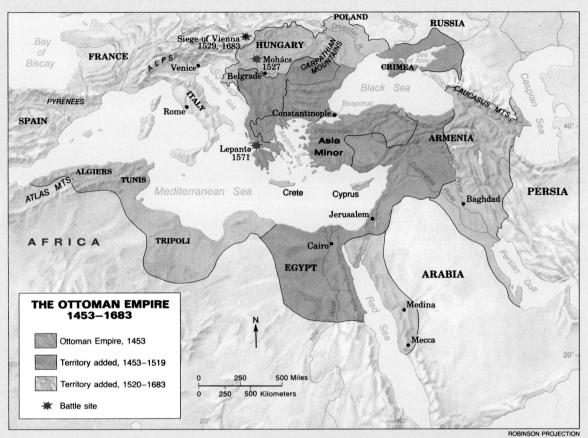

THE OTTOMAN EMPIRE
1453–1683

- Ottoman Empire, 1453
- Territory added, 1453–1519
- Territory added, 1520–1683
- ✳ Battle site

| 0 | 250 | 500 Miles |
| 0 | 250 | 500 Kilometers |

N

ROBINSON PROJECTION

Labels on map: POLAND, RUSSIA, Bay of Biscay, FRANCE, HUNGARY, Siege of Vienna 1529, 1683, Mohács 1527, Belgrade, Venice, ALPS, CARPATHIAN MOUNTAINS, CRIMEA, Sea of Azov, Danube River, Dnieper R., CAUCASUS MTS., ITALY, Rome, Adriatic Sea, Constantinople, Black Sea, Bosporus, PYRENEES, SPAIN, Lepanto 1571, Asia Minor, Dardanelles, Aegean Sea, ARMENIA, Caspian Sea, 40°, ALGIERS, TUNIS, ATLAS MTS., Mediterranean Sea, Crete, Cyprus, Jerusalem, Tigris River, Euphrates River, Baghdad, PERSIA, AFRICA, TRIPOLI, Cairo, EGYPT, Nile River, ARABIA, Red Sea, Medina, Mecca, Persian Gulf, 20°, 40°

EUROPE IN 1763

- Possessions of the Austrian Habsburgs
- Possessions of the Hohenzollerns

| 0 | 150 | 300 Miles |
| 0 | 150 | 300 Kilometers |

N

AZIMUTHAL EQUAL AREA PROJECTION

Labels on map: SWEDEN, St. Petersburg, Stockholm, RUSSIA, Baltic Sea, KINGDOM OF DENMARK AND NORWAY, EAST PRUSSIA, KINGDOM OF GREAT BRITAIN AND IRELAND, North Sea, PRUSSIA, POLAND, HANOVER, Berlin, Warsaw, Vistula River, London, UNITED NETHERLANDS, SAXONY, SILESIA, ATLANTIC OCEAN, English Channel, AUSTRIAN NETHERLANDS, LESSER GERMAN STATES, BOHEMIA, Rhine, Paris, BAVARIA, Vienna, LORRAINE, Buda, Pest, HUNGARY, Bay of Biscay, FRANCE, SWITZERLAND, AUSTRIA, Danube River, Black Sea, SAVOY, MILAN, VENETIAN REPUBLIC, Adriatic Sea, 30°, PARMA, Avignon, TUSCANY, PAPAL STATES, MONTENEGRO, OTTOMAN, GENOA, Constantinople, KINGDOM OF SARDINIA, Corsica, Rome, PORTUGAL, Madrid, Minorca (BR.), Sardinia, KINGDOM OF NAPLES, EMPIRE, Aegean Sea, 40°, SPAIN, BALEARIC ISLANDS (SP.), Gibraltar (BR.), Mediterranean Sea, Sicily, Crete, AFRICA, 10°, 20°, 50°

NAPOLEONIC EUROPE, 1805–1815

- Empire of the French, 1812
- States controlled by Napoleon, 1812
- States allied with Napoleon, 1812
- States allied against Napoleon, 1812
- Neutral states, 1812
- ★ Battle site

St. Petersburg

SWEDEN

KINGDOM OF DENMARK AND NORWAY

Baltic Sea

Niemen River

Moscow

Borodino 1812 ★

Route of the Grand Army 1812

RUSSIAN EMPIRE

GREAT BRITAIN

North Sea

ATLANTIC OCEAN

London

English Channel

Waterloo 1815 ★

Paris

EMPIRE OF THE FRENCH

KINGDOM OF WESTPHALIA

Berlin

Rhine River

PRUSSIA

GRAND DUCHY OF WARSAW

Leipzig 1813 ★

SAXONY

CONFEDERATION OF THE RHINE

Austerlitz 1805 ★

Vienna

AUSTRIAN EMPIRE

SWITZERLAND

KINGDOM OF ITALY

Venice

ILLYRIAN PROVINCES

Danube River

Black Sea

Adriatic Sea

OTTOMAN

Constantinople

MONTENEGRO

N ↑

0   150   300 Miles
0   150   300 Kilometers

PORTUGAL

Lisbon

Madrid

SPAIN

Corsica

Elba

Rome

KINGDOM OF SARDINIA

BALEARIC ISLANDS

KINGDOM OF NAPLES

Corfu

IONIAN ISLANDS (British)

EMPIRE

ASIA

Aegean Sea

Crete

Strait of Gibraltar

Trafalgar 1805 ★

GIBRALTAR (BR.)

Mediterranean Sea

AFRICA

MALTA (BR.)

KINGDOM OF SICILY

AZIMUTHAL EQUAL AREA PROJECTION

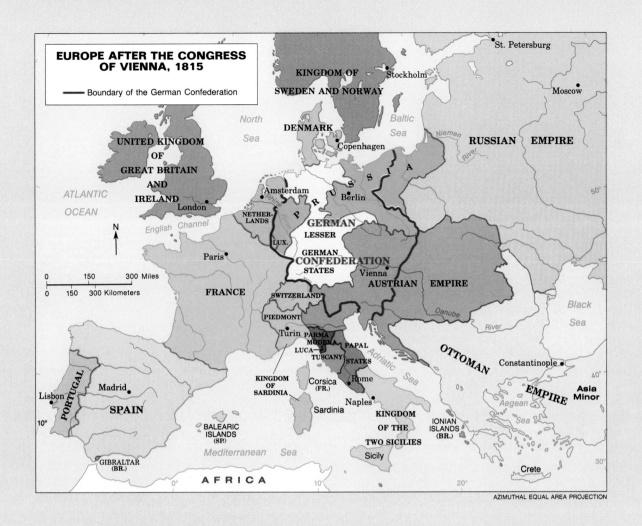

EUROPE AFTER THE CONGRESS OF VIENNA, 1815

—— Boundary of the German Confederation

St. Petersburg

KINGDOM OF
SWEDEN AND NORWAY

Stockholm

Moscow

DENMARK

Baltic Sea

Copenhagen

North Sea

RUSSIAN EMPIRE

UNITED KINGDOM
OF
GREAT BRITAIN
AND
IRELAND

Amsterdam

Berlin

P R U S S I A

ATLANTIC OCEAN

London

Niemen River

50°

NETHER-LANDS

GERMAN

English Channel

N

LESSER

LUX.

GERMAN

Paris

CONFEDERATION

STATES

Vienna

0   150   300 Miles
0   150   300 Kilometers

FRANCE

SWITZERLAND

AUSTRIAN   EMPIRE

Danube River

Black Sea

PIEDMONT

Turin   PARMA
MODENA

LUCA   TUSCANY

Adriatic Sea

OTTOMAN

Constantinople

KINGDOM OF
SARDINIA

Corsica
(FR.)

PAPAL
STATES

Rome

EMPIRE

Asia Minor

40°

PORTUGAL

Madrid

SPAIN

Sardinia

Naples

KINGDOM

Aegean Sea

Lisbon

10°

BALEARIC
ISLANDS
(SP.)

OF THE

TWO SICILIES

IONIAN
ISLANDS
(BR.)

30°

Mediterranean   Sea

Sicily

GIBRALTAR
(BR.)

0°

AFRICA

10°

Crete

20°

AZIMUTHAL EQUAL AREA PROJECTION

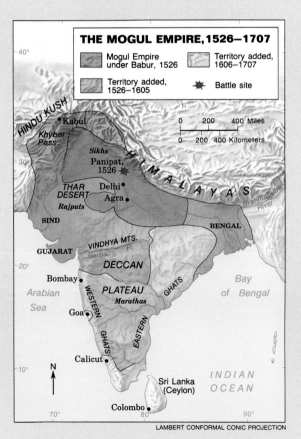

THE MOGUL EMPIRE, 1526–1707

▨ Mogul Empire
under Babur, 1526

▨ Territory added,
1606–1707

▨ Territory added,
1526–1605

✸ Battle site

0   200   400 Miles
0   200   400 Kilometers

40°

HINDU KUSH

Kabul

Khyber
Pass

Sikhs
Panipat,
1526

H I M A L A Y A S

30°

THAR
DESERT

Delhi

Agra

Rajputs

SIND

BENGAL

GUJARAT

VINDHYA MTS.

Narbada

Brahmaputra River

Ganges

Bombay

DECCAN

Bay
of Bengal

20°

PLATEAU

Marathas

WESTERN

EASTERN

GHATS

Goa

GHATS

Arabian
Sea

Calicut

10°

Sri Lanka
(Ceylon)

INDIAN
OCEAN

Colombo

70°   80°   90°

LAMBERT CONFORMAL CONIC PROJECTION

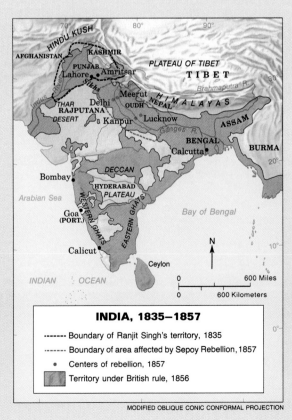

70°   80°   90°

HINDU KUSH

KASHMIR

AFGHANISTAN

PUNJAB

PLATEAU OF TIBET

Lahore

Amritsar

T I B E T

Sikhs

30°

Brahmaputra R.

THAR
RAJPUTANA
DESERT

Meerut

Delhi

NEPAL

H I M A L A Y A S

OUDH

Kanpur

Lucknow

ASSAM

Ganges R.

BENGAL

BURMA

Bombay

DECCAN

Calcutta

20°

Arabian Sea

HYDERABAD
PLATEAU

WESTERN GHATS

Goa
(PORT.)

EASTERN GHATS

Bay of Bengal

N

Calicut

10°

Ceylon

INDIAN   OCEAN

0   600 Miles
0   600 Kilometers

0°

INDIA, 1835–1857

---- Boundary of Ranjit Singh's territory, 1835

----- Boundary of area affected by Sepoy Rebellion, 1857

• Centers of rebellion, 1857

▨ Territory under British rule, 1856

MODIFIED OBLIQUE CONIC CONFORMAL PROJECTION

LATIN AMERICA, 1790

Spanish territory

Portuguese territory

British territory

French territory

Dutch territory

DISPUTED TERRITORY
(SPAIN VS. RUSSIA)

SPANISH LOUISIANA

UNITED STATES

Monterrey

VICEROYALTY OF NEW SPAIN

Monterrey

Guadalajara

Mérida

México

Veracruz

WEST FLORIDA

EAST FLORIDA

Gulf of Mexico

BAHAMAS (BR.)

ATLANTIC OCEAN

Havana

CAPTAINCY-GENERAL OF CUBA

Cuba

Jamaica

Puerto Rico

Hispaniola

Haiti

Santo Domingo

WEST INDIES

BRITISH HONDURAS

CAPTAINCY-GENERAL OF GUATEMALA

Caribbean Sea

Cartagena

Caracas

Cumaná

CAPTAINCY-GENERAL OF VENEZUELA

GUIANAS

PACIFIC OCEAN

ISTHMUS OF PANAMA

Bogotá

Popayán

Quito

Guayaquil

VICEROYALTY OF NEW GRANADA

Amazon River

Trujillo

ANDES

Lima

Cuzco

BRAZIL

Arequipa

La Paz

BRAZILIAN HIGHLANDS

VICEROYALTY OF PERU

VICEROYALTY OF

Salta

Asunción

Tucumán

Corrientes

RÍO DE LA PLATA

Santiago

Buenos Aires

Montevideo

Concepción

PAMPAS

Río de la Plata

ANDES

Strait of Magellan

FALKLAND ISLANDS (ISLAS MALVINAS)

Cape Horn

N

0   500   1000 Miles

0   500   1000 Kilometers

MILLER CYLINDRICAL PROJECTION

OREGON COUNTRY
(disputed: U.S. vs. Britain)

UNITED STATES

MÉXICO, 1821

ATLANTIC

OCEAN

Missouri River

Mississippi

Colorado River

Rio Grande

Gulf of
Mexico

BAHAMAS
(BR.)

México Veracruz

W E S T

CUBA
(SP.)

HAITI, 1803

PUERTO RICO
(SP.)

BRITISH
HONDURAS
(BR.)

JAMAICA
(BR.)

I N D I E S

Guatemala City

MOSQUITO
COAST
(BR.)

Caribbean
Sea

TRINIDAD
(BR.)

Caracas

UNITED
PROVINCES
OF
CENTRAL
AMERICA
1823

ISTHMUS OF
PANAMA

**GREAT COLOMBIA
1819–1830**

G U I A N A S

(BR.)

(NETH.)

(FR.)

Bogotá

PACIFIC

OCEAN

Quito

DISPUTED
TERRITORY

Amazon River

N

PERU, 1821

EMPIRE OF BRAZIL, 1822

Lima

Salvador

La Paz
BOLIVIA, 1825

Chuquisaca
(Sucre)

0   500   1000 Miles

0   500   1000 Kilometers

**PARAGUAY
1811**

São Paulo

Asunción

Rio de Janeiro

Paraná River

**NEW NATIONS IN
LATIN AMERICA, 1828**

**URUGUAY
1828**

Santiago

Buenos Aires

Montevideo

**CHILE
1817**

**UNITED
PROVINCES
OF
LA PLATA, 1816
(ARGENTINA)**

Río de
la Plata

FALKLAND ISLANDS
(ISLAS MALVINAS)

Strait of
Magellan

Cape Horn

MILLER CYLINDRICAL PROJECTION

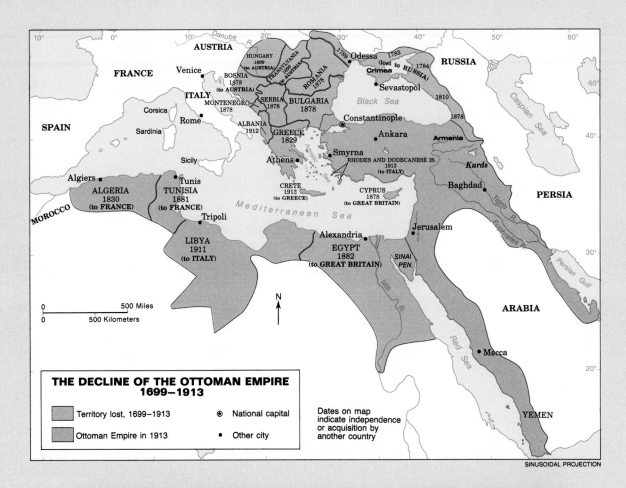

THE DECLINE OF THE OTTOMAN EMPIRE 1699–1913

- Territory lost, 1699–1913
- Ottoman Empire in 1913

⊛ National capital
• Other city

Dates on map indicate independence or acquisition by another country

SINUSOIDAL PROJECTION

Map labels:

AUSTRIA
FRANCE
Venice
ITALY
Corsica
Rome
SPAIN
Sardinia
Sicily
MOROCCO
Algiers
Tunis
ALGERIA 1830 (to FRANCE)
TUNISIA 1881 (to FRANCE)
Tripoli
LIBYA 1911 (to ITALY)
HUNGARY 1699 (lost to AUSTRIA)
TRANSYLVANIA (to AUSTRIA)
BOSNIA 1878 (to AUSTRIA)
SERBIA 1878
MONTENEGRO 1878
ALBANIA 1912
GREECE 1829
ROMANIA 1878
BULGARIA 1878
Athens
CRETE 1913 (to GREECE)
Mediterranean Sea
Odessa 1789
Crimea 1783
1784 (lost to RUSSIA)
RUSSIA
Sevastopol 1810
Black Sea
Constantinople
Ankara
Armenia
Kurds
Baghdad
PERSIA
Smyrna
RHODES AND DODECANESE IS. 1913 (to ITALY)
CYPRUS 1878 (to GREAT BRITAIN)
Alexandria
Jerusalem
EGYPT 1882 (to GREAT BRITAIN)
SINAI PEN.
Nile R.
Tigris R.
Euphrates R.
Caspian Sea
Persian Gulf
ARABIA
Red Sea
Mecca
YEMEN
Danube R.

500 Miles
500 Kilometers
N

Colonialism and Independence in Africa

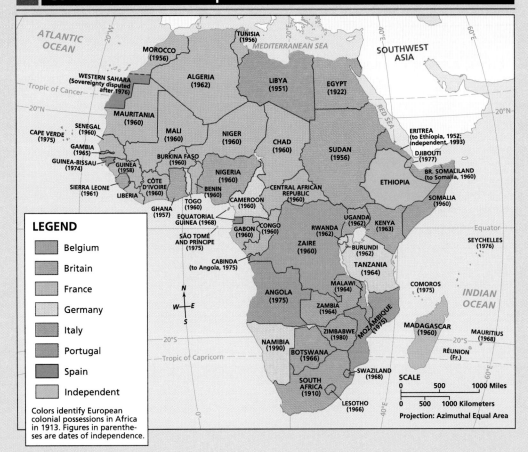

LEGEND

- Belgium
- Britain
- France
- Germany
- Italy
- Portugal
- Spain
- Independent

Colors identify European colonial possessions in Africa in 1913. Figures in parentheses are dates of independence.

Map labels:

ATLANTIC OCEAN
MEDITERRANEAN SEA
SOUTHWEST ASIA
TUNISIA (1956)
MOROCCO (1956)
WESTERN SAHARA (Sovereignty disputed after 1976)
ALGERIA (1962)
LIBYA (1951)
EGYPT (1922)
Tropic of Cancer
MAURITANIA (1960)
SENEGAL (1960)
CAPE VERDE (1975)
GAMBIA (1965)
GUINEA-BISSAU (1974)
MALI (1960)
GUINEA (1958)
SIERRA LEONE (1961)
BURKINA FASO (1960)
CÔTE D'IVOIRE (1960)
LIBERIA
GHANA (1957)
TOGO (1960)
BENIN (1960)
NIGER (1960)
NIGERIA (1960)
CHAD (1960)
SUDAN (1956)
ERITREA (to Ethiopia, 1952; independent, 1993)
DJIBOUTI (1977)
BR. SOMALILAND (to Somalia, 1960)
ETHIOPIA
CAMEROON (1960)
CENTRAL AFRICAN REPUBLIC (1960)
EQUATORIAL GUINEA (1968)
SÃO TOMÉ AND PRÍNCIPE (1975)
GABON (1960)
CONGO (1960)
CABINDA (to Angola, 1975)
ZAIRE (1960)
RWANDA (1962)
BURUNDI (1962)
UGANDA (1962)
KENYA (1963)
SOMALIA (1960)
SEYCHELLES (1976)
Equator
TANZANIA (1964)
ANGOLA (1975)
ZAMBIA (1964)
MALAWI (1964)
COMOROS (1975)
INDIAN OCEAN
MADAGASCAR (1960)
MAURITIUS (1968)
NAMIBIA (1990)
ZIMBABWE (1980)
MOZAMBIQUE (1975)
RÉUNION (Fr.)
BOTSWANA (1966)
SWAZILAND (1968)
SOUTH AFRICA (1910)
LESOTHO (1966)
Tropic of Capricorn

N W E S

SCALE
0 500 1000 Miles
0 500 1000 Kilometers
Projection: Azimuthal Equal Area

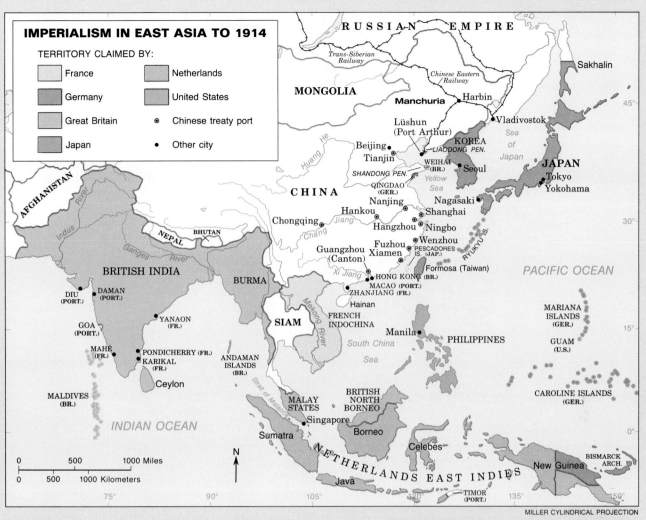

IMPERIALISM IN EAST ASIA TO 1914

TERRITORY CLAIMED BY:

- France
- Netherlands
- Germany
- United States
- Great Britain
- ⊙ Chinese treaty port
- Japan
- • Other city

RUSSIAN EMPIRE

MONGOLIA

Trans-Siberian Railway
Chinese Eastern Railway

Manchuria
Harbin
Sakhalin

Lüshun (Port Arthur)
Vladivostok
LIAODONG PEN.
KOREA
Sea of Japan

Beijing
Tianjin
WEIHAI (BR.)
SHANDONG PEN.
Seoul
JAPAN
Tokyo
Yokohama

Huang He

CHINA
QINGDAO (GER.)
Yellow Sea

Nanjing
Nagasaki

Hankou
Shanghai
Chongqing
Chang Jiang
Hangzhou
Ningbo

AFGHANISTAN
Indus River
Ganges River

NEPAL
BHUTAN

Guangzhou (Canton)
Fuzhou
Wenzhou
Xiamen
PESCADORES IS. (JAP.)
RYUKYU IS.

BRITISH INDIA
BURMA

Xi Jiang
HONG KONG (BR.)
MACAO (PORT.)
ZHANJIANG (FR.)
Formosa (Taiwan)

PACIFIC OCEAN

DIU (PORT.)
DAMAN (PORT.)

Hainan

SIAM
FRENCH INDOCHINA

GOA (PORT.)
YANAON (FR.)

Mekong River

MARIANA ISLANDS (GER.)

Manila
PHILIPPINES

GUAM (U.S.)

MAHÉ (FR.)
PONDICHERRY (FR.)
KARIKAL (FR.)

ANDAMAN ISLANDS (BR.)

South China Sea

MALDIVES (BR.)

Ceylon

INDIAN OCEAN

MALAY STATES
Singapore

BRITISH NORTH BORNEO

CAROLINE ISLANDS (GER.)

Sumatra

Borneo

Celebes

NETHERLANDS EAST INDIES

New Guinea
BISMARCK ARCH.

Java
TIMOR (PORT.)

0   500   1000 Miles
0   500   1000 Kilometers

N

MILLER CYLINDRICAL PROJECTION

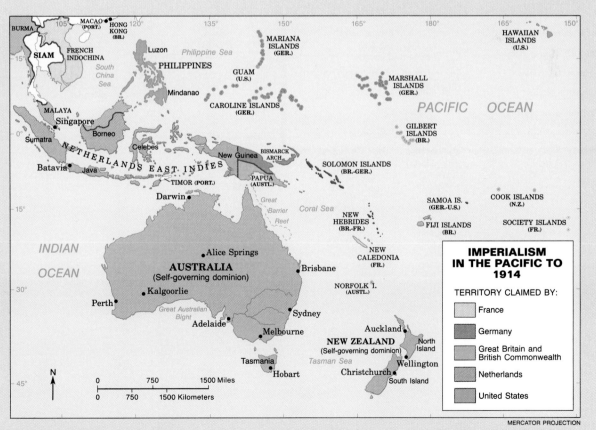

IMPERIALISM IN THE PACIFIC TO 1914

TERRITORY CLAIMED BY:

- France
- Germany
- Great Britain and British Commonwealth
- Netherlands
- United States

BURMA
MACAO (PORT.)
HONG KONG (BR.)

SIAM
FRENCH INDOCHINA

Luzon

MARIANA ISLANDS (GER.)

HAWAIIAN ISLANDS (U.S.)

Philippine Sea

PHILIPPINES

South China Sea

GUAM (U.S.)

MARSHALL ISLANDS (GER.)

PACIFIC OCEAN

Mindanao

CAROLINE ISLANDS (GER.)

MALAYA
Singapore
Borneo

GILBERT ISLANDS (BR.)

Sumatra

NETHERLANDS EAST INDIES

Celebes

New Guinea
BISMARCK ARCH.

SOLOMON ISLANDS (BR.-GER.)

Batavia
Java
TIMOR (PORT.)
PAPUA (AUSTL.)

SAMOA IS. (GER.-U.S.)
COOK ISLANDS (N.Z.)

Darwin

Great Barrier Reef
Coral Sea

NEW HEBRIDES (BR.-FR.)

FIJI ISLANDS (BR.)

SOCIETY ISLANDS (FR.)

INDIAN OCEAN

Alice Springs

NEW CALEDONIA (FR.)

AUSTRALIA (Self-governing dominion)

Brisbane

NORFOLK I. (AUSTL.)

Kalgoorlie

Perth

Great Australian Bight

Adelaide
Sydney

Auckland
North Island

Melbourne

NEW ZEALAND (Self-governing dominion)

Tasmania
Hobart

Tasman Sea

Christchurch
Wellington
South Island

N

0   750   1500 Miles
0   750   1500 Kilometers

MERCATOR PROJECTION

World War I, 1914–1917

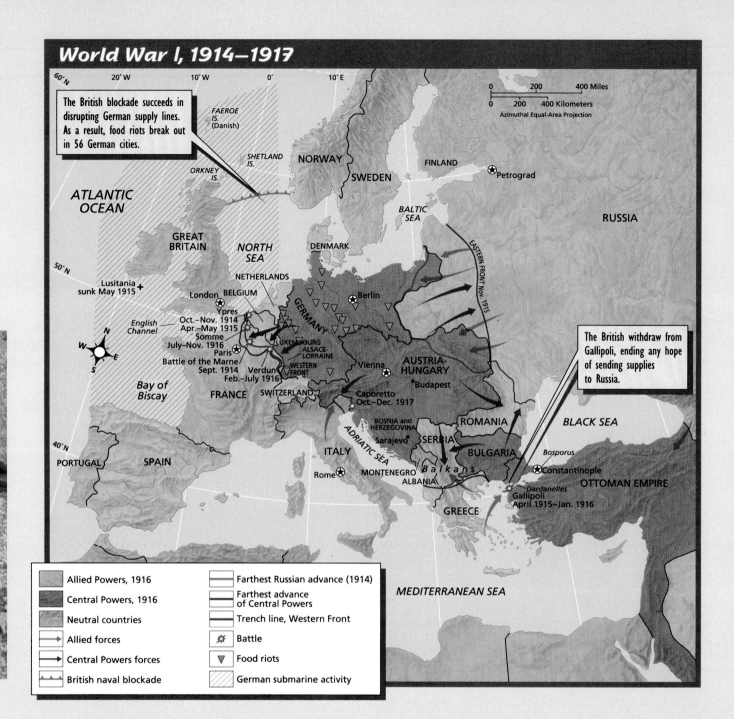

The British blockade succeeds in disrupting German supply lines. As a result, food riots break out in 56 German cities.

The British withdraw from Gallipoli, ending any hope of sending supplies to Russia.

60°N
20°W
10°W
0°
10°E

0   200   400 Miles
0   200   400 Kilometers
Azimuthal Equal-Area Projection

FAEROE IS. (Danish)

SHETLAND IS.

ORKNEY IS.

NORWAY

SWEDEN

FINLAND

*Petrograd

BALTIC SEA

RUSSIA

ATLANTIC OCEAN

50°N

GREAT BRITAIN

NORTH SEA

DENMARK

Lusitania sunk May 1915 +

London

NETHERLANDS

BELGIUM

Berlin

EASTERN FRONT Nov. 1915

English Channel

Ypres
Oct.–Nov. 1914
Apr.–May 1915
Somme
July–Nov. 1916
Paris

GERMANY

LUXEMBOURG
ALSACE-LORRAINE

WESTERN FRONT

Battle of the Marne
Sept. 1914

Verdun
Feb.–July 1916

Vienna

AUSTRIA-HUNGARY

Budapest

Bay of Biscay

FRANCE

SWITZERLAND

Caporetto
Oct.–Dec. 1917

BLACK SEA

40°N

PORTUGAL

SPAIN

ITALY

ADRIATIC SEA

BOSNIA and HERZEGOVINA

Sarajevo

SERBIA

Balkans

ROMANIA

BULGARIA

Bosporus

Constantinople

OTTOMAN EMPIRE

Rome

MONTENEGRO

ALBANIA

Dardanelles
Gallipoli
April 1915–Jan. 1916

GREECE

MEDITERRANEAN SEA

N
W E
S

Legend

▢	Allied Powers, 1916
▢	Central Powers, 1916
▢	Neutral countries
→	Allied forces
→	Central Powers forces
∿	British naval blockade
⎯	Farthest Russian advance (1914)
⎯	Farthest advance of Central Powers
⎯	Trench line, Western Front
✸	Battle
▽	Food riots
▨	German submarine activity

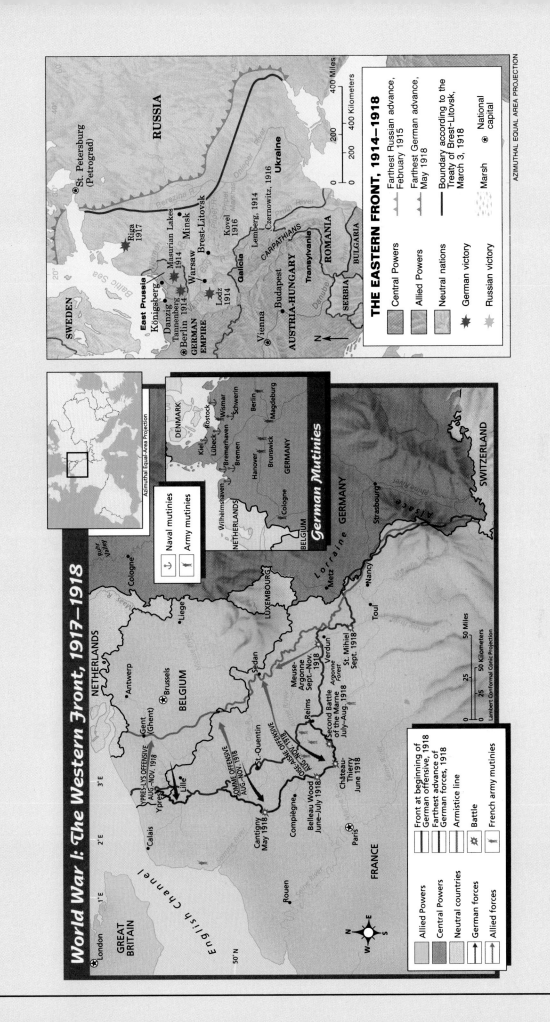

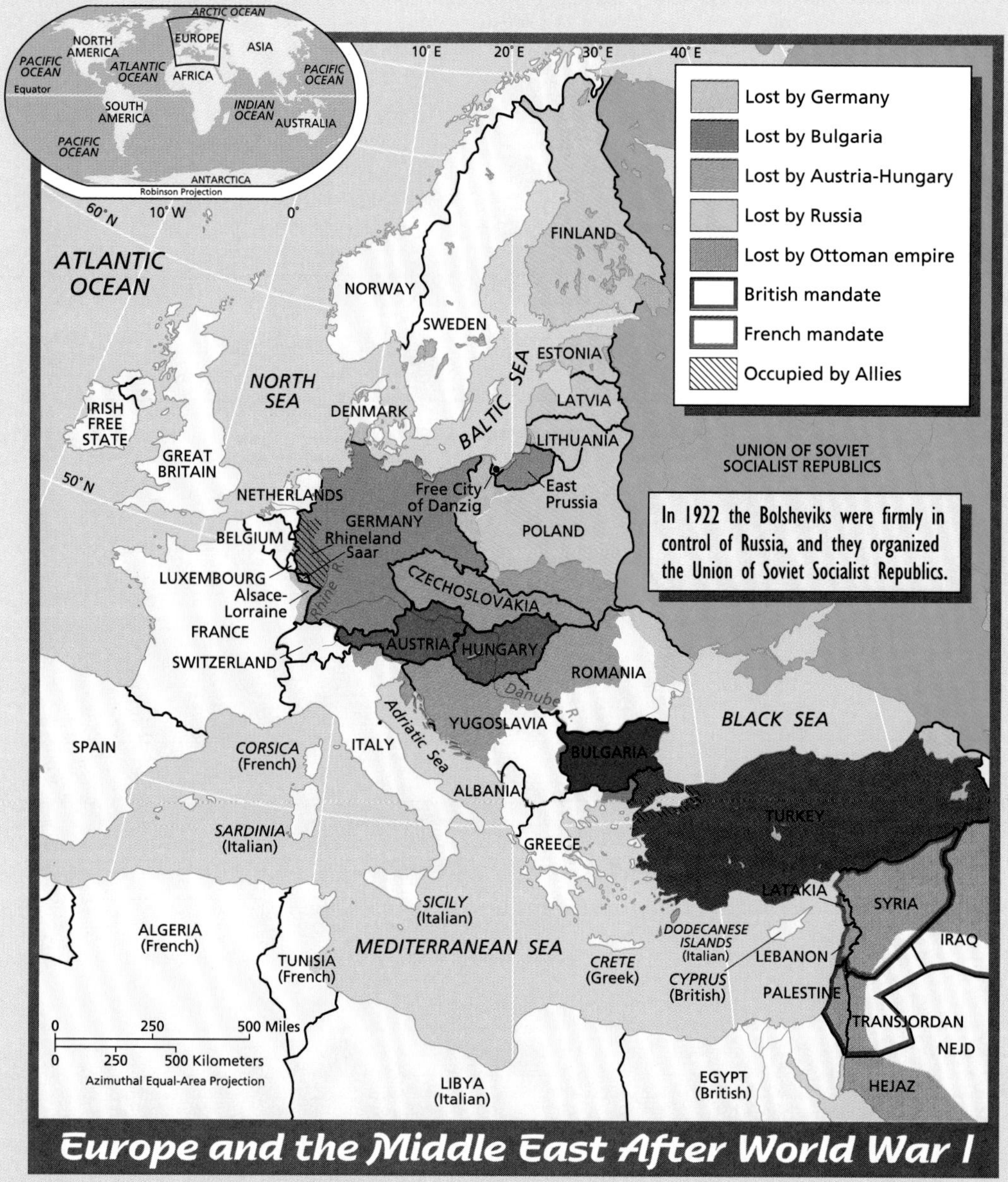
Lost by Germany
Lost by Bulgaria
Lost by Austria-Hungary
Lost by Russia
Lost by Ottoman empire
British mandate
French mandate
Occupied by Allies
In 1922 the Bolsheviks were firmly in control of Russia, and they organized the Union of Soviet Socialist Republics.
ATLANTIC OCEAN
NORTH SEA
BALTIC SEA
BLACK SEA
MEDITERRANEAN SEA
Adriatic Sea
IRISH FREE STATE
GREAT BRITAIN
NORWAY
SWEDEN
FINLAND
ESTONIA
LATVIA
LITHUANIA
DENMARK
NETHERLANDS
BELGIUM
LUXEMBOURG
GERMANY
Rhineland
Saar
Alsace-Lorraine
FRANCE
SWITZERLAND
Free City of Danzig
East Prussia
POLAND
CZECHOSLOVAKIA
AUSTRIA
HUNGARY
ROMANIA
YUGOSLAVIA
BULGARIA
ALBANIA
GREECE
ITALY
SPAIN
CORSICA (French)
SARDINIA (Italian)
SICILY (Italian)
UNION OF SOVIET SOCIALIST REPUBLICS
TURKEY
LATAKIA
SYRIA
IRAQ
LEBANON
PALESTINE
TRANSJORDAN
NEJD
HEJAZ
DODECANESE ISLANDS (Italian)
CRETE (Greek)
CYPRUS (British)
ALGERIA (French)
TUNISIA (French)
LIBYA (Italian)
EGYPT (British)
0 250 500 Miles
0 250 500 Kilometers
Azimuthal Equal-Area Projection
ARCTIC OCEAN
NORTH AMERICA
EUROPE
ASIA
PACIFIC OCEAN
ATLANTIC OCEAN
AFRICA
SOUTH AMERICA
INDIAN OCEAN
AUSTRALIA
ANTARCTICA
Equator
Robinson Projection

Europe and the Middle East After World War I

MAJOR BATTLES

1 — Britain, Aug.–Oct. 1940
2 — Leningrad, Sept. 1941–Jan. 1944
3 — El Alamein, Oct.–Nov. 1942
4 — Stalingrad, Nov. 1942–Feb. 1943
5 — Anzio, Jan.–Mar. 1944
6 — D-Day, June 6, 1944
7 — Minsk, June–Aug. 1944
8 — Battle of the Bulge, Dec. 1944
9 — Warsaw, Aug. 1944–Jan. 1945
10 — Berlin, Apr.–May, 1945

WORLD WAR II IN EUROPE AND NORTH AFRICA, 1939–1945

Allied countries
Axis countries
Axis-controlled territory at its greatest extent, 1942
Neutral countries
Allied advance
Axis advance

★ Major battle
⊛ National capital
• Other city

AZIMUTHAL EQUAL AREA PROJECTION

ATLANTIC OCEAN

Murmansk
Narvik
NORWAY
SWEDEN
Oslo
Stockholm
FINLAND
Helsinki
Leningrad
ESTONIA
LATVIA
LITHUANIA
Moscow
Voronezh
SOVIET UNION
Volga R.
Stalingrad
Caspian Sea
IRELAND
GREAT BRITAIN
London
North Sea
DENMARK
Hamburg
Königsberg
Danzig
EAST PRUSSIA
Minsk
Dnieper R.
English Channel
NETH.
BEL.
Antwerp
Berlin
Torgau
Warsaw
POLAND
Paris
FRANCE
LUX.
GERMANY
Remagen
Prague
SLOVAKIA
Vienna
Budapest
HUNGARY
ROMANIA
Bucharest
Ploesti
Black Sea
Vichy
VICHY FRANCE 1940–1942
SWITZ.
YUGOSLAVIA
BULGARIA
Istanbul
Ankara
TURKEY
IRAN
Lisbon
PORTUGAL
Madrid
SPAIN
Corsica
Rome
ITALY
Naples
ALBANIA
GREECE
Crete
Cyprus
SYRIA (FR.)
IRAQ
Sardinia
Sicily
Malta
Mediterranean Sea
SP. MOR.
Oran
Algiers
Tunis
TUNISIA (FR.)
MOROCCO (FR.)
ALGERIA (FR.)
LIBYA (IT.)
Tobruk
EGYPT
PALESTINE (BR.)
TRANS-JORDAN (BR.)
SAUDI ARABIA
Nile R.

0   300   600 Miles
0   300   600 Kilometers
N

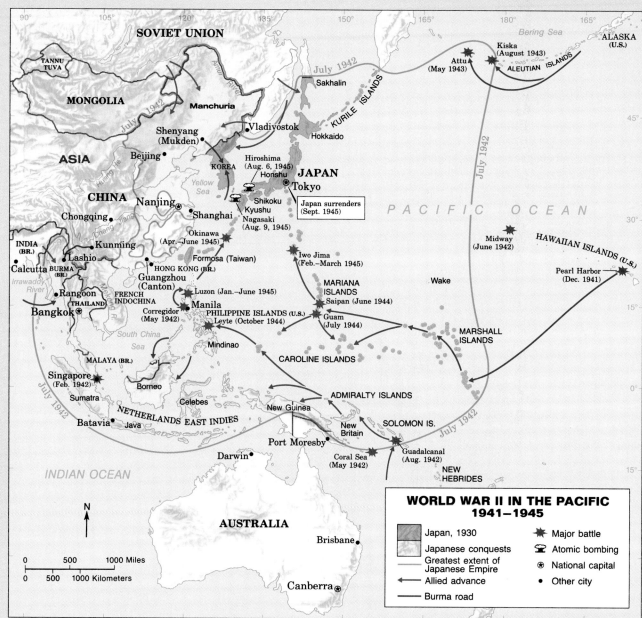

WORLD WAR II IN THE PACIFIC
1941–1945

Japan, 1930

Japanese conquests

Greatest extent of Japanese Empire

← Allied advance

Burma road

✦ Major battle

☁ Atomic bombing

⊛ National capital

• Other city

SOVIET UNION

TANNU TUVA

MONGOLIA

Manchuria

ASIA

Shenyang (Mukden)

Beijing

CHINA

Nanjing

Chongqing

Shanghai

Yellow Sea

KOREA

Hiroshima (Aug. 6, 1945)

Honshu

JAPAN

Tokyo

Shikoku

Kyushu

Nagasaki (Aug. 9, 1945)

Japan surrenders (Sept. 1945)

Vladivostok

Sakhalin

Hokkaido

KURILE ISLANDS

July 1942

Attu (May 1943)

Kiska (August 1943)

ALEUTIAN ISLANDS

ALASKA (U.S.)

Bering Sea

PACIFIC OCEAN

Okinawa (Apr.–June 1945)

Formosa (Taiwan)

INDIA (BR.)

Lashio

Kunming

Calcutta

BURMA (BR.)

Irrawaddy River

Rangoon

THAILAND

Bangkok

HONG KONG (BR.)

Guangzhou (Canton)

FRENCH INDOCHINA

Luzon (Jan.–June 1945)

Manila

Corregidor (May 1942)

PHILIPPINE ISLANDS (U.S.)

Leyte (October 1944)

South China Sea

Iwo Jima (Feb.–March 1945)

MARIANA ISLANDS

Saipan (June 1944)

Guam (July 1944)

Wake

Midway (June 1942)

HAWAIIAN ISLANDS (U.S.)

Pearl Harbor (Dec. 1941)

MARSHALL ISLANDS

CAROLINE ISLANDS

Mindinao

MALAYA (BR.)

Singapore (Feb. 1942)

Sumatra

Batavia

Java

Borneo

Celebes

NETHERLANDS EAST INDIES

New Guinea

Port Moresby

New Britain

ADMIRALTY ISLANDS

SOLOMON IS.

Coral Sea (May 1942)

Guadalcanal (Aug. 1942)

NEW HEBRIDES

July 1942

Darwin

INDIAN OCEAN

N

0   500   1000 Miles

0   500   1000 Kilometers

AUSTRALIA

Brisbane

Canberra

MERCATOR PROJECTION

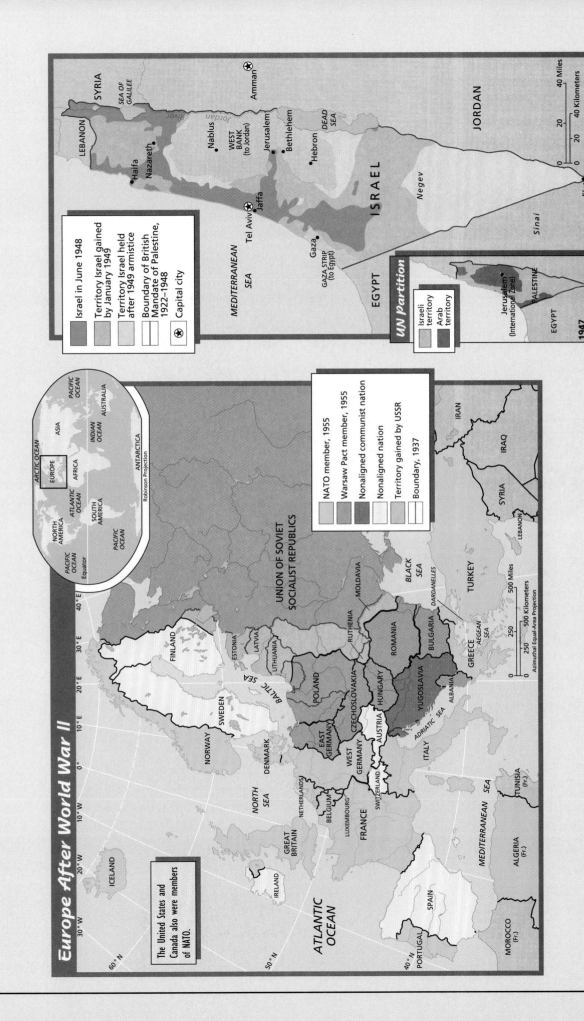

Israel, 1949

Israel, 1949 (map legend)
- Israel in June 1948
- Territory Israel gained by January 1949
- Territory Israel held after 1949 armistice
- Boundary of British Mandate of Palestine, 1922–1948
- ✪ Capital city

SYRIA
SEA OF GALILEE
LEBANON
Jordan River
Nazareth
Haifa
Nablus
WEST BANK (to Jordan)
Jerusalem
Bethlehem
Hebron
DEAD SEA
✪ Amman
JORDAN
Tel Aviv
Jaffa
MEDITERRANEAN SEA
Gaza
GAZA STRIP (to Egypt)
ISRAEL
Negev
Sinai
EGYPT
Elat

40 Miles
40 Kilometers
20
20
Lambert Conformal Conic Projection

UN Partition
1947
- Israeli territory
- Arab territory

Jerusalem (International Zone)
PALESTINE
EGYPT

Europe After World War II

The United States and Canada also were members of NATO.

(map legend)
- NATO member, 1955
- Warsaw Pact member, 1955
- Nonaligned communist nation
- Nonaligned nation
- Territory gained by USSR
- Boundary, 1937

ICELAND
NORWAY
SWEDEN
FINLAND
ESTONIA
LATVIA
LITHUANIA
UNION OF SOVIET SOCIALIST REPUBLICS
RUTHENIA
MOLDAVIA
DENMARK
NORTH SEA
BALTIC SEA
IRELAND
GREAT BRITAIN
NETHERLANDS
BELGIUM
LUXEMBOURG
EAST GERMANY
WEST GERMANY
POLAND
CZECHOSLOVAKIA
AUSTRIA
HUNGARY
ROMANIA
SWITZERLAND
FRANCE
PORTUGAL
SPAIN
ITALY
YUGOSLAVIA
ADRIATIC SEA
ALBANIA
BULGARIA
BLACK SEA
GREECE
AEGEAN SEA
DARDANELLES
TURKEY
IRAN
IRAQ
SYRIA
LEBANON
MEDITERRANEAN SEA
ATLANTIC OCEAN
MOROCCO (Fr.)
ALGERIA (Fr.)
TUNISIA (Fr.)

60° N
50° N
40° N
30° W
20° W
10° W
0°
10° E
20° E
30° E
40° E

0   250   500 Miles
0   250   500 Kilometers
Azimuthal Equal-Area Projection

ARCTIC OCEAN
NORTH AMERICA
EUROPE
ASIA
AFRICA
SOUTH AMERICA
AUSTRALIA
ANTARCTICA
PACIFIC OCEAN
ATLANTIC OCEAN
INDIAN OCEAN
Equator
Robinson Projection

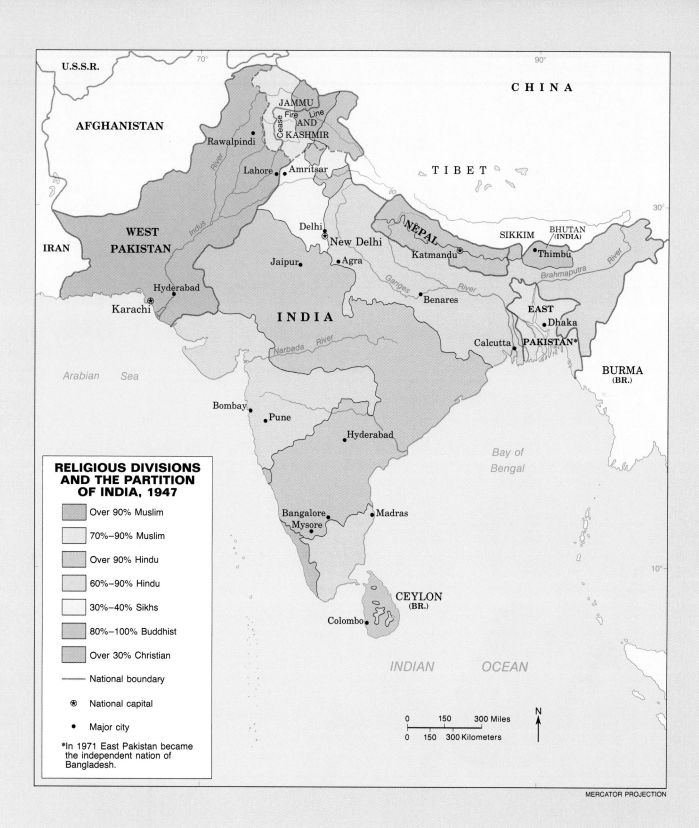

U.S.S.R.

AFGHANISTAN

IRAN

CHINA

TIBET

Rawalpindi

Indus River

WEST
PAKISTAN

Lahore • Amritsar

JAMMU
Cease Fire Line
AND
KASHMIR

Delhi
⊛ New Delhi

Jaipur • • Agra

NEPAL

Katmandu ⊛

SIKKIM

BHUTAN
(INDIA)

• Thimbú

Ganges River

Brahmaputra River

Hyderabad

Karachi ⊛

INDIA

Benares

EAST

• Dhaka

Calcutta • PAKISTAN*

BURMA
(BR.)

Narbada River

Arabian Sea

Bombay •
• Pune

• Hyderabad

Bay of
Bengal

Bangalore •
Mysore •

• Madras

CEYLON
(BR.)

Colombo •

INDIAN OCEAN

RELIGIOUS DIVISIONS AND THE PARTITION OF INDIA, 1947

Over 90% Muslim

70%–90% Muslim

Over 90% Hindu

60%–90% Hindu

30%–40% Sikhs

80%–100% Buddhist

Over 30% Christian

National boundary

⊛ National capital

• Major city

*In 1971 East Pakistan became
the independent nation of
Bangladesh.

0   150   300 Miles

0   150   300 Kilometers

N

MERCATOR PROJECTION

INDEPENDENT NATIONS IN SOUTHEAST ASIA, 1946–1984

- ⊛ National capital
- • Other city
- —— National boundary
- ✹ Battle site
- 1945 Date of independence
- Continuously independent

0 250 500 Miles
0 250 500 Kilometers

N

CHINA

INDIA

TAIWAN

BURMA
1948
• Mandalay

Red R.

Dien Bien Phu
1954
⊛ Hanoi

LAOS
1949

Gulf of
Tonkin

Irrawaddy R.
Salween R.
ANNAM CORDILLERA
Mekong R.

Vientiane ⊛

Rangoon ⊛

THAILAND

Bangkok ⊛

Andaman
Sea

Gulf of
Thailand

VIETNAM
1945

CAMBODIA
1953

⊛ Phnom Penh
• Ho Chi Minh City
(Saigon)

South
China
Sea

Luzon

Quezon City •
Manila ⊛

PHILIPPINES
1946

Sulu
Sea

Mindanao

PACIFIC
OCEAN

MALAY
PENINSULA

MALAYSIA
1957

Bandar Seri
Begawan ⊛
BRUNEI
1984

SABAH
(1963: Joined
Malaysia)

Kuala
Lumpur ⊛

Strait of Malacca

Singapore
1965

SARAWAK
(1963: Joined Malaysia)

Borneo

Celebes
Sea

BARISAN MTS.

Sumatra

I N D O N E S I A
1 9 4 5

GREATER SUNDA IS.

Java Sea

Celebes

Molucca
Sea

M O L U C C A S

Ceram Sea

New Guinea

MAOKE MTS.

IRIAN JAYA
(1963: Transfered
to Indonesia)

Jakarta ⊛
Bandung •   Java   • Surabaya
Bali

INDIAN OCEAN

LESSER SUNDA IS.

Banda Sea

Arafura
Sea

Timor   PORT. TIMOR
(1975: Transfered
to Indonesia)

AUSTRALIA

MERCATOR PROJECTION

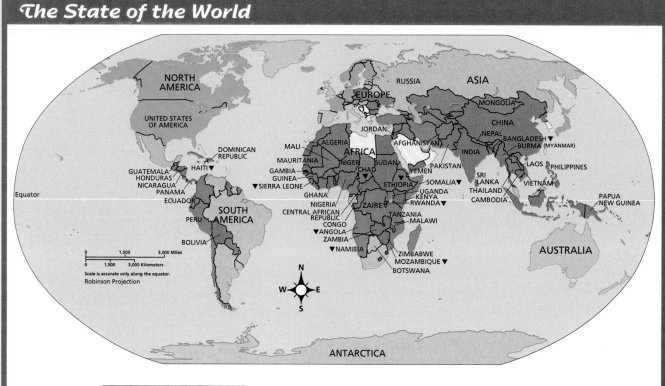

Infant Mortality Rates for Selected Nations
(deaths per 1,000 live births)

Netherlands	11
United States	18
Romania	35
China	55
Brazil	94
Algeria	128
India	139
Gabon	227

Rich Nations and Poor Nations, 1991

Per Capita GNP, 1991

Less than $300	$6,001–$9,000
$300–$750	$9,001–$20,000
$751–$2,500	$20,001–$30,000
$2,501–$6,000	

▼ Calorie supply 25% below recommended levels, 1988

Estimated Cumulative Adult HIV Infections, 1992

North America	1 million +
Central America, South America, & Caribbean	1 million +
Western Europe	500,000
North Africa & Middle East	75,000 +
Sub-Saharan Africa	7.5 million +
Australia, New Zealand, & Indonesia	25,000 +
India & Southeast Asia	1.5 million +
China, Japan, & Pacific	25,000 +
Eastern Europe, Russia, & Central Asia	50,000

Population, 1990
total population: 5,289,000,000 (growth rate: 1.7%)

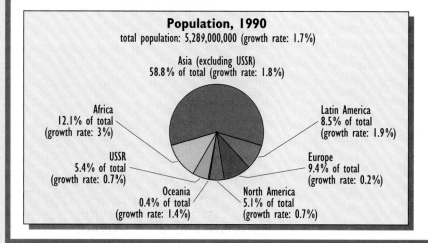

Asia (excluding USSR)
58.8% of total (growth rate: 1.8%)

Africa
12.1% of total
(growth rate: 3%)

Latin America
8.5% of total
(growth rate: 1.9%)

USSR
5.4% of total
(growth rate: 0.7%)

Europe
9.4% of total
(growth rate: 0.2%)

Oceania
0.4% of total
(growth rate: 1.4%)

North America
5.1% of total
(growth rate: 0.7%)

AMERICAN HISTORY

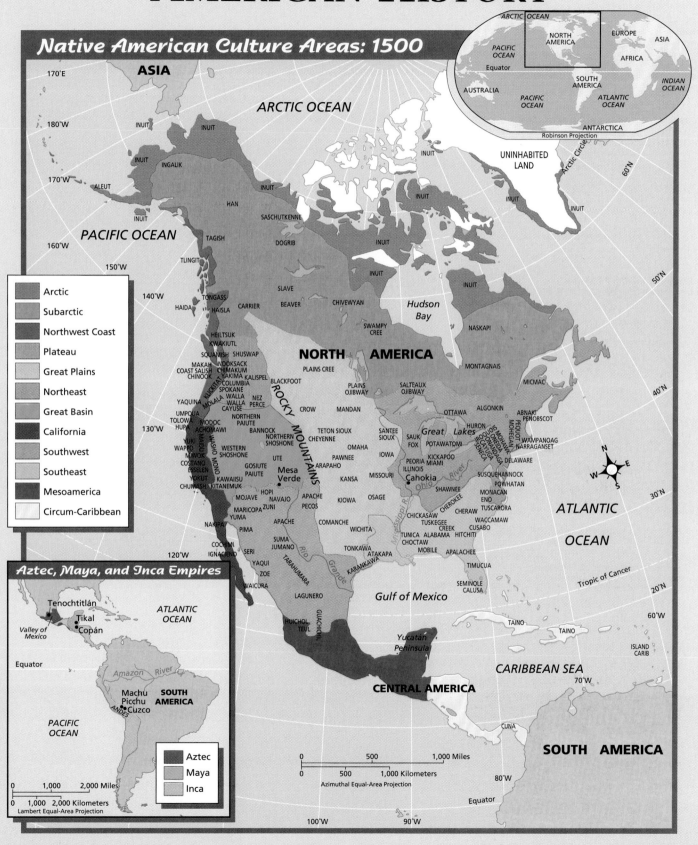

Native American Culture Areas: 1500

Legend:
- Arctic
- Subarctic
- Northwest Coast
- Plateau
- Great Plains
- Northeast
- Great Basin
- California
- Southwest
- Southeast
- Mesoamerica
- Circum-Caribbean

Aztec, Maya, and Inca Empires

- Aztec
- Maya
- Inca

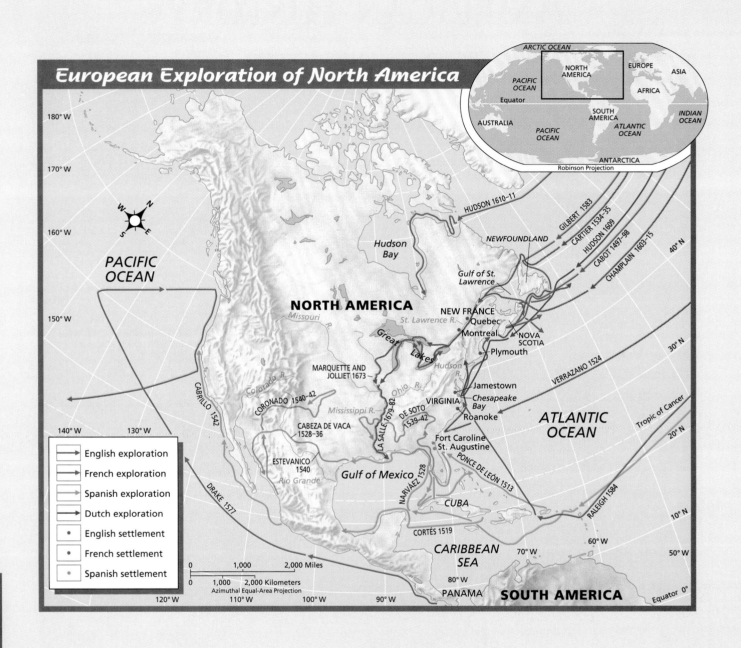

European Exploration of North America

Legend:
- → English exploration
- → French exploration
- → Spanish exploration
- → Dutch exploration
- • English settlement
- • French settlement
- • Spanish settlement

0 | 1,000 | 2,000 Miles
0 | 1,000 | 2,000 Kilometers
Azimuthal Equal-Area Projection

Map labels:

PACIFIC OCEAN

NORTH AMERICA

Hudson Bay

HUDSON 1610–11

NEWFOUNDLAND

GILBERT 1583
CARTIER 1534–35
HUDSON 1609
CABOT 1497–98
CHAMPLAIN 1603–15

Gulf of St. Lawrence

NEW FRANCE
St. Lawrence R.
Quebec
Montreal
NOVA SCOTIA
Plymouth

Missouri

Great Lakes

Hudson R.

MARQUETTE AND JOLLIET 1673

Ohio R.

Jamestown
Chesapeake Bay
VIRGINIA
Roanoke

VERRAZANO 1524

ATLANTIC OCEAN

Colorado R.

CORONADO 1540–42

Mississippi R.

CABEZA DE VACA 1528–36

LA SALLE 1679–82

DE SOTO 1539–42

Fort Caroline
St. Augustine

Tropic of Cancer

CABRILLO 1542

ESTEVANICO 1540

Rio Grande

Gulf of Mexico

NARVÁEZ 1528

PONCE DE LEÓN 1513

DRAKE 1577

CORTÉS 1519

CUBA

RALEIGH 1584

CARIBBEAN SEA

PANAMA

SOUTH AMERICA

Inset map:
ARCTIC OCEAN
NORTH AMERICA
EUROPE
ASIA
PACIFIC OCEAN
AFRICA
Equator
SOUTH AMERICA
AUSTRALIA
PACIFIC OCEAN
ATLANTIC OCEAN
INDIAN OCEAN
ANTARCTICA
Robinson Projection

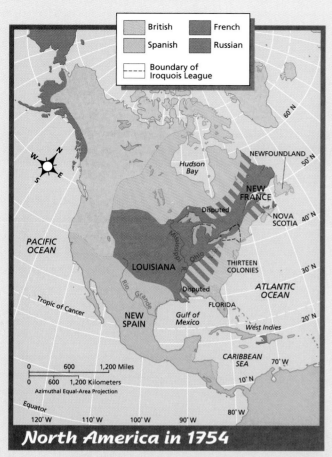

North America in 1754

Legend:
- British
- Spanish
- French
- Russian
- Boundary of Iroquois League

North America in 1763

Legend:
- Russian
- British
- French
- Spanish
- Pontiac's Rebellion
- Proclamation Line of 1763

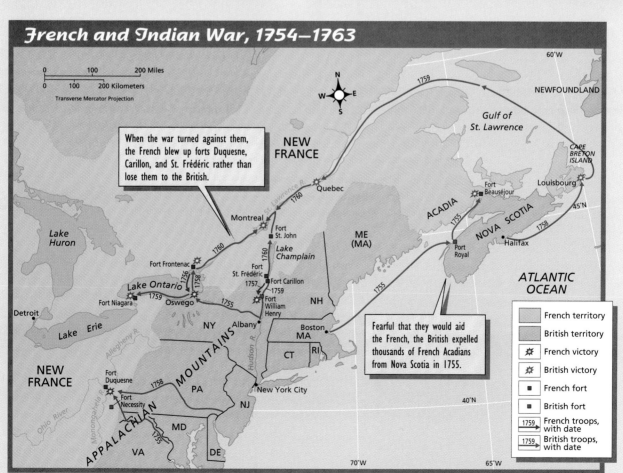

French and Indian War, 1754–1763

When the war turned against them, the French blew up forts Duquesne, Carillon, and St. Frédéric rather than lose them to the British.

Fearful that they would aid the French, the British expelled thousands of French Acadians from Nova Scotia in 1755.

Legend:
- French territory
- British territory
- French victory
- British victory
- French fort
- British fort
- 1759 → French troops, with date
- 1759 → British troops, with date

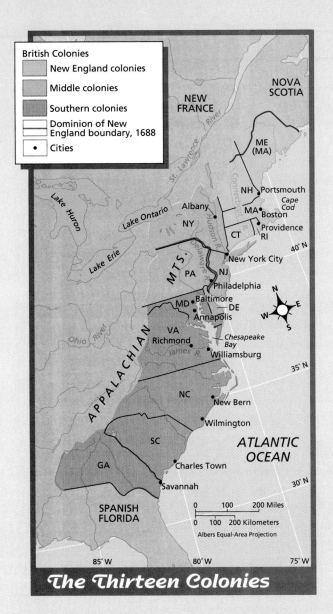

The Thirteen Colonies

British Colonies
- New England colonies
- Middle colonies
- Southern colonies
- Dominion of New England boundary, 1688
- • Cities

NOVA SCOTIA

NEW FRANCE

ME (MA)

NH Portsmouth
Cape Cod
MA Boston
Providence
CT RI

Albany
NY

New York City
NJ
Philadelphia
PA
MD Baltimore DE
Annapolis

VA
Richmond
Williamsburg
Chesapeake Bay

APPALACHIAN MTS.

NC
New Bern
Wilmington

SC

GA
Charles Town
Savannah

SPANISH FLORIDA

ATLANTIC OCEAN

Lake Huron
Lake Erie
Lake Ontario
St. Lawrence River
Hudson R.
Delaware R.
Ohio River
James R.
Connecticut R.

40° N
35° N
30° N
85° W
80° W
75° W

0   100   200 Miles
0   100   200 Kilometers
Albers Equal-Area Projection

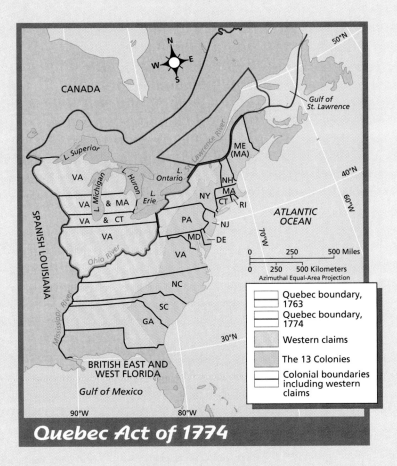

Quebec Act of 1774

CANADA

SPANISH LOUISIANA

VA
VA & MA
VA & CT
VA

L. Superior
L. Michigan
L. Huron
L. Ontario
L. Erie

ME (MA)
NH
MA
CT RI
NY
PA
NJ
MD DE
VA
NC
SC
GA

ATLANTIC OCEAN

Gulf of St. Lawrence

BRITISH EAST AND WEST FLORIDA

Gulf of Mexico

Mississippi River
Ohio River
St. Lawrence River

50°N
40°N
30°N
90°W
80°W
70°W
60°W

0   250   500 Miles
0   250   500 Kilometers
Azimuthal Equal-Area Projection

- Quebec boundary, 1763
- Quebec boundary, 1774
- Western claims
- The 13 Colonies
- Colonial boundaries including western claims

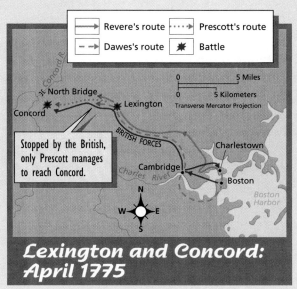

Lexington and Concord: April 1775

→ Revere's route   ⋯▸ Prescott's route
--▸ Dawes's route   ✳ Battle

0   5 Miles
0   5 Kilometers
Transverse Mercator Projection

North Bridge
Concord
Lexington

Stopped by the British, only Prescott manages to reach Concord.

BRITISH FORCES

Charlestown
Cambridge
Boston
Charles River
Boston Harbor
Concord R.

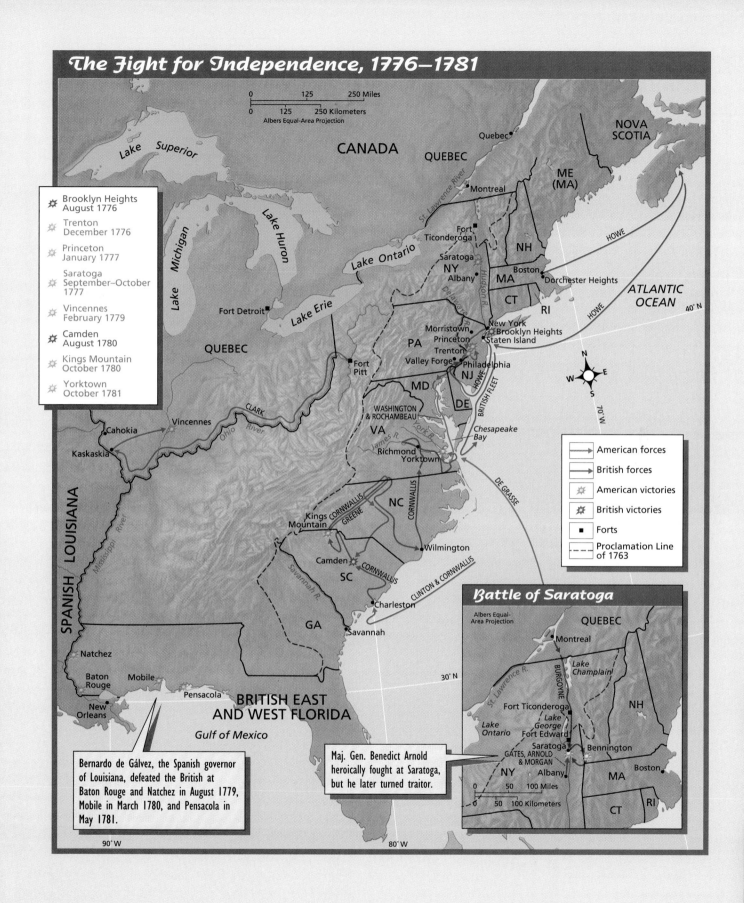

The Fight for Independence, 1776–1781

0   125   250 Miles
0   125   250 Kilometers
Albers Equal-Area Projection

Brooklyn Heights
August 1776

Trenton
December 1776

Princeton
January 1777

Saratoga
September–October
1777

Vincennes
February 1779

Camden
August 1780

Kings Mountain
October 1780

Yorktown
October 1781

Lake Superior

CANADA

Lake Michigan

Lake Huron

QUEBEC

Quebec

NOVA SCOTIA

Montreal

St. Lawrence River

ME (MA)

Fort Ticonderoga

Lake Ontario

Saratoga

NY

Albany

NH

Boston

MA

Dorchester Heights

HOWE

Lake Erie

Fort Detroit

QUEBEC

CT

RI

ATLANTIC OCEAN

40° N

Morristown

New York

Brooklyn Heights

Staten Island

Hudson R.

Delaware R.

PA

Princeton

Trenton

Valley Forge

Philadelphia

NJ

HOWE

N

W   E

S

70° W

CLARK

Fort Pitt

MD

DE

Ohio River

WASHINGTON & ROCHAMBEAU

VA

James R.

Richmond

Yorktown

York R.

Chesapeake Bay

BRITISH FLEET

Cahokia

Vincennes

Kaskaskia

DE GRASSE

Kings Mountain

CORNWALLIS

GREENE

NC

CORNWALLIS

Wilmington

Camden

CORNWALLIS

SC

Charleston

CLINTON & CORNWALLIS

SPANISH LOUISIANA

Mississippi River

Savannah R.

GA

Savannah

Natchez

Baton Rouge

Mobile

Pensacola

New Orleans

BRITISH EAST AND WEST FLORIDA

Gulf of Mexico

Bernardo de Gálvez, the Spanish governor of Louisiana, defeated the British at Baton Rouge and Natchez in August 1779, Mobile in March 1780, and Pensacola in May 1781.

Maj. Gen. Benedict Arnold heroically fought at Saratoga, but he later turned traitor.

American forces

British forces

American victories

British victories

Forts

Proclamation Line of 1763

30° N

90° W   80° W

Battle of Saratoga

Albers Equal-Area Projection

QUEBEC

Montreal

St. Lawrence R.

BURGOYNE

Lake Champlain

Fort Ticonderoga

Lake George

Lake Ontario

Fort Edward

NH

Saratoga

GATES, ARNOLD & MORGAN

Bennington

NY

Albany

MA

Boston

0   50   100 Miles
0   50   100 Kilometers

CT   RI

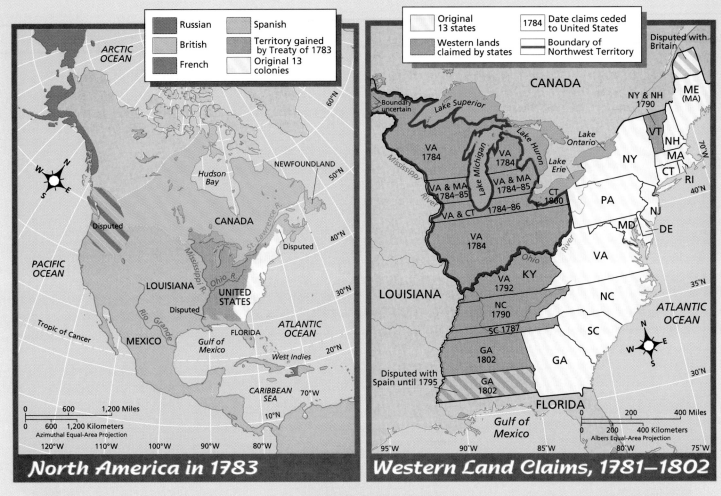

North America in 1783

Legend:
- Russian
- British
- French
- Spanish
- Territory gained by Treaty of 1783
- Original 13 colonies

ARCTIC OCEAN

Hudson Bay

NEWFOUNDLAND

CANADA

Disputed

PACIFIC OCEAN

Disputed

LOUISIANA

Disputed

Tropic of Cancer

MEXICO

Disputed

UNITED STATES

FLORIDA

Gulf of Mexico

ATLANTIC OCEAN

West Indies

CARIBBEAN SEA

St. Lawrence R.

Mississippi R.

Ohio R.

Rio Grande

60°N
50°N
40°N
30°N
20°N
10°N
70°W

120°W 110°W 100°W 90°W 80°W

0   600   1,200 Miles
0   600   1,200 Kilometers
Azimuthal Equal-Area Projection

Western Land Claims, 1781–1802

Legend:
- Original 13 states
- Western lands claimed by states
- 1784 Date claims ceded to United States
- Boundary of Northwest Territory

CANADA

Boundary uncertain

Lake Superior
Lake Michigan
Lake Huron
Lake Ontario
Lake Erie

Mississippi River

VA 1784
VA 1784
VA & MA 1784-85
VA & MA 1784-85
VA & CT 1784-86
CT 1800
VA 1784
VA 1792
KY
NC 1790
SC 1787
GA 1802
GA 1802

Disputed with Spain until 1795

LOUISIANA

Ohio River

NY & NH 1790
VT
NH
MA
CT
RI
NY
PA
NJ
MD
DE
VA
NC
SC
GA

Disputed with Britain

ME (MA)

ATLANTIC OCEAN

FLORIDA

Gulf of Mexico

95°W 90°W 85°W 80°W 75°W
40°N
35°N
30°N
70°W

0   200   400 Miles
0   200   400 Kilometers
Albers Equal-Area Projection

The Louisiana Purchase

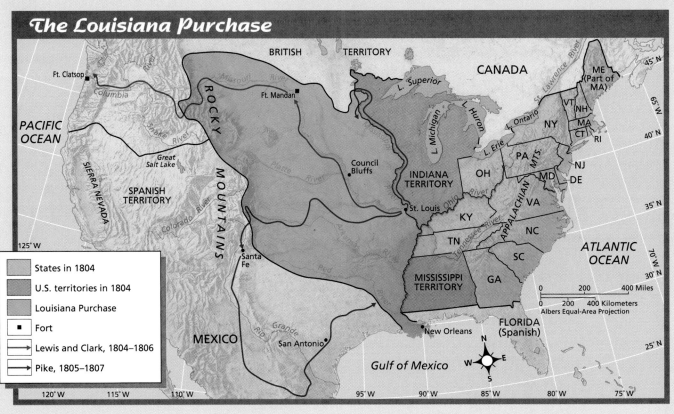

Legend:
- States in 1804
- U.S. territories in 1804
- Louisiana Purchase
- ■ Fort
- → Lewis and Clark, 1804–1806
- → Pike, 1805–1807

BRITISH TERRITORY

CANADA

Ft. Clatsop

Ft. Mandan

PACIFIC OCEAN

ROCKY MOUNTAINS

Columbia River
Snake River
Great Salt Lake
SIERRA NEVADA
SPANISH TERRITORY
Colorado River
Missouri River
Platte River
Council Bluffs
St. Louis
INDIANA TERRITORY
OH
KY
TN
Arkansas River
Red River
Santa Fe
MISSISSIPPI TERRITORY
GA
New Orleans
MEXICO
San Antonio
Rio Grande
Gulf of Mexico

L. Superior
L. Michigan
L. Huron
L. Ontario
L. Erie

St. Lawrence River
Ohio River
Tennessee River

APPALACHIAN MTS.

ME (Part of MA)
VT
NH
MA
CT
RI
NY
PA
NJ
MD
DE
VA
NC
SC

ATLANTIC OCEAN

FLORIDA (Spanish)

125°W 120°W 115°W 110°W 95°W 90°W 85°W 80°W 75°W
45°N
40°N
35°N
30°N
25°N
65°W
70°W

0   200   400 Miles
0   200   400 Kilometers
Albers Equal-Area Projection

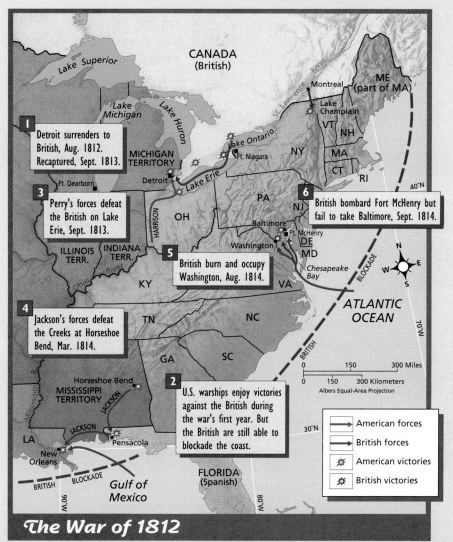

The War of 1812

CANADA
(British)

Lake Superior

Lake Michigan

Lake Huron

1 Detroit surrenders to British, Aug. 1812. Recaptured, Sept. 1813.

MICHIGAN TERRITORY

Ft. Dearborn

Detroit

Lake Erie

Lake Ontario

Ft. Niagara

Montreal

Lake Champlain

St. Lawrence River

ME (part of MA)

VT

NH

NY

MA

CT

RI

3 Perry's forces defeat the British on Lake Erie, Sept. 1813.

HARRISON

OH

PA

NJ

DE

MD

Baltimore

Ft. McHenry

Washington

6 British bombard Fort McHenry but fail to take Baltimore, Sept. 1814.

ILLINOIS TERR.

INDIANA TERR.

KY

VA

5 British burn and occupy Washington, Aug. 1814.

Ohio River

Chesapeake Bay

BLOCKADE

ATLANTIC OCEAN

40°N

70°W

4 Jackson's forces defeat the Creeks at Horseshoe Bend, Mar. 1814.

TN

NC

GA

SC

Horseshoe Bend

MISSISSIPPI TERRITORY

JACKSON

Mississippi R.

LA

New Orleans

Pensacola

JACKSON

2 U.S. warships enjoy victories against the British during the war's first year. But the British are still able to blockade the coast.

30°N

150 / 300 Miles
150 / 300 Kilometers
Albers Equal-Area Projection

BRITISH

BRITISH BLOCKADE

Gulf of Mexico

FLORIDA (Spanish)

90°W

80°W

→ American forces
→ British forces
✦ American victories
✦ British victories

U.S. Boundaries, 1820

Albers Equal-Area Projection

Claimed by U.S., ceded to Great Britain in 1818

British Territory

49th Parallel

Lake of the Woods

49° N

Disputed

ME

PACIFIC OCEAN

Oregon Country

ROCKY MOUNTAINS

42nd Parallel

Unorganized Territory

Great Lakes

Michigan Territory

VT

NH

NY

MA

CT

RI

42° N

40° N

The United States and Great Britain jointly occupied Oregon Country until 1846, long past the 10 years called for by the Convention of 1818.

Spanish Territory

Mississippi R.

PA

NJ

MD

DE

IL

IN

OH

VA

Missouri Territory

Arkansas River

KY

TN

NC

APPALACHIAN MOUNTAINS

SC

ATLANTIC OCEAN

70° W

Red River

Arkansas Territory

MS

AL

GA

Sabine R.

LA

By the terms of the Adams-Onís Treaty, Spain ceded East Florida to the United States and gave up all claims to West Florida.

Unorganized Territory

120° W

225 / 450 Miles
225 / 450 Kilometers

Gulf of Mexico

90° W

80° W

▬ Convention of 1818
▨ Adams-Onís Treaty of 1819
▨ Louisiana Purchase
▨ Florida Cession
▨ British Cession of 1818

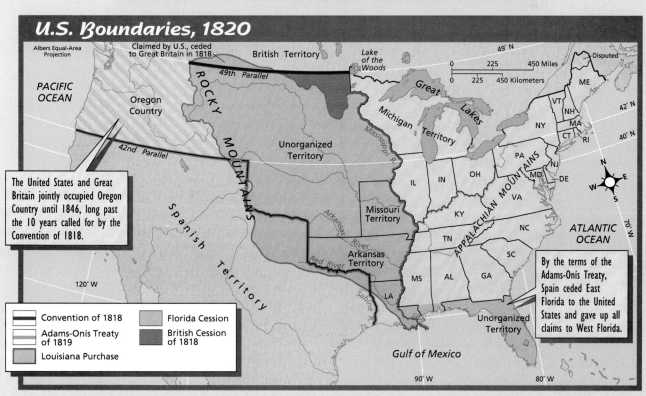

Missouri Compromise: 1820

Legend:
- Free state
- Free territory
- Slave state
- Slave territory

OREGON COUNTRY
MAINE
MISSOURI
Missouri Compromise Line 36° 30' N

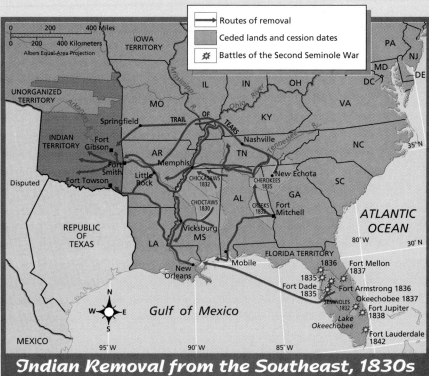

Indian Removal from the Southeast, 1830s

Legend:
- Routes of removal
- Ceded lands and cession dates
- Battles of the Second Seminole War

IOWA TERRITORY
UNORGANIZED TERRITORY
PA
NJ
MD
DE
IL
IN
OH
DC
MO
VA
KY
Springfield
TRAIL
OF
Nashville
NC
35° N
INDIAN TERRITORY
Fort Gibson
AR
TEARS
Memphis
TN
Fort Smith
Little Rock
CHICKASAWS 1832
New Echota
SC
Disputed
Fort Towson
CHOCTAWS 1830
CHEROKEES 1835
GA
AL
CREEKS 1832
Fort Mitchell
ATLANTIC OCEAN
REPUBLIC OF TEXAS
Vicksburg
MS
LA
80° W
30° N
FLORIDA TERRITORY
1836
Fort Mellon 1837
New Orleans
Mobile
1835
Fort Dade 1835
Fort Armstrong 1836
Okeechobee 1837
SEMINOLES 1832
Fort Jupiter 1838
Gulf of Mexico
Lake Okeechobee
MEXICO
Fort Lauderdale 1842
95° W
90° W
85° W

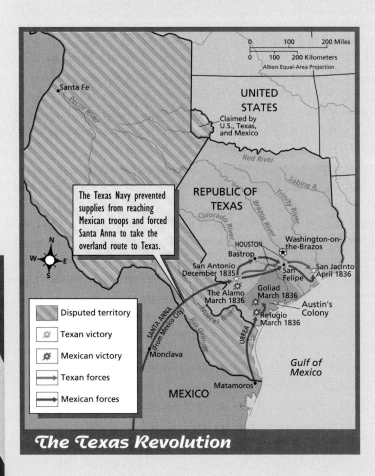

The Texas Revolution

Legend:
- Disputed territory
- Texan victory
- Mexican victory
- Texan forces
- Mexican forces

Santa Fe
UNITED STATES
Claimed by U.S., Texas, and Mexico
Red River
REPUBLIC OF TEXAS
Sabine R.
Trinity River
Brazos River
The Texas Navy prevented supplies from reaching Mexican troops and forced Santa Anna to take the overland route to Texas.
Colorado River
HOUSTON
Bastrop
Washington-on-the-Brazos
San Antonio December 1835
San Felipe
San Jacinto April 1836
The Alamo March 1836
Goliad March 1836
Austin's Colony
SANTA ANNA (from Mexico City)
Refugio March 1836
URREA
Nueces River
Monclava
Rio Grande
Gulf of Mexico
MEXICO
Matamoros

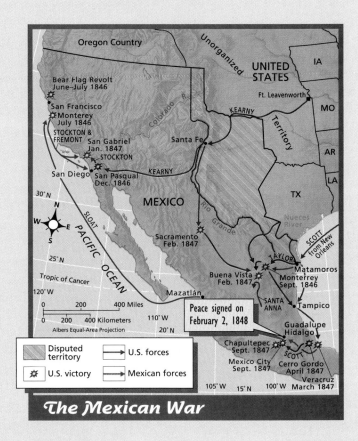

The Mexican War

Legend:
- Disputed territory
- U.S. victory
- U.S. forces
- Mexican forces

Oregon Country
Unorganized
UNITED STATES
IA
Bear Flag Revolt June–July 1846
San Francisco
Monterey July 1846
STOCKTON & FREMONT
San Gabriel Jan. 1847
KEARNY
Ft. Leavenworth
MO
Santa Fe
STOCKTON
San Diego
San Pasqual Dec. 1846
KEARNY
AR
LA
30° N
MEXICO
TX
Colorado R.
Rio Grande
Nueces River
PACIFIC OCEAN
SLOAT
25° N
Sacramento Feb. 1847
SCOTT from New Orleans
Tropic of Cancer
120° W
Mazatlán
Buena Vista Feb. 1847
TAYLOR
Matamoros
Monterrey Sept. 1846
Peace signed on February 2, 1848
SANTA ANNA
Tampico
Guadalupe Hidalgo
Chapultepec Sept. 1847
Mexico City Sept. 1847
Cerro Gordo April 1847
Veracruz March 1847
110° W
20° N
105° W
15° N
100° W

U.S. Boundaries, 1853

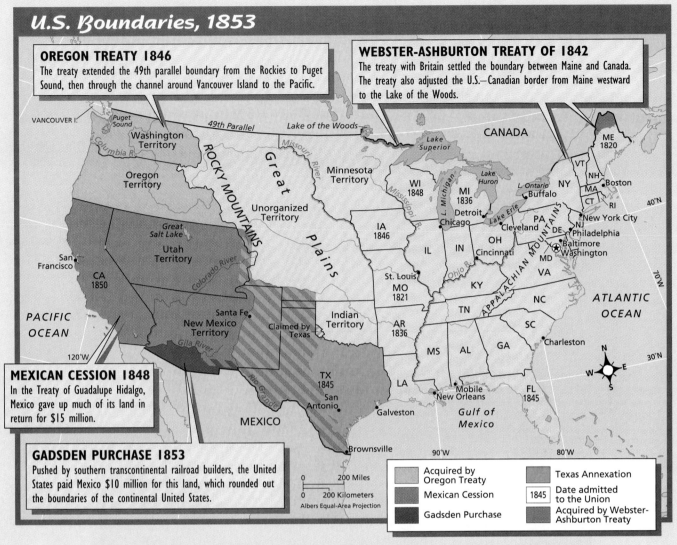

OREGON TREATY 1846
The treaty extended the 49th parallel boundary from the Rockies to Puget Sound, then through the channel around Vancouver Island to the Pacific.

WEBSTER-ASHBURTON TREATY OF 1842
The treaty with Britain settled the boundary between Maine and Canada. The treaty also adjusted the U.S.–Canadian border from Maine westward to the Lake of the Woods.

MEXICAN CESSION 1848
In the Treaty of Guadalupe Hidalgo, Mexico gave up much of its land in return for $15 million.

GADSDEN PURCHASE 1853
Pushed by southern transcontinental railroad builders, the United States paid Mexico $10 million for this land, which rounded out the boundaries of the continental United States.

VANCOUVER I. · Puget Sound · 49th Parallel · Lake of the Woods · CANADA · ME 1820

Washington Territory · Columbia R. · ROCKY MOUNTAINS · Missouri River · Minnesota Territory · Lake Superior · WI 1848 · L. Michigan · MI 1836 · Lake Huron · L. Ontario · NY · VT · NH · MA · Boston

Oregon Territory · Great Plains · Unorganized Territory · IA 1846 · Detroit · Lake Erie · Chicago · Cleveland · PA · RI · CT · New York City

Great Salt Lake · Utah Territory · IL · IN · OH · Cincinnati · NJ · Philadelphia · DE · Baltimore · Washington · MD

San Francisco · CA 1850 · Colorado River · St. Louis · MO 1821 · Ohio R. · KY · VA · APPALACHIAN MOUNTAINS

PACIFIC OCEAN · Santa Fe · New Mexico Territory · Claimed by Texas · Indian Territory · AR 1836 · TN · NC · ATLANTIC OCEAN

120°W · Gila River · Rio Grande · TX 1845 · San Antonio · LA · MS · AL · GA · SC · Charleston

MEXICO · Galveston · New Orleans · Mobile · Gulf of Mexico · FL 1845

Brownsville · 90°W · 80°W · 70°W · 40°N · 30°N

200 Miles · 200 Kilometers · Albers Equal-Area Projection

Legend:
- Acquired by Oregon Treaty
- Mexican Cession
- Gadsden Purchase
- Texas Annexation
- 1845 Date admitted to the Union
- Acquired by Webster-Ashburton Treaty

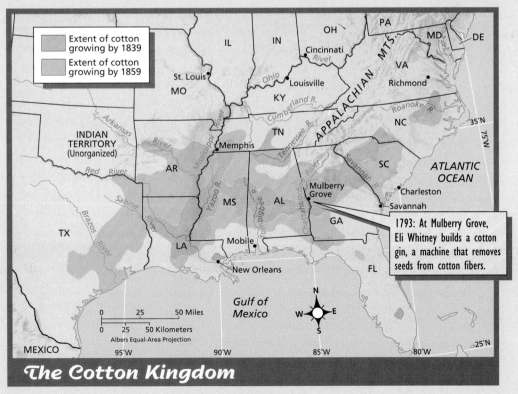

Legend:
- Extent of cotton growing by 1839
- Extent of cotton growing by 1859

IL · IN · OH · PA · MD · DE

St. Louis · MO · Cincinnati · Ohio River · Louisville · KY · VA · Richmond · APPALACHIAN MTS. · Roanoke R.

INDIAN TERRITORY (Unorganized) · Arkansas River · Cumberland R. · TN · Tennessee R. · NC · 35°N · 75°W

Red River · AR · Memphis · Mississippi River · Yazoo R. · Savannah River · SC · ATLANTIC OCEAN

Sabine River · Brazos River · TX · MS · AL · Tombigbee R. · Chattahoochee R. · Mulberry Grove · GA · Charleston · Savannah

LA · Mobile · FL

1793: At Mulberry Grove, Eli Whitney builds a cotton gin, a machine that removes seeds from cotton fibers.

New Orleans · Gulf of Mexico

MEXICO · 95°W · 90°W · 85°W · 80°W · 25°N

25 · 50 Miles · 25 · 50 Kilometers · Albers Equal-Area Projection

The Cotton Kingdom

Slave vs. Free Territory, 1850 and 1854

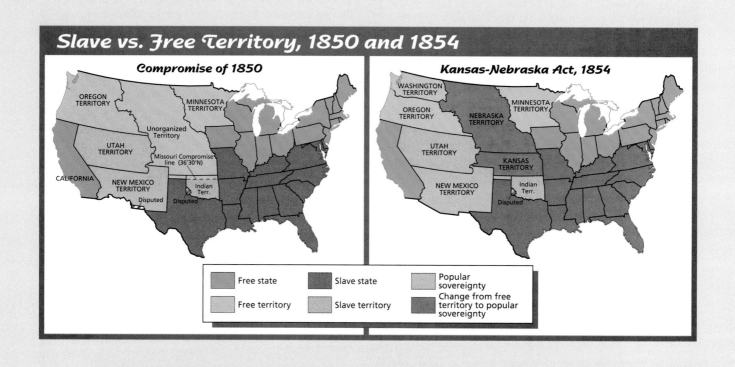

Compromise of 1850

OREGON TERRITORY
MINNESOTA TERRITORY
Unorganized Territory
UTAH TERRITORY
Missouri Compromise line (36°30'N)
CALIFORNIA
NEW MEXICO TERRITORY
Indian Terr.
Disputed
Disputed

Kansas-Nebraska Act, 1854

WASHINGTON TERRITORY
OREGON TERRITORY
NEBRASKA TERRITORY
MINNESOTA TERRITORY
UTAH TERRITORY
KANSAS TERRITORY
NEW MEXICO TERRITORY
Indian Terr.
Disputed

- Free state
- Free territory
- Slave state
- Slave territory
- Popular sovereignty
- Change from free territory to popular sovereignty

The Union and the Confederacy, 1861

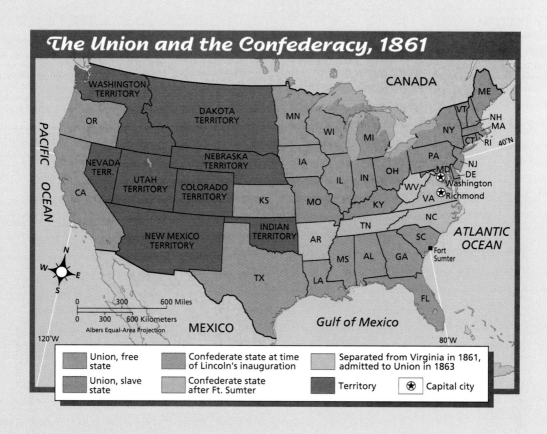

WASHINGTON TERRITORY
CANADA
OR
DAKOTA TERRITORY
MN
ME
VT
NH
MA
WI
MI
NY
CT
RI
40°N
NEVADA TERR.
NEBRASKA TERRITORY
IA
PA
NJ
PACIFIC OCEAN
CA
UTAH TERRITORY
COLORADO TERRITORY
KS
IL
IN
OH
MD
DE
Washington
WV
VA
Richmond
MO
KY
NEW MEXICO TERRITORY
INDIAN TERRITORY
AR
TN
NC
SC
ATLANTIC OCEAN
Fort Sumter
MS
AL
GA
TX
LA
FL

120°W
MEXICO
Gulf of Mexico
80°W

0   300   600 Miles
0   300   600 Kilometers
Albers Equal-Area Projection

- Union, free state
- Union, slave state
- Confederate state at time of Lincoln's inauguration
- Confederate state after Ft. Sumter
- Separated from Virginia in 1861, admitted to Union in 1863
- Territory
- Capital city

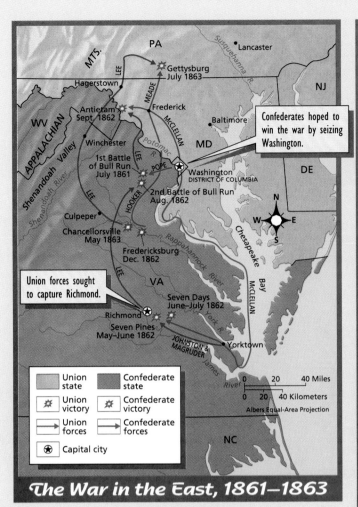

The War in the East, 1861–1863

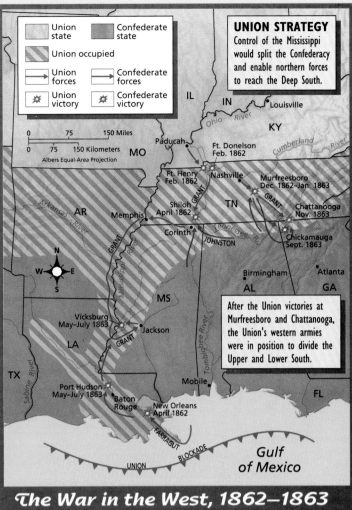

The War in the West, 1862–1863

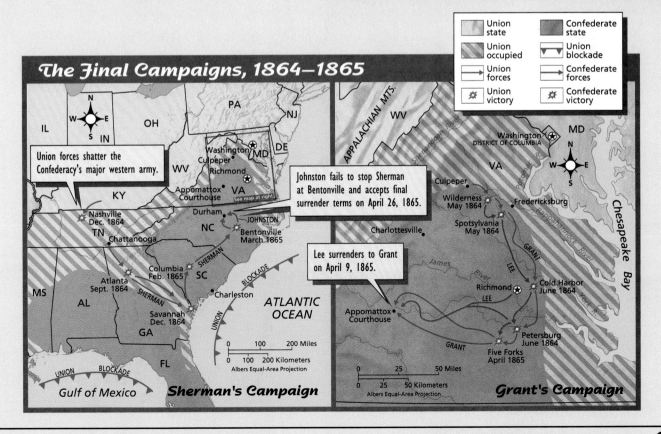

The Final Campaigns, 1864–1865

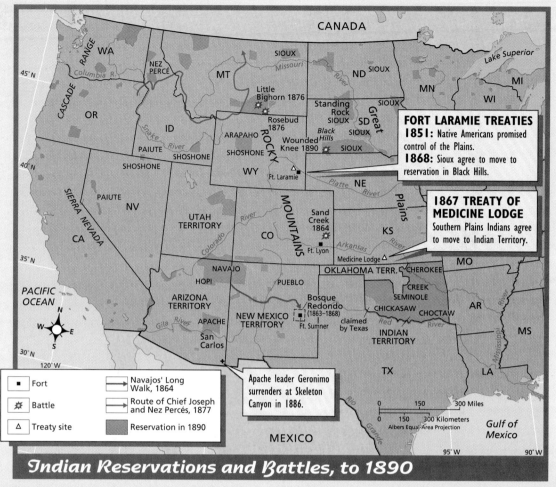

Indian Reservations and Battles, to 1890

FORT LARAMIE TREATIES
1851: Native Americans promised control of the Plains.
1868: Sioux agree to move to reservation in Black Hills.

1867 TREATY OF MEDICINE LODGE
Southern Plains Indians agree to move to Indian Territory.

Apache leader Geronimo surrenders at Skeleton Canyon in 1886.

■ Fort	→ Navajos' Long Walk, 1864
✸ Battle	→ Route of Chief Joseph and Nez Percés, 1877
△ Treaty site	Reservation in 1890

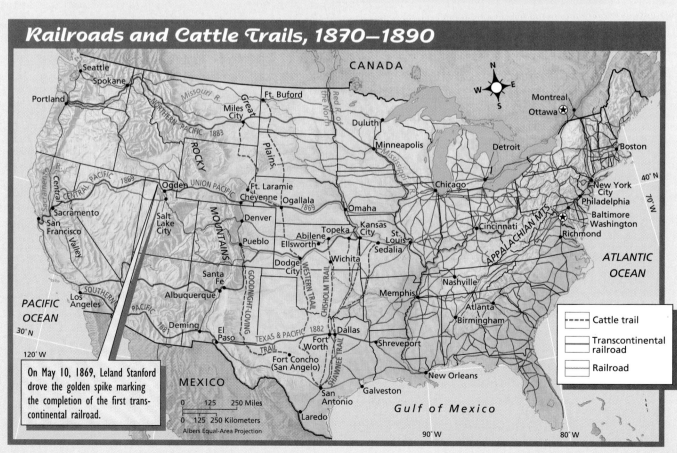

Railroads and Cattle Trails, 1870–1890

On May 10, 1869, Leland Stanford drove the golden spike marking the completion of the first transcontinental railroad.

- - - -	Cattle trail
────	Transcontinental railroad
······	Railroad

Labor Strikes, 1870–1900

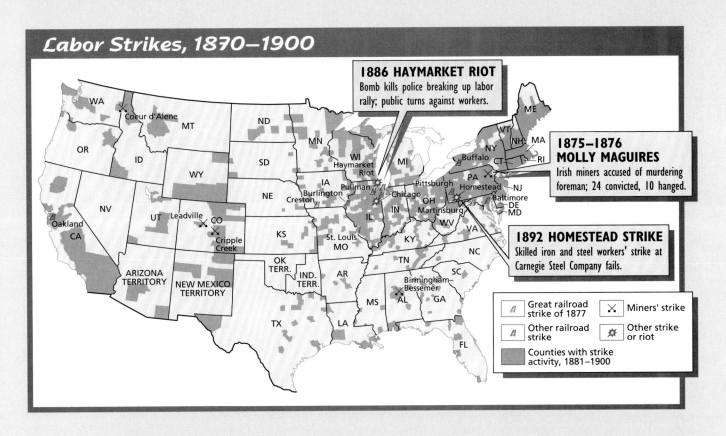

1886 HAYMARKET RIOT
Bomb kills police breaking up labor rally; public turns against workers.

1875–1876 MOLLY MAGUIRES
Irish miners accused of murdering foreman; 24 convicted, 10 hanged.

1892 HOMESTEAD STRIKE
Skilled iron and steel workers' strike at Carnegie Steel Company fails.

Great railroad strike of 1877

Other railroad strike

Counties with strike activity, 1881–1900

Miners' strike

Other strike or riot

Spanish-American War, 1898

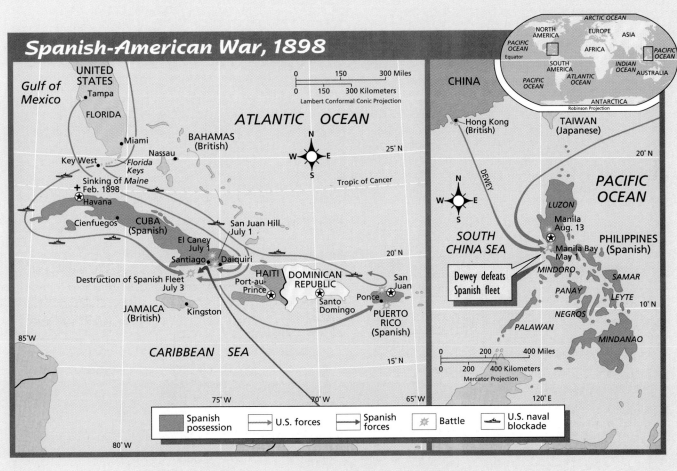

Spanish possession
U.S. forces
Spanish forces
Battle
U.S. naval blockade

U.S. Territories in the Pacific

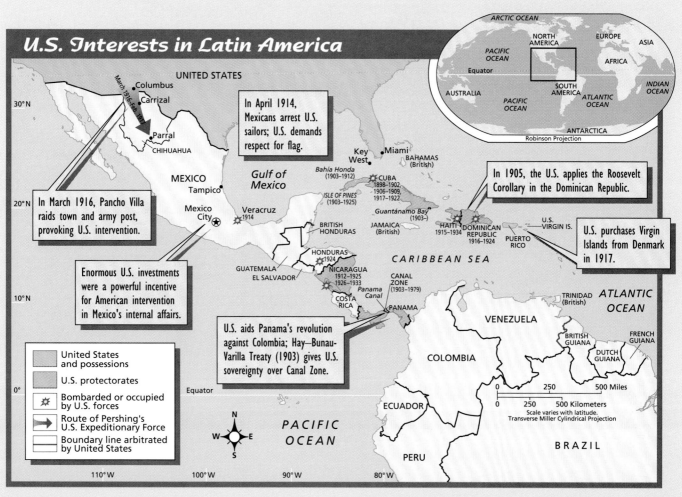

U.S. Interests in Latin America

In April 1914, Mexicans arrest U.S. sailors; U.S. demands respect for flag.

In 1905, the U.S. applies the Roosevelt Corollary in the Dominican Republic.

In March 1916, Pancho Villa raids town and army post, provoking U.S. intervention.

U.S. purchases Virgin Islands from Denmark in 1917.

Enormous U.S. investments were a powerful incentive for American intervention in Mexico's internal affairs.

U.S. aids Panama's revolution against Colombia; Hay–Bunau-Varilla Treaty (1903) gives U.S. sovereignty over Canal Zone.

United States and possessions
U.S. protectorates
Bombarded or occupied by U.S. forces
Route of Pershing's U.S. Expeditionary Force
Boundary line arbitrated by United States

The Global Depression

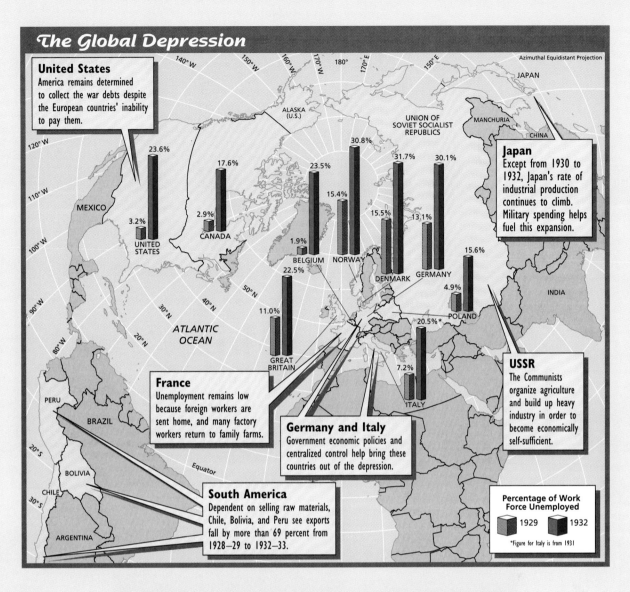

United States
America remains determined to collect the war debts despite the European countries' inability to pay them.

Japan
Except from 1930 to 1932, Japan's rate of industrial production continues to climb. Military spending helps fuel this expansion.

France
Unemployment remains low because foreign workers are sent home, and many factory workers return to family farms.

Germany and Italy
Government economic policies and centralized control help bring these countries out of the depression.

USSR
The Communists organize agriculture and build up heavy industry in order to become economically self-sufficient.

South America
Dependent on selling raw materials, Chile, Bolivia, and Peru see exports fall by more than 69 percent from 1928–29 to 1932–33.

Azimuthal Equidistant Projection

UNITED STATES 3.2% / 23.6%
CANADA 2.9% / 17.6%
BELGIUM 1.9% / 23.5%
NORWAY 15.4% / 30.8%
DENMARK 15.5% / 31.7%
GERMANY 13.1% / 30.1%
POLAND 4.9% / 15.6%
GREAT BRITAIN 11.0% / 22.5%
ITALY 7.2% / 20.5%*
MEXICO
ATLANTIC OCEAN
PERU
BRAZIL
BOLIVIA
CHILE
ARGENTINA
Equator
ALASKA (U.S.)
UNION OF SOVIET SOCIALIST REPUBLICS
MANCHURIA
CHINA
JAPAN
INDIA

Percentage of Work Force Unemployed
☐ 1929   ■ 1932

*Figure for Italy is from 1931

Unemployment Relief: 1934

ND 29%
SD 41%
OK 28%
NM 31%
AZ

WA, OR, MT, ID, WY, NV, CA, UT, CO, NE, KS, MN, IA, WI, MI, IL, IN, OH, MO, KY, TN, AR, MS, AL, GA, SC, NC, TX, LA, FL, PA, NY, WV, VA, NJ, DE, MD, DC, VT, ME, NH, MA, RI, CT

Percentage of Total State Population Receiving Unemployment Relief
■ More than 25 percent
■ 21-25 percent
■ 16-20 percent
□ 11-15 percent
□ Less than 11 percent

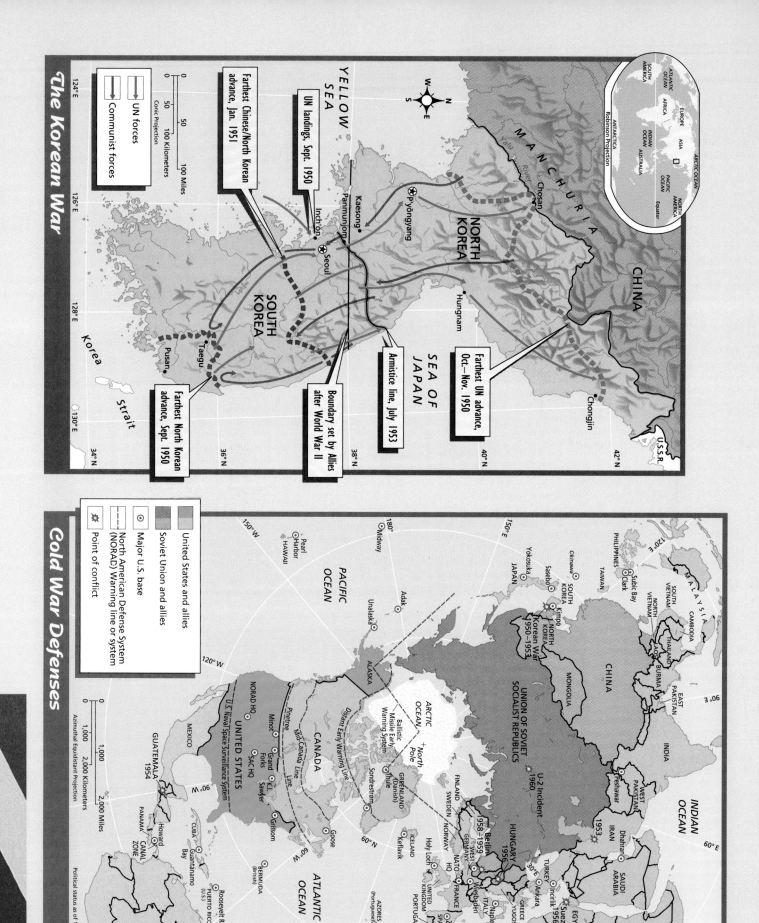

The Korean War

Farthest Chinese/North Korean advance, Jan. 1951

UN landings, Sept. 1950

Farthest North Korean advance, Sept. 1950

Boundary set by Allies after World War II

Armistice line, July 1953

Farthest UN advance, Oct.–Nov. 1950

UN forces

Communist forces

0 50 100 Kilometers
0 50 100 Miles
Conic Projection

124° E
126° E
128° E
130° E
34° N
36° N
38° N
40° N
42° N

YELLOW SEA

Kaesong
Inchon
Seoul
Panmunjom
Pyŏngyang
NORTH KOREA
SOUTH KOREA
Pusan
Taegu
Hungnam
Chosan
Chongjin
MANCHURIA
CHINA
U.S.S.R.
Yalu River
SEA OF JAPAN
Korea Strait

ANTARCTICA
SOUTH AMERICA
ATLANTIC OCEAN
AFRICA
EUROPE
ASIA
ARCTIC OCEAN
INDIAN OCEAN
AUSTRALIA
PACIFIC OCEAN
NORTH AMERICA
Equator
Robinson Projection

Cold War Defenses

Point of conflict
Major U.S. base
Soviet Union and allies
United States and allies
North American Defense System (NORAD) Warning line or system

0 1,000 2,000 Kilometers
0 1,000 2,000 Miles
Azimuthal Equidistant Projection
Political status as of 1960.

PACIFIC OCEAN
ATLANTIC OCEAN
ARCTIC OCEAN
INDIAN OCEAN

Pearl Harbor
HAWAII
Midway
Adak
Unalaska
ALASKA
North Pole
Ballistic Missile Early Warning System
Distant Early Warning Line
Mid-Canada Line
Pinetree Line
NORAD HQ
Minot
Grand Forks
Sawyer
SAC HQ
Grissom
U.S. Naval Space Surveillance System
UNITED STATES
CANADA
MEXICO
GUATEMALA 1954
PANAMA CANAL ZONE
Howard
CUBA
Guantanamo Bay
PUERTO RICO (U.S.)
Roosevelt Roads
BERMUDA (British)
Goose
Sondrestrom
GREENLAND (Danish)
Thule
Keflavik
ICELAND
AZORES (Portuguese) Lajes
UNITED KINGDOM
Holy Loch
PORTUGAL
SPAIN
Zaragoza
MOROCCO
ALGERIA (French)
LIBYA
Wheelus
FINLAND
SWEDEN
NORWAY
UNION OF SOVIET SOCIALIST REPUBLICS
U-2 Incident 1960
MONGOLIA
CHINA
NORTH KOREA
SOUTH KOREA
Korean War 1950–1953
Kimpo
Sasebo
Yokosuka
Okinawa
JAPAN
Subic Bay
Clark
PHILIPPINES
TAIWAN
NORTH VIETNAM
SOUTH VIETNAM
CAMBODIA
LAOS
THAILAND
BURMA
MALAYSIA
INDIA
EAST PAKISTAN
WEST PAKISTAN
Peshawar
IRAN
Dhahran
SAUDI ARABIA
EGYPT
Suez Canal 1956
GREECE
YUGOSLAVIA
Incirlik 1956
TURKEY
Ankara
1953
HUNGARY 1956
Berlin 1958–1959
WEST GERMANY
Wiesbaden
NATO HQ
FRANCE
ITALY
Naples
Holy Loch
150° W
180°
150° E
120° W
120° E
90° E
90° W
60° W
60° N
30° N
30° W
30° E
60° E
0°
90° E

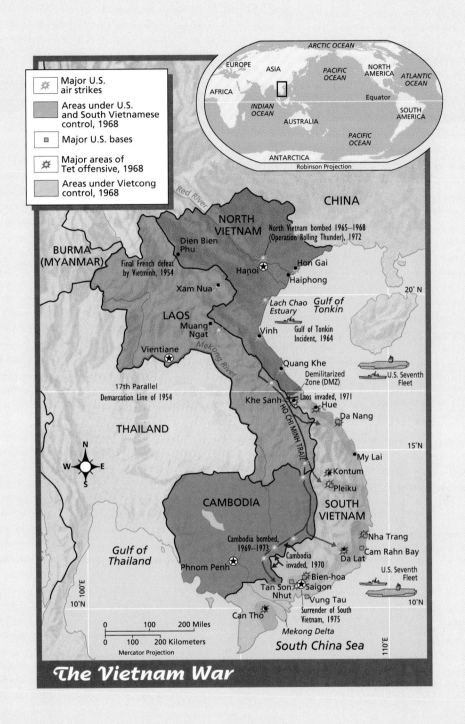

Major U.S. air strikes

Areas under U.S. and South Vietnamese control, 1968

Major U.S. bases

Major areas of Tet offensive, 1968

Areas under Vietcong control, 1968

ARCTIC OCEAN

EUROPE

ASIA

PACIFIC OCEAN

NORTH AMERICA

ATLANTIC OCEAN

AFRICA

INDIAN OCEAN

Equator

SOUTH AMERICA

AUSTRALIA

PACIFIC OCEAN

ANTARCTICA

Robinson Projection

Red River

CHINA

NORTH VIETNAM

North Vietnam bombed 1965–1968 (Operation Rolling Thunder), 1972

BURMA (MYANMAR)

Dien Bien Phu

Final French defeat by Vietminh, 1954

Hon Gai

Hanoi

Haiphong

Xam Nua

20° N

LAOS

Lach Chao Estuary

Gulf of Tonkin

Muang Ngat

Vinh

Gulf of Tonkin Incident, 1964

Vientiane

Mekong River

Quang Khe

Demilitarized Zone (DMZ)

U.S. Seventh Fleet

17th Parallel Demarcation Line of 1954

Khe Sanh

Laos invaded, 1971

Hue

THAILAND

Da Nang

HO CHI MINH TRAIL

15°N

N
W   E
S

My Lai

Kontum

Pleiku

CAMBODIA

SOUTH VIETNAM

Cambodia bombed, 1969–1973

Nha Trang

Cam Rahn Bay

Phnom Penh

Cambodia invaded, 1970

Da Lat

U.S. Seventh Fleet

Gulf of Thailand

Bien-hoa

Tan Son Nhut

Saigon

Vung Tau

10°N

100°E

10°N

Can Tho

Surrender of South Vietnam, 1975

0   100   200 Miles

0   100   200 Kilometers

Mercator Projection

Mekong Delta

South China Sea

110°E

The Vietnam War

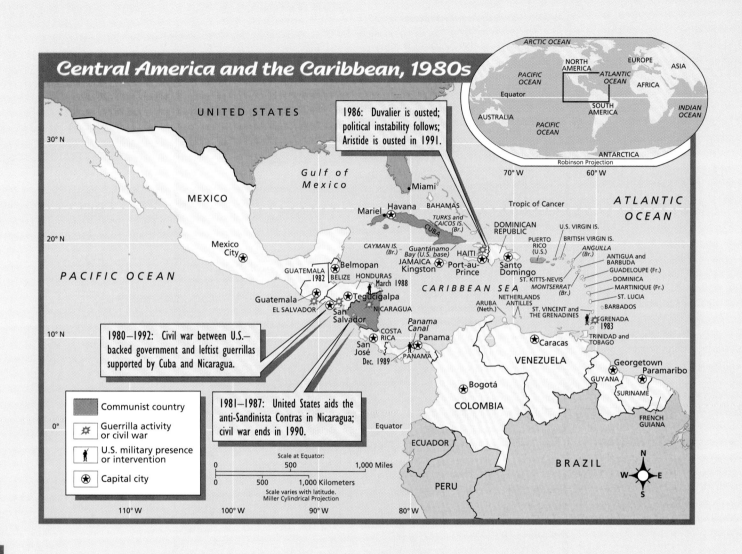

Central America and the Caribbean, 1980s

1986: Duvalier is ousted; political instability follows; Aristide is ousted in 1991.

1980–1992: Civil war between U.S.–backed government and leftist guerrillas supported by Cuba and Nicaragua.

1981–1987: United States aids the anti-Sandinista Contras in Nicaragua; civil war ends in 1990.

Legend

- Communist country
- Guerrilla activity or civil war
- U.S. military presence or intervention
- Capital city

UNITED STATES

Gulf of Mexico

MEXICO

Mexico City

PACIFIC OCEAN

Miami

Mariel
Havana
CUBA

BAHAMAS

TURKS and CAICOS IS. (Br.)

CAYMAN IS. (Br.)

Guantánamo Bay (U.S. base)

JAMAICA
Kingston

HAITI

Port-au-Prince

DOMINICAN REPUBLIC

Santo Domingo

PUERTO RICO (U.S.)

U.S. VIRGIN IS.
BRITISH VIRGIN IS.

ANGUILLA (Br.)
ANTIGUA and BARBUDA
GUADELOUPE (Fr.)
ST. KITTS-NEVIS
MONTSERRAT (Br.)
DOMINICA
MARTINIQUE (Fr.)
ST. LUCIA
BARBADOS

ARUBA (Neth.)
NETHERLANDS ANTILLES

ST. VINCENT and THE GRENADINES

GRENADA 1983

TRINIDAD and TOBAGO

CARIBBEAN SEA

Tropic of Cancer

ATLANTIC OCEAN

GUATEMALA 1982
Belmopan
BELIZE
HONDURAS
March 1988
Guatemala
Tegucigalpa
EL SALVADOR
San Salvador
NICARAGUA

COSTA RICA
San José
Dec. 1989

Panama Canal
Panama
PANAMA

Caracas

VENEZUELA

Bogotá

COLOMBIA

Equator

ECUADOR

PERU

BRAZIL

Georgetown
Paramaribo
GUYANA
SURINAME
FRENCH GUIANA

Scale at Equator:
0   500   1,000 Miles
0   500   1,000 Kilometers
Scale varies with latitude.
Miller Cylindrical Projection

30° N
20° N
10° N
0°

110° W   100° W   90° W   80° W

ARCTIC OCEAN
NORTH AMERICA
PACIFIC OCEAN
ATLANTIC OCEAN
EUROPE
ASIA
AFRICA
Equator
AUSTRALIA
PACIFIC OCEAN
SOUTH AMERICA
INDIAN OCEAN
ANTARCTICA
Robinson Projection

70° W   60° W

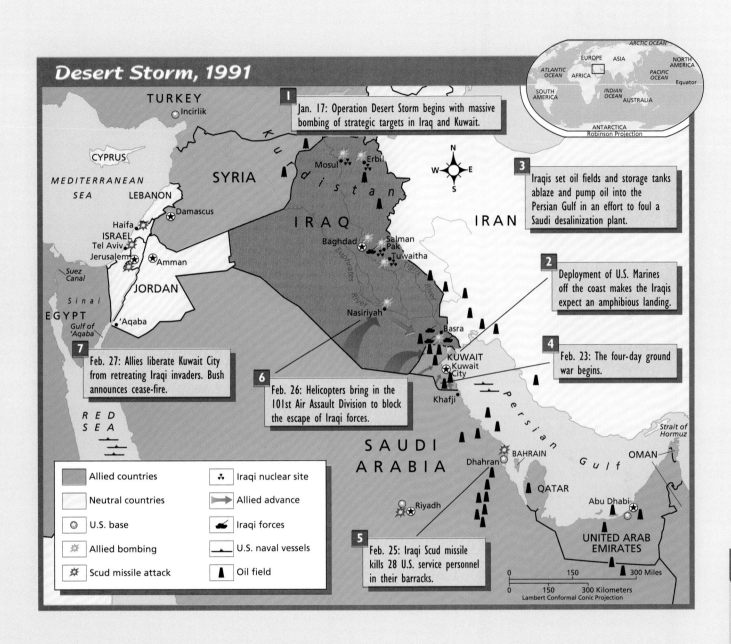

Desert Storm, 1991

TURKEY
Incirlik

CYPRUS

MEDITERRANEAN
SEA
LEBANON

SYRIA
Damascus

Haifa
ISRAEL
Tel Aviv
Jerusalem
Amman

Suez
Canal
JORDAN

Sinai
EGYPT
Gulf of
'Aqaba
'Aqaba

RED
SEA

Kudistan

Mosul   Erbil

IRAQ

Baghdad   Salman
Pak
Tuwaitha

Euphrates River

Nasiriyah

Tigris River

Basra

KUWAIT
Kuwait
City

Khafji

IRAN

SAUDI
ARABIA

Dhahran   BAHRAIN

Riyadh

Persian   Gulf   OMAN

Strait of
Hormuz

QATAR

Abu Dhabi

UNITED ARAB
EMIRATES

1 Jan. 17: Operation Desert Storm begins with massive bombing of strategic targets in Iraq and Kuwait.

3 Iraqis set oil fields and storage tanks ablaze and pump oil into the Persian Gulf in an effort to foul a Saudi desalinization plant.

2 Deployment of U.S. Marines off the coast makes the Iraqis expect an amphibious landing.

4 Feb. 23: The four-day ground war begins.

7 Feb. 27: Allies liberate Kuwait City from retreating Iraqi invaders. Bush announces cease-fire.

6 Feb. 26: Helicopters bring in the 101st Air Assault Division to block the escape of Iraqi forces.

5 Feb. 25: Iraqi Scud missile kills 28 U.S. service personnel in their barracks.

N
W   E
S

ARCTIC OCEAN
EUROPE   ASIA   NORTH
AMERICA
ATLANTIC
OCEAN   AFRICA   PACIFIC
OCEAN
SOUTH   INDIAN   Equator
AMERICA   OCEAN   AUSTRALIA
ANTARCTICA
Robinson Projection

Legend:
- Allied countries
- Neutral countries
- U.S. base
- Allied bombing
- Scud missile attack
- Iraqi nuclear site
- Allied advance
- Iraqi forces
- U.S. naval vessels
- Oil field

0   150   300 Miles
0   150   300 Kilometers
Lambert Conformal Conic Projection

A MULTI-CULTURAL COUNTRY

■■

EVEN before the founding of the United States, immigrants flocked to America from around the world. The origins of the immigrants have changed over time, however. The original Native Americans emigrated from Asia across Beringia. In colonial times the vast majority of immigrants came from Europe and Africa. Although Europe continued to provide the bulk of immigrants throughout the 19th century, more and more were from southern and eastern Europe. After World War II, immigration patterns changed dramatically as more people began to come from Latin America and from Asia. All of these immigrant groups have contributed to the diversity of American culture.

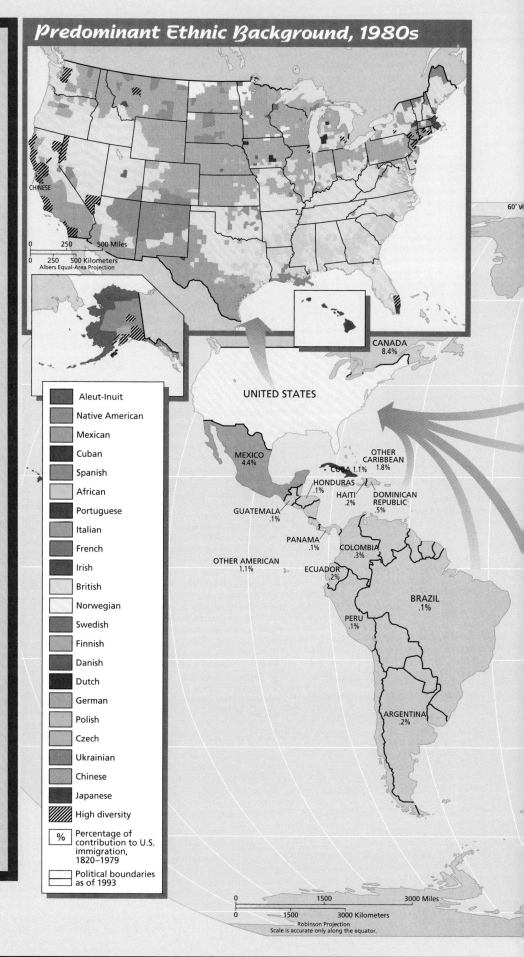

Predominant Ethnic Background, 1980s

CHINESE

0   250   500 Miles
0 250   500 Kilometers
Albers Equal-Area Projection

Aleut-Inuit
Native American
Mexican
Cuban
Spanish
African
Portuguese
Italian
French
Irish
British
Norwegian
Swedish
Finnish
Danish
Dutch
German
Polish
Czech
Ukrainian
Chinese
Japanese
High diversity

% Percentage of contribution to U.S. immigration, 1820–1979

Political boundaries as of 1993

UNITED STATES

CANADA
8.4%

MEXICO
4.4%

OTHER CARIBBEAN
1.8%

CUBA 1.1%

HONDURAS
.1%

HAITI
.2%

DOMINICAN REPUBLIC
.5%

GUATEMALA
.1%

PANAMA
.1%

COLOMBIA
.3%

OTHER AMERICAN
1.1%

ECUADOR
.2%

BRAZIL
.1%

PERU
.1%

ARGENTINA
.2%

60° W

0   1500   3000 Miles
0   1500   3000 Kilometers
Robinson Projection
Scale is accurate only along the equator.

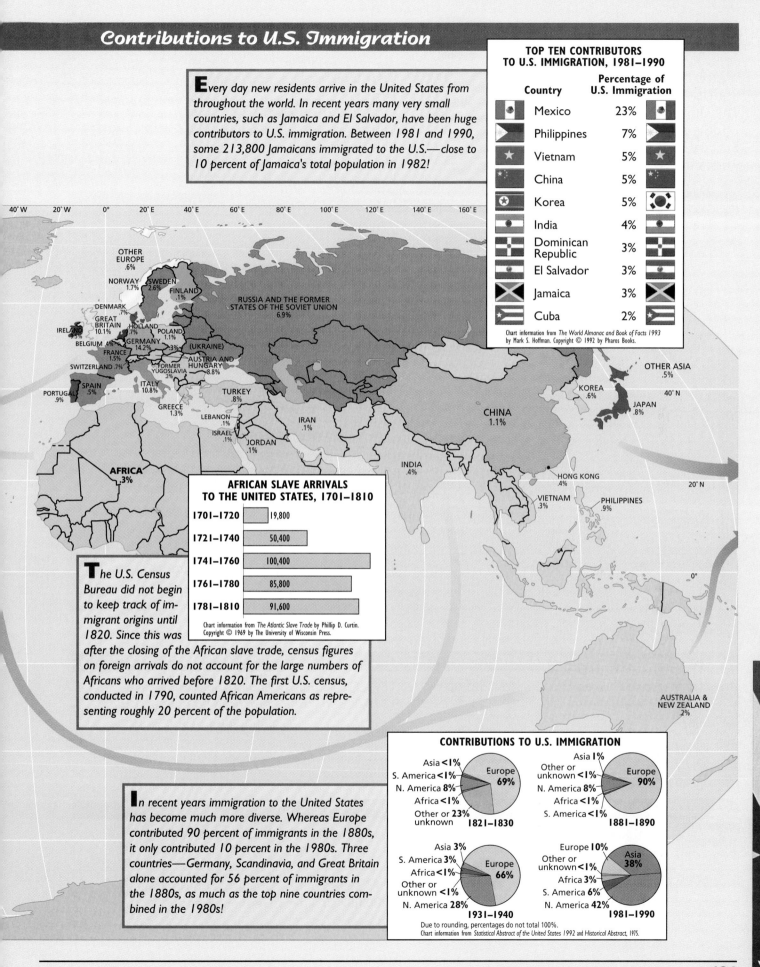

Every day new residents arrive in the United States from throughout the world. In recent years many very small countries, such as Jamaica and El Salvador, have been huge contributors to U.S. immigration. Between 1981 and 1990, some 213,800 Jamaicans immigrated to the U.S.—close to 10 percent of Jamaica's total population in 1982!

TOP TEN CONTRIBUTORS TO U.S. IMMIGRATION, 1981–1990

Country	Percentage of U.S. Immigration	
Mexico	23%	
Philippines	7%	
Vietnam	5%	
China	5%	
Korea	5%	
India	4%	
Dominican Republic	3%	
El Salvador	3%	
Jamaica	3%	
Cuba	2%	

Chart information from *The World Almanac and Book of Facts 1993* by Mark S. Hoffman. Copyright © 1992 by Pharos Books.

OTHER EUROPE .6%
NORWAY 1.7%
SWEDEN 2.6%
FINLAND .1%
DENMARK .7%
GREAT BRITAIN 10.1%
IRELAND 9.5%
HOLLAND .7%
BELGIUM .4%
GERMANY 14.2%
POLAND 1.1%
(UKRAINE) .3%
FRANCE 1.5%
SWITZERLAND .7%
FORMER YUGOSLAVIA .2%
AUSTRIA AND HUNGARY 8.8%
SPAIN .5%
PORTUGAL .9%
ITALY 10.8%
GREECE 1.3%
TURKEY .8%
LEBANON .1%
ISRAEL .1%
JORDAN .1%
IRAN .1%
RUSSIA AND THE FORMER STATES OF THE SOVIET UNION 6.9%
AFRICA .3%
INDIA .4%
CHINA 1.1%
HONG KONG .4%
VIETNAM .3%
PHILIPPINES .9%
KOREA .6%
JAPAN .8%
OTHER ASIA .5%
AUSTRALIA & NEW ZEALAND .2%

40° W 20° W 0° 20° E 40° E 60° E 80° E 100° E 120° E 140° E 160° E
40° N 20° N 0°

AFRICAN SLAVE ARRIVALS TO THE UNITED STATES, 1701–1810

1701–1720	19,800
1721–1740	50,400
1741–1760	100,400
1761–1780	85,800
1781–1810	91,600

Chart information from *The Atlantic Slave Trade* by Phillip D. Curtin. Copyright © 1969 by The University of Wisconsin Press.

The U.S. Census Bureau did not begin to keep track of immigrant origins until 1820. Since this was after the closing of the African slave trade, census figures on foreign arrivals do not account for the large numbers of Africans who arrived before 1820. The first U.S. census, conducted in 1790, counted African Americans as representing roughly 20 percent of the population.

CONTRIBUTIONS TO U.S. IMMIGRATION

1821–1830
Asia <1%
S. America <1%
N. America 8%
Africa <1%
Other or unknown 23%
Europe 69%

1881–1890
Asia 1%
Other or unknown <1%
N. America 8%
Africa <1%
S. America <1%
Europe 90%

1931–1940
Asia 3%
S. America 3%
Africa <1%
Other or unknown <1%
N. America 28%
Europe 66%

1981–1990
Europe 10%
Other or unknown <1%
Africa 3%
S. America 6%
N. America 42%
Asia 38%

Due to rounding, percentages do not total 100%.
Chart information from *Statistical Abstract of the United States 1992* and *Historical Abstract, 1975.*

In recent years immigration to the United States has become much more diverse. Whereas Europe contributed 90 percent of immigrants in the 1880s, it only contributed 10 percent in the 1980s. Three countries—Germany, Scandinavia, and Great Britain alone accounted for 56 percent of immigrants in the 1880s, as much as the top nine countries combined in the 1980s!

APPENDIX

Metric Conversion Table

	If you have	multiply by	to get
LENGTH	miles	1.609	kilometers
	kilometers	.62	miles
	feet	.3048	meters
	meters	39.37, then divide by 12	feet
	inches	2.54	centimeters
	centimeters	.39	inches
	pounds	.454	kilograms
	kilograms	2.2046	pounds
AREA	acres	.405	hectares
	hectares	2.47	acres
	square miles	2.59	square kilometers
	square kilometers	.3861	square miles
CAPACITY	quarts	.946	liters
	liters	1.057	quarts
TEMPERATURE	degrees Fahrenheit	subtract 32, then multiply by $5/9$	degrees Celsius
	degrees Celsius	multiply by $9/5$, then add 32	degrees Fahrenheit

Country ★ Capital	Population (1992)	Land Area (1992)	Principal Languages
THE UNITED STATES AND CANADA			
United States ★ Washington, D.C.	254,521,000	3,679,192 sq. mi. 9,529,063 sq. km	English, Spanish, Native American languages, other languages of the world
Canada ★ Ottawa	27,351,509	3,849,675 sq. mi. 9,970,610 sq. km	English, French
MIDDLE AND SOUTH AMERICA			
Antigua and Barbuda ★ St. John's	64,110	171 sq. mi. 442 sq. km	English, local dialects
Argentina ★ Buenos Aires	32,901,234	1,073,399 sq. mi. 2,780,092 sq. km	Spanish, English, Italian, German, French

	Country ★ Capital	Population (1992)	Land Area (1992)	Principal Languages
	Bahamas ★ Nassau	255,811	5,382 sq. mi. 13,939 sq. km	English, Creole
	Barbados ★ Bridgetown	254,934	166 sq. mi. 430 sq. km	English
	Belize ★ Belmopan	229,143	8,867 sq. mi. 22,965 sq. km	English, Spanish, Maya, Garifuna (Carib)
	Bolivia ★ La Paz ★ Sucre	7,323,048	424,164 sq. mi. 1,098,581 sq. km	Spanish, Quechua, Aymara,
	Brazil ★ Brasília	158,202,019	3,286,488 sq. mi. 8,511,965 sq. km	Portuguese, Spanish, English, French
	Chile ★ Santiago	13,528,945	292,135 sq. mi. 756,626 sq. km	Spanish
	Colombia ★ Bogotá	34,296,941	440,831 sq. mi. 1,141,748 sq. km	Spanish
	Costa Rica ★ San José	3,187,085	19,730 sq. mi. 51,100 sq. km	Spanish, English
	Cuba ★ Havana	10,846,821	42,804 sq. mi. 110,861 sq. km	Spanish
	Dominica ★ Roseau	87,035	290 sq. mi. 750 sq. km	English, French patois
	Dominican Republic ★ Santo Domingo	7,515,892	18,704 sq. mi. 48,443 sq. km	Spanish
	Ecuador ★ Quito	10,933,143	104,505 sq. mi. 270,667 sq. km	Spanish, Quechua and other Native American languages
	El Salvador ★ San Salvador	5,574,279	8,124 sq. mi. 21,041 sq. km	Spanish, Nahuatl
	Grenada ★ St. George's	83,556	133 sq. mi. 345 sq. km	English, French patois
	Guatemala ★ Guatemala City	9,784,275	42,042 sq. mi. 108,889 sq. km	Spanish, Native American dialects
	Guyana ★ Georgetown	739,431	83,044 sq. mi. 215,083 sq. km	English, Native American dialects
	Haiti ★ Port-au-Prince	6,431,977	10,579 sq. mi. 27,400 sq. km	French, Creole

Country ★ Capital	Population (1992)	Land Area (1992)	Principal Languages
Honduras ★ Tegucigalpa	5,092,776	43,277 sq. mi. 112,088 sq. km	Spanish, Native American dialects
Jamaica ★ Kingston	2,506,701	4,244 sq. mi. 10,991 sq. km	English, Creole
Mexico ★ Mexico City	92,380,721	756,066 sq. mi. 1,958,201 sq. km	Spanish, Mayan dialects
Nicaragua ★ Managua	3,878,150	50,464 sq. mi. 130,700 sq. km	Spanish, English, Native American languages
Panama ★ Panama City	2,529,902	29,157 sq. mi. 75,517 sq. km	Spanish, English
Paraguay ★ Asunción	4,929,446	157,048 sq. mi. 406,752 sq. km	Spanish, Guaraní
Peru ★ Lima	22,767,543	496,225 sq. mi. 1,285,216 sq. km	Spanish, Quechua, Aymara
St. Kitts and Nevis ★ Basseterre	40,061	104 sq. mi. 269 sq. km	English
St. Lucia ★ Castries	151,774	238 sq. mi. 617 sq. km	English, French patois
St. Vincent and the Grenadines ★ Kingstown	115,339	150 sq. mi. 389 sq. km	English, French patois
Suriname ★ Paramaribo	410,016	63,251 sq. mi. 163,820 sq. km	Dutch, English, Surinamese, Hindi, Javanese
Trinidad and Tobago ★ Port-of-Spain	1,299,301	1,980 sq. mi. 5,128 sq. km	English, Hindi, French, Spanish
Uruguay ★ Montevideo	3,141,533	68,037 sq. mi. 176,215 sq. km	Spanish
Venezuela ★ Caracas	20,675,970	352,144 sq. mi. 912,050 sq. km	Spanish, Native American dialects

EUROPE

Country ★ Capital	Population (1992)	Land Area (1992)	Principal Languages
Albania ★ Tiranë	3,285,224	11,100 sq. mi. 28,748 sq. km	Albanian, Greek
Andorra ★ Andorra la Vella	54,428	181 sq. mi. 468 sq. km	Catalan, French, Castilian

Country ★ Capital	Population (1992)	Land Area (1992)	Principal Languages
Austria ★ Vienna	7,867,541	32,377 sq. mi. 83,856 sq. km	German
Belgium ★ Brussels	10,016,623	11,783 sq. mi. 30,518 sq. km	Flemish (Dutch), French, German
Bosnia and Herzegovina ★ Sarajevo	4,364,000	19,781 sq. mi. 51,233 sq. km	Serbo-Croatian
Bulgaria ★ Sofia	8,869,161	42,855 sq. mi. 110,994 sq. km	Bulgarian, Turkish
Croatia ★ Zagreb	4,784,000	21,829 sq. mi. 56,538 sq. km	Serbo-Croatian
Czech Republic ★ Prague	10,365,000	30,450 sq. mi. 78,864 sq. km	Czech, Slovak, German
Denmark ★ Copenhagen	5,163,955	16,638 sq. mi. 43,093 sq. km	Danish, Faroese, Greenlandic, German
Estonia ★ Tallinn	1,607,349	17,413 sq. mi. 45,100 sq. km	Estonian, Latvian, Lithuanian, Russian
Finland ★ Helsinki	5,004,273	130,559 sq. mi. 338,145 sq. km	Finnish, Swedish, Lapp, Russian
France ★ Paris	57,287,258	210,026 sq. mi. 543,965 sq. km	French, regional dialects
Germany ★ Berlin	80,387,283	137,820 sq. mi. 356,954 sq. km	German
Greece ★ Athens	10,064,250	50,949 sq. mi. 131,957 sq. km	Greek, English, French
Hungary ★ Budapest	10,333,327	35,920 sq. mi. 93,033 sq. km	Hungarian
Iceland ★ Reykjavik	259,012	39,699 sq. mi. 102,819 sq. km	Icelandic
Ireland ★ Dublin	3,521,207	27,137 sq. mi. 70,285 sq. km	English, Irish (Gaelic)
Italy ★ Rome	57,904,628	116,324 sq. mi. 301,277 sq. km	Italian, German, French, Slovene
Latvia ★ Riga	2,728,937	24,900 sq. mi. 64,500 sq. km	Latvian, Lithuanian, Russian

Country ★ Capital	Population (1992)	Land Area (1992)	Principal Languages
Liechtenstein ★ Vaduz	28,642	62 sq. mi. 160 sq. km	German, Alemannic dialect
Lithuania ★ Vilnius	3,788,542	25,213 sq. mi. 65,301 sq. km	Lithuanian, Polish, Russian
Luxembourg ★ Luxembourg	392,405	999 sq. mi. 2,586 sq. km	Luxembourgisch, German, French, English
Macedonia ★ Skopje	2,174,000	9,781 sq. mi. 25,333 sq. km	Macedonian, Albanian, Turkish, Serbo-Croatian
Malta ★ Valletta	359,231	122 sq. mi. 316 sq. km	Maltese, English
Monaco ★ Monaco	29,965	.75 sq. mi. 1.95 sq. km	French, English, Italian, Monegasque
Netherlands ★ Amsterdam ★ The Hague	15,112,064	16,163 sq. mi. 41,863 sq. km	Dutch
Norway ★ Oslo	4,294,876	125,050 sq. mi. 323,878 sq. km	Norwegian, Lapp, Finnish
Poland ★ Warsaw	38,385,617	120,727 sq. mi. 312,683 sq. km	Polish
Portugal ★ Lisbon	10,448,509	35,672 sq. mi. 92,389 sq. km	Portuguese
Romania ★ Bucharest	23,169,914	91,699 sq. mi. 237,500 sq. km	Romanian, Hungarian, German
San Marino ★ San Marino	23,404	24 sq. mi. 61 sq. km	Italian
Slovakia ★ Bratislava	5,310,000	18,932 sq. mi. 49,035 sq. km	Slovak, Czech, Hungarian
Slovenia ★ Ljubljana	1,963,000	7,836 sq. mi. 20,296 sq. km	Slovenian, Serbo-Croatian
Spain ★ Madrid	39,118,399	194,898 sq. mi. 504,783 sq. km	Castilian, Spanish, Catalan, Galician, Basque
Sweden ★ Stockholm	8,602,157	173,732 sq. mi. 449,964 sq. km	Swedish, Lapp, Finnish
Switzerland ★ Bern	6,828,023	15,943 sq. mi. 41,293 sq. km	German, French, Italian, Romansh

Country ★ Capital	Population (1992)	Land Area (1992)	Principal Languages
United Kingdom ★ London	57,797,514	94,251 sq. mi. 244,110 sq. km	English, Welsh, Scottish, Gaelic
Yugoslavia (Serbia and Montenegro) ★ Belgrade	10,642,000	39,517 sq. mi. 102,350 sq. km	Serbo-Croatian
Vatican City ★ Vatican City	802	0.169 sq. mi. 0.438 sq. km	Italian, Latin, other languages of the world

RUSSIA AND NORTHERN EURASIA

Country ★ Capital	Population (1992)	Land Area (1992)	Principal Languages
Armenia ★ Yerevan	3,415,566	11,500 sq. mi. 29,800 sq. km	Armenian, Russian
Azerbaijan ★ Baki	7,450,787	33,400 sq. mi. 86,600 sq. km	Azeri, Russian, Armenian
Belarus ★ Minsk	10,373,881	80,200 sq. mi. 207,600 sq. km	Byelorusian, Russian
Georgia ★ T'bilisi	5,570,978	26,900 sq. mi. 69,700 sq. km	Georgian, Russian, Armenian, Azerbaijani
Kazakhstan ★ Almaty	17,103,927	1,049,200 sq. mi. 2,717,300 sq. km	Kazakh, Russian
Kyrgyzstan ★ Bishkek	4,567,875	76,600 sq. mi. 198,500 sq. km	Kyrgyz
Moldova ★ Chişinău	4,458,435	13,000 sq. mi. 33,700 sq. km	Moldovan, Romanian, Russian
Russia ★ Moscow	149,527,479	6,592,800 sq. mi. 17,075,400 sq. km	Russian, Estonian, Latvian, Lithuanian
Tajikistan ★ Dushanbe	5,680,242	55,300 sq. mi. 143,100 sq. km	Tajik
Turkmenistan ★ Ashgabat	3,838,108	188,500 sq. mi. 488,100 sq. km	Turkmen, Russian, Uzbek
Ukraine ★ Kyyiv	51,940,426	233,100 sq. mi. 603,700 sq. km	Ukrainian, Russian, Romanian, Polish
Uzbekistan ★ Toshkent	21,626,784	172,700 sq. mi. 447,400 sq. km	Uzbek, Russian

SOUTHWEST ASIA

Country ★ Capital	Population (1992)	Land Area (1992)	Principal Languages
Afghanistan ★ Kabul	16,095,664	251,825 sq. mi. 652,225 sq. km	Pashtu, Afghan Persian, Uzbek, Turkmen

Country ★ Capital	Population (1992)	Land Area (1992)	Principal Languages
Bahrain ★ Manama	551,513	267 sq. mi. 692 sq. km	Arabic, English, Farsi, Urdu
Cyprus ★ Nicosia	716,492	3,572 sq. mi. 9,251 sq. km	Greek, Turkish, English
Iran ★ Tehran	61,183,138	636,372 sq. mi. 1,648,196 sq. km	Persian and Persian dialects, Turkic dialects, Kurdish, Luri, Baloch, Arabic, Turkish
Iraq ★ Baghdad	18,445,847	167,975 sq. mi. 435,052 sq. km	Arabic, Kurdish, Assyrian, Armenian
Israel ★ Jerusalem	4,748,059	7,992 sq. mi. 20,700 sq. km	Hebrew, Arabic, English
Jordan ★ Amman	3,557,304	34,343 sq. mi. 88,946 sq. km	Arabic, English
Kuwait ★ Kuwait City	1,378,613	6,880 sq. mi. 17,818 sq. km	Arabic, English
Lebanon ★ Beirut	3,439,115	3,950 sq. mi. 10,230 sq. km	Arabic, French, Armenian, English
Oman ★ Muscat	1,587,581	120,000 sq. mi. 300,000 sq. km	Arabic, English, Balochi, Urdu, Indian dialects
Qatar ★ Doha	484,387	4,412 sq. mi. 11,427 sq. km	Arabic, English
Saudi Arabia ★ Riyadh	17,050,934	865,000 sq. mi. 2,240,000 sq. km	Arabic
Syria ★ Damascus	13,730,436	71,498 sq. mi. 185,180 sq. km	Arabic, Kurdish, Armenian, Aramaic, Circassian, French
Turkey ★ Ankara	59,640,143	300,948 sq. mi. 779,452 sq. km	Turkish, Kurdish, Arabic
United Arab Emirates ★ Abu Dhabi	2,522,315	30,000 sq. mi. 77,700 sq. km	Arabic, Persian, English, Hindi, Urdu
Yemen ★ Sanaa	10,394,749	205,356 sq. mi. 531,869 sq. km	Arabic

AFRICA

Country ★ Capital	Population (1992)	Land Area (1992)	Principal Languages
Algeria ★ Algiers	26,666,921	919,595 sq. mi. 2,381,741 sq. km	Arabic, French, Berber dialects

Country ★ Capital	Population (1992)	Land Area (1992)	Principal Languages
Angola ★ Luanda	8,902,076	481,354 sq. mi. 1,246,700 sq. km	Portuguese, Bantu dialects
Benin ★ Porto-Novo	4,997,599	43,450 sq. mi. 112,600 sq. km	French, Fon, Yoruba, other local languages
Botswana ★ Gaborone	1,292,210	224,607 sq. mi. 581,730 sq. km	English, Setswana
Burkina Faso ★ Ouagadougou	9,653,672	105,869 sq. mi. 274,200 sq. km	French, local languages
Burundi ★ Bujumbura	6,022,341	10,740 sq. mi. 27,817 sq. km	Kirundi, French, Swahili
Cameroon ★ Yaoundé	12,658,439	179,714 sq. mi. 465,458 sq. km	English, French, African languages
Cape Verde ★ Praia	398,276	1,557 sq. mi. 4,033 sq. km	Portuguese, Crioulo
Central African Republic ★ Bangui	3,029,080	240,324 sq. mi. 622,436 sq. km	French, Sangho, Arabic, Hunsa, Swahili
Chad ★ N'Djamena	5,238,908	495,755 sq. mi. 1,284,000 sq. km	French, Arabic, Sara, Sango
Comoros ★ Moroni	493,853	719 sq. mi. 1,862 sq. km	Arabic, French, Comoran
Congo ★ Brazzaville	2,376,687	132,047 sq. mi. 342,000 sq. km	French, Lingala, Kikongo, other African languages
Côte d'Ivoire ★ Yamoussoukro	13,497,153	123,847 sq. mi. 320,763 sq. km	French, Dioula, native dialects
Djibouti ★ Djibouti	390,906	8,950 sq. mi. 23,200 sq. km	French, Arabic, Somali, Afar
Egypt ★ Cairo	56,368,950	385,229 sq. mi. 997,739 sq. km	Arabic, English, French
Equatorial Guinea ★ Malabo	388,799	10,831 sq. mi. 28,051 sq. km	Spanish, pidgin English, Fang, Bubi, Ibo
Eritrea ★ Asmara	3,500,000 (est.)	48,649 sq. mi. 126,000 sq. km	Tigrinya, other Afro-Asiatic languages
Ethiopia ★ Addis Ababa	54,270,464	472,400 sq. mi. 1,223,500 sq. km	Amharic, Tigrinya, Orominga, Guaraginga, Somali, Arabic, English

Country ★ Capital	Population (1992)	Land Area (1992)	Principal Languages
Gabon ★ Libreville	1,106,355	103,347 sq. mi. 267,667 sq. km	French, Fang, Myene, Bateke, Bapounou/Eschira, Bandjabi
Gambia ★ Banjul	902,089	4,127 sq. mi. 10,689 sq. km	English, Mandinka, Wolof, Fula
Ghana ★ Accra	16,185,351	92,098 sq. mi. 238,533 sq. km	English, Akan, Moshi-Dagomba, Ewe, Ga
Guinea ★ Conakry	7,783,926	94,926 sq. mi. 245,857 sq. km	French, local languages
Guinea-Bissau ★ Bissau	1,047,137	13,948 sq. mi. 36,125 sq. km	Portuguese, Criolo, African languages
Kenya ★ Nairobi	26,164,473	224,961 sq. mi. 582,646 sq. km	English, Swahili, local languages
Lesotho ★ Maseru	1,848,925	11,720 sq. mi. 30,355 sq. km	Sesotho, English, Zulu, Xhosa
Liberia ★ Monrovia	2,462,276	38,250 sq. mi. 99,067 sq. km	English, Niger-Congo languages
Libya ★ Tripoli	4,484,795	678,400 sq. mi. 1,757,000 sq. km	Arabic, Italian, English
Madagascar ★ Antananarivo	12,596,263	226,658 sq. mi. 587,041 sq. km	French, Malagasy
Malawi ★ Lilongwe	9,605,342	45,747 sq. mi. 118,484 sq. km	English, Chichewa, other regional languages
Mali ★ Bamako	8,641,178	478,841 sq. mi. 1,240,192 sq. km	French, Bambara, African languages
Mauritania ★ Nouakchott	2,059,187	398,000 sq. mi. 1,030,700 sq. km	Hasaniya, Arabic, Pular, Soninke, Wolof
Mauritius ★ Port Louis	1,092,130	788 sq. mi. 2,040 sq. km	English, Creole, French, Hindi, Urdu, Hakka, Bojpoori
Morocco ★ Rabat	26,708,587	177,117 sq. mi. 458,730 sq. km	Arabic, Berber dialects, French
Mozambique ★ Maputo	15,469,150	313,661 sq. mi. 812,379 sq. km	Portuguese, many local dialects
Namibia ★ Windhoek	1,574,927	317,818 sq. mi. 823,144 sq. km	English, Afrikaans, German, local languages

Country ★ Capital	Population (1992)	Land Area (1992)	Principal Languages
Niger ★ Niamey	8,052,945	458,075 sq. mi. 1,186,408 sq. km	French, Hausa, Djerma
Nigeria ★ Abuja	126,274,589	356,669 sq. mi. 923,768 sq. km	English, Hausa, Yoruba, Ibo, Fulani
Rwanda ★ Kigali	8,206,446	10,169 sq. mi. 26,338 sq. km	Kinyarwanda, French, Kiswahili
São Tomé and Príncipe ★ São Tomé	132,338	386 sq. mi. 1,001 sq. km	Portuguese
Senegal ★ Dakar	8,205,058	75,955 sq. mi. 196,722 sq. km	French, Wolof, Pulaar, Diola, Mandingo
Seychelles ★ Victoria	69,519	175 sq. mi. 453 sq. km	English, French, Creole
Sierra Leone ★ Freetown	4,456,737	27,699 sq. mi. 71,740 sq. km	English, Mende, Temne, Krio
Somalia ★ Mogadishu	7,235,226	246,000 sq. mi. 637,000 sq. km	Somali, Arabic, Italian, English
South Africa ★ Pretoria	41,688,360	473,290 sq. mi. 1,225,815 sq. km	Afrikaans, English, Zulu, Xhosa, North and South Sotho, Tswana
Sudan ★ Khartoum	28,305,046	966,757 sq. mi. 2,503,890 sq. km	Arabic; Nubian; Ta Bedawie; various dialects of Nilotic, Nilo-Hamitic, and Sudanic languages; English
Swaziland ★ Mbabane	913,008	6,704 sq. mi. 17,364 sq. km	English, siSwati
Tanzania ★ Dar es Salaam	27,791,552	364,017 sq. mi. 942,799 sq. km	Swahili, English, local languages
Togo ★ Lomé	3,958,863	21,925 sq. mi. 56,785 sq. km	French, Ewe, Mina, Dagomba, Kabyè
Tunisia ★ Tūnis	8,445,656	59,664 sq. mi. 154,530 sq. km	Arabic, French
Uganda ★ Kampala	19,386,104	93,070 sq. mi. 241,040 sq. km	English, Luganda, Swahili, other Bantu and Nilotic languages
Zaire ★ Kinshasa	39,084,400	905,446 sq. mi. 2,345,095 sq. km	French, Lingala, Swahili, Kingwana, Kikongo, Tshiluba

Country ★ Capital	Population (1992)	Land Area (1992)	Principal Languages
Zambia ★ Lusaka	8,745,284	290,586 sq. mi. 752,614 sq. km	English, local languages
Zimbabwe ★ Harare	11,033,376	150,873 sq. mi. 390,759 sq. km	English, Shona, Sindebele

EAST AND SOUTHEAST ASIA

Country ★ Capital	Population (1992)	Land Area (1992)	Principal Languages
Brunei ★ Bandar Seri Begawan	269,319	2,226 sq. mi. 5,765 sq. km	Malay, English, Chinese
Burma (Myanmar) ★ Rangoon (Yangon)	42,642,418	261,228 sq. mi. 676,577 sq. km	Burmese, local languages
Cambodia ★ Phnom Penh	7,295,706	70,238 sq. mi. 181,916 sq. km	Khmer, French
China ★ Beijing	1,169,619,601	3,696,100 sq. mi. 9,572,900 sq. km	Mandarin Chinese, other Chinese dialects
Indonesia ★ Jakarta	195,683,531	752,410 sq. mi. 1,948,732 sq. km	Bahasa Indonesia, English, Dutch, Javanese and other local dialects
Japan ★ Tokyo	124,460,481	145,883 sq. mi. 377,835 sq. km	Japanese
Laos ★ Vientiane	4,440,213	91,400 sq. mi. 236,800 sq. km	Lao, French, English
Malaysia ★ Kuala Lumpur	18,410,920	127,584 sq. mi. 330,442 sq. km	Malay, English, Chinese dialects, Tamil
Mongolia ★ Ulaanbaatar	2,305,516	604,800 sq. mi. 1,566,500 sq. km	Khalkha Mongol, Russian, Chinese, Turkic languages
North Korea ★ P'yŏngyang	22,227,303	47,400 sq. mi. 122,762 sq. km	Korean
Philippines ★ Manila	67,114,060	115,800 sq. mi. 300,000 sq. km	Pilipino, English, Tagalog
Singapore ★ Singapore	2,792,092	240 sq. mi. 622 sq. km	Chinese, Malay, Tamil, English
South Korea ★ Seoul	44,149,199	38,326 sq. mi. 99,263 sq. km	Korean
Taiwan ★ T'aipei	20,878,556	13,969 sq. mi. 36,179 sq. km	Mandarin Chinese, Taiwanese (Miu) and Hakka dialects

Country ★ Capital	Population (1992)	Land Area (1992)	Principal Languages
Thailand ★ Bangkok	57,624,180	198,115 sq. mi. 513,115 sq. km	Thai, English, regional dialects
Vietnam ★ Hanoi	68,964,018	127,246 sq. mi. 329,566 sq. km	Vietnamese, French, Chinese, English, Khmer

SOUTH ASIA

Country ★ Capital	Population (1992)	Land Area (1992)	Principal Languages
Bangladesh ★ Dhaka	119,411,711	55,598 sq. mi. 143,998 sq. km	Bangla, English
Bhutan ★ Thimphu	1,660,167	18,150 sq. mi. 47,000 sq. km	Dzongkha, other Tibetan dialects, Nepalese dialects
India ★ New Delhi	886,362,180	1,222,559 sq. mi. 3,166,414 sq. km	Hindi, English, Hindustani, local languages
Maldives ★ Male	234,371	115 sq. mi. 298 sq. km	Divehi, English
Nepal ★ Kathmandu	20,086,455	56,827 sq. mi. 147,181 sq. km	Nepali, local dialect
Pakistan ★ Islamabad	121,664,539	339,697 sq. mi. 879,811 sq. km	Urdu, English, Punjabi, Sindhi, Pashtu
Sri Lanka ★ Colombo	17,631,528	25,332 sq. mi. 65,610 sq. km	Sinhala, Tamil, English

THE PACIFIC WORLD

Country ★ Capital	Population (1992)	Land Area (1992)	Principal Languages
Australia ★ Canberra	17,576,354	2,966,200 sq. mi. 7,682,300 sq. km	English, local languages
Fiji ★ Suva	749,946	7,056 sq. mi. 18,274 sq. km	English, Fijian, Hindustani
Kiribati ★ Tarawa	74,788	320 sq. mi. 830 sq. km	English, Gilbertese
Marshall Islands ★ Majuro	50,004	70 sq. mi. 181 sq. km	English, Marshallese dialects, Japanese
Micronesia, Federated States of ★ Palikir	114,694	271 sq. mi. 702 sq. km	English, Austronesian languages, Polynesian languages
Nauru ★ Yaren District	9,460	8.2 sq. mi. 21.2 sq. km	Nauruan, English

	Country ★ Capital	Population (1992)	Land Area (1992)	Principal Languages
	New Zealand ★ Wellington	3,347,369	104,454 sq. mi. 270,534 sq. km	English, Maori
	Papua New Guinea ★ Port Moresby	4,006,509	178,704 sq. mi. 462,840 sq. km	local languages, English, pidgin English, Motu
	Solomon Islands ★ Honiara	360,010	10,954 sq. mi. 28,370 sq. km	local languages, Melanesian pidgin, English
	Tonga ★ Nuku'alofa	103,114	301 sq. mi. 780 sq. km	Tongan, English
	Tuvalu ★ Funafuti	9,494	9.3 sq. mi. 24 sq. km	Tuvaluan, English
	Vanuatu ★ Port-Vila	174,574	4,707 sq. mi. 12,190 sq. km	English, French pidgin
	Western Samoa ★ Apia	194,992	1,093 sq. mi. 2,831 sq. km	Samoan (Polynesian), English

THE UNITED STATES

State	Capital	Date entered Union	State	Capital	Date entered Union
Alabama	Montgomery	1819	**Montana**	Helena	1889
Alaska	Juneau	1959	**Nebraska**	Lincoln	1867
Arizona	Phoenix	1912	**Nevada**	Carson City	1864
Arkansas	Little Rock	1836	**New Hampshire**	Concord	1788
California	Sacramento	1850	**New Jersey**	Trenton	1787
Colorado	Denver	1876	**New Mexico**	Santa Fe	1912
Connecticut	Hartford	1788	**New York**	Albany	1788
Delaware	Dover	1787	**North Carolina**	Raleigh	1789
Florida	Tallahassee	1845	**North Dakota**	Bismarck	1889
Georgia	Atlanta	1788	**Ohio**	Columbus	1803
Hawaii	Honolulu	1959	**Oklahoma**	Oklahoma City	1907
Idaho	Boise	1890	**Oregon**	Salem	1859
Illinois	Springfield	1818	**Pennsylvania**	Harrisburg	1787
Indiana	Indianapolis	1816	**Rhode Island**	Providence	1790
Iowa	Des Moines	1846	**South Carolina**	Columbia	1788
Kansas	Topeka	1861	**South Dakota**	Pierre	1889
Kentucky	Frankfort	1792	**Tennessee**	Nashville	1796
Louisiana	Baton Rouge	1812	**Texas**	Austin	1845
Maine	Augusta	1820	**Utah**	Salt Lake City	1896
Maryland	Annapolis	1788	**Vermont**	Montpelier	1791
Massachusetts	Boston	1788	**Virginia**	Richmond	1788
Michigan	Lansing	1837	**Washington**	Olympia	1889
Minnesota	St. Paul	1858	**West Virginia**	Charleston	1863
Mississippi	Jackson	1817	**Wisconsin**	Madison	1848
Missouri	Jefferson City	1821	**Wyoming**	Cheyenne	1890

INDEX

(def.) indicates definition
Dates are in italic.